MARKED MEN

Marked Men

*Black Politicians and the
Racialization of Scandal*

Nyron N. Crawford

NEW YORK UNIVERSITY PRESS
New York

NEW YORK UNIVERSITY PRESS
New York
www.nyupress.org

© 2024 by New York University
All rights reserved

Please contact the Library of Congress for Cataloging-in-Publication data.

ISBN: 9781479816323 (hardback)
ISBN: 9781479816330 (paperback)
ISBN: 9781479816354 (library ebook)
ISBN: 9781479816347 (consumer ebook)

This book is printed on acid-free paper, and its binding materials are chosen for strength and durability. We strive to use environmentally responsible suppliers and materials to the greatest extent possible in publishing our books.

Manufactured in the United States of America

10 9 8 7 6 5 4 3 2 1

Also available as an ebook

For Gwen,

daydreamer, poet, and heaven's newest storyteller

Blessed and Free

So, when they continued asking him, he lifted up himself, and said unto them, "He that is without sin among you, let him first cast a stone at her."
—John 8:7

CONTENTS

Dramatis Personae   xi

Prologue   xiii

Introduction: Is There Vice in This City?   1

1. Perilous Negro Rule: Framing Black Politics as Corrupt   25

2. Black Suspicion, Black Protection: An Experimental Test   61

3. "Bitch Set Me Up": The Suspecting Harassment of Marion Barry   83

Conclusion: Black Power Failure: Toward a Critical Black Protectionism   107

Epilogue   117

Acknowledgments   127

Appendix   131

Notes   145

Bibliography   163

Index   177

About the Author   187

DRAMATIS PERSONAE

Marion S. Barry Jr.—Second and fourth mayor of the District of Columbia, serving from 1979 to 1991 and from 1995 to 1999.

Tom Bradley—Thirty-eighth mayor and first African American mayor of Los Angeles, serving from 1973 to 1993, the longest tenure in the city's history.

Byron W. Brown—First African American mayor of Buffalo, New York, elected in 2006.

Sheila Dixon—First woman mayor of the City of Baltimore, serving from 2007 to 2010.

Kenneth Gibson—First African American mayor of Newark, New Jersey.

Andrew Gillum—126th mayor of Tallahassee, Florida, serving from 2014 to 2018.

Vincent Gray—Seventh mayor of the District of Columbia, in office from 2011 to 2015.

Alcee L. Hastings—First African American federal judge in the state of Florida. Elected to the U.S. House of Representatives in 1992.

Sharpe James—Thirty-seventh mayor of Newark, New Jersey, serving simultaneously as state senator for the Twenty-Ninth Legislative District.

Kwame Kilpatrick—Seventy-second mayor of Detroit, Michigan, serving from 2002 to 2008.

Marilyn Mosby—Twenty-fifth state's attorney for Baltimore, Maryland, and youngest chief prosecutor of any American city.

Richard Nixon—Thirty-seventh president of the United States, serving from 1969 to 1974.

Adam Clayton Powell Jr.—American Baptist pastor and first African American to represent New York in the U.S. Congress.

Catherine Pugh—Fiftieth mayor of Baltimore, Maryland, serving from 2016 to 2019.

Charles R. Rangel—Member of the U.S. House of Representatives for districts in New York from 1971 to 2017.

Carl Stokes—First African American mayor of Cleveland, Ohio, serving from 1967 to 1971.

John F. Street—Second African American mayor of Philadelphia, Pennsylvania, serving from 2000 to 2008.

Donald J. Trump—Forty-fifth president of the United States.

Coleman Young—First African American mayor of Detroit, Michigan, serving from 1974 to 1994.

PROLOGUE

"Is Philadelphia the most corrupt city in America?" That was the question posed by Aaron Kase in *Vice* in 2017.[1] "Move over, Chicago. Back of the line, Detroit. Be easy, Big Easy," Kase declared, "this is Philly: machine politics, pay to play, and blatant nepotism are the norm." This City of Brotherly Love (and Sisterly Affection), where I live, has a well-earned reputation for political corruption. "Other American cities, no matter how bad their own conditions may be," warned Lincoln Steffens in 1902, "all point with scorn to Philadelphia as worse."[2]

It is understandable to think so. Rapid-fire allegations, investigations, indictments, and convictions of the city's leaders do not inspire confidence. Two Philadelphia city council members, Bobby Henon and Kenyatta Johnson, were indicted on federal bribery charges in 2019 and 2020, respectively.[3] Henon was convicted; Johnson's case was declared a mistrial (though prosecutors are planning another round of charges).[4] The city's former district attorney, Seth Williams, pled guilty to bribery in the summer of 2017, a year after the corruption conviction of Chaka Fattah, one of Philadelphia's longtime members of Congress. A parking-ticket-fixing scandal ended with indictments against nine Philadelphia Traffic Court judges in 2013, leading state officials to disband the body after a federal investigation.[5] Three of the city's elected sheriffs have faced allegations of improper conduct ranging from sexual harassment to bribery, landing the latter in prison.[6] The list goes on.

However, casting the city as the "most corrupt" makes it an easy target. When President Donald J. Trump protested the election results in 2020, he declared that "Philadelphia and Detroit" are "two of the corrupt political places anywhere in our country." His comments serviced what has become known as the Big Lie, a deceit that massive voter fraud in

U.S. cities allowed Democrats to steal the election, that *he* had won. His allegations were unfounded and, not surprisingly given Trump's record of duplicitousness, seemed to boomerang back as confession of his own misdeeds. "Bad things happen in Philadelphia," the president lamented. Trump's contemptuous remark trended on Twitter and became an internet meme. His insults of the city and failed maneuvering within it even inspired what came to be known as the Fraud Street Run, a play on the city's popular ten-mile Broad Street Run.[7] The route for Philly's Fraud Street Run poked fun at Trump lawyer and former New York mayor Rudy Giuliani, who hastily and mistakenly organized a press conference regarding voting fraud in the city at Four Seasons Total Landscaping instead of the better-known, luxurious Four Seasons Hotel.

At the same time, it is true: bad things *do* happen here. But they are random, not regular, incidents of official malfeasance that defined a different era. For example, voter fraud is statistically rare and does not happen at a scale that would significantly change the outcome of an election.[8] We should wonder what then earns this city the label "*most* corrupt"? Some political observers offer that one answer is race, considering the president "was accused of singling-out Black cities as politically corrupt places."[9] The trouble is, some readers might recoil in exasperation, even rolling their eyes, at the last two sentences. It is not hard to imagine you muttering to yourself, *why is it always race?*, as if I pulled it from a deck of imaginary racial grievances, to cloak one from ever being held accountable. But you can look at the balance of evidence in the distance, rightly reluctant to supply sympathy, and find yourself struggling with whether to ignore the possibility that racism colors who and what is seen as corrupt.

And if we do ignore it, we fall for the illusion, even when we know the trick. We take for granted that "allegations of voter fraud routinely invoke and strengthen racist stereotypes" and that they work to "exclude African Americans, who some still believe are endemically prone to criminality," from political power.[10] "Time is an odd sort of currency" in that way, to borrow from John Koenig.[11] Accusing Black voters and Black officials of stuffing ballots and repeat voting goes as far back as the Reconstruction era. Of course, race is not the only factor (party, gender) that structures perceptions of election fraud.[12] While political parties have weaponized corruption prosecution, the role of race has played a significant but underappreciated role as well. Black leaders have been surveilled and prosecuted by the U.S. government for alleged transgressions at disproportionate rates, for instance. If that is not convincing, consider former president Trump, who faces forty-four federal charges, forty-seven state charges, and civil liabilities, calling the three Black prosecutors in New York and Georgia racist for bringing charges against him. His brand of political and racial harassment is tried and true: caricature Black elected officials as corrupt.[13] Meanwhile, Trump also represents the very double standard about which Black political leaders have long complained.

There is good reason to doubt whether any of these claims are made in good faith in one instance, especially in view of egregious misconduct, and to carefully consider the possibility of racial harassment in a second instance. And yet I do not need you, the reader, to believe that race is a meaningful factor at play. I am unlikely to convince you. Even if I tell you that many of the Philadelphia politicians discussed above were Black or that the media coverage I witnessed felt racially uneven to my eyes, the familiar reader might be right to dismiss those examples as cherry-picked. Because of course White politicians get convicted of crimes too (see Bobby Henon). That response misunderstands the broader empirical demonstration that Black political leaders are disproportionally targeted for legal attention.[14] It is true of Black laypersons, and it is true of the Black elite.

A Racial Politics of Scandal

We might wonder to what extent African American voters do suspect harassment, and why. Because eventually a scandalized Black elected official may proffer a racial defense to "defend themselves against what they see as a racist attack."[15] That is exactly what Philadelphia mayor John F. Street was accused of doing in 2003, four weeks before a municipal election in which he was a candidate for a second term, after local police discovered a listening device in his City Hall office. Before then, in speculating about the future of Philadelphia politics, political scientist Richard Keiser wondered whether "a sizable segment of the Black community [would] take a stand for a good-government candidate against a Black mayor," concluding that "unless there [was] a huge scandal . . . dissent [would] be minimal."[16] But the bug in the mayor's office was a huge scandal, one that instead seemed to hasten voters' support of the beleaguered mayor. Although the FBI had planted the bug as part of an ongoing criminal probe, the mayor was incredulous: "You'd like to think you have a certain amount of privacy in your own office, and when you don't, you feel violated," Street said after the device was found.[17] In an interview with *Today*'s Katie Couric, the mayor mused further, "I think there will continue to be a huge amount of speculation and concern that some of this is racially motivated. We live in the greatest country in the world, but it is not a perfect country." In an unlikely turn of events, the bug turned into a boon for the incumbent. The event invited the suspicion of Philadelphians.[18] A poll in the *Philadelphia Inquirer* found that "thirty-nine percent of [B]lack voters said that news of the federal probe made them 'more likely' to vote to re-elect the mayor."[19]

And indeed they did: the incumbent John F. Street won a second term with 58 percent of the vote. A set of circumstances that might have otherwise tanked a candidate's electoral fortunes proved to be beneficial for Philadelphia's mayor. Some news observers speculated that the mayor's success was partly because he "was joined by many members of the city's large African American population in saying the bug was another misguided federal effort to embarrass an important leader."[20]

This book is about why, how, and in what manner Black voters take this protective position. Hence, this book is about African American political thought in the context of Black politics—a politics of and for

Black people—and the protectionism it encourages. It is not a book about whether White Americans believe Black politicians are corrupt (though I will describe in the next chapter that they do). Neither is it a racial comparison of the misdeeds of local elected officials. Juxtaposing a beleaguered White politician like former Providence, Rhode Island, mayor Buddy Cianci to a Black politician like former Washington, D.C., mayor Marion Barry would be provocative and the conventional way forward, but that is not our task here. Such comparisons tend to confuse and construct false equivalence, seldom taking seriously the claim that Black political leaders have been treated unfairly. Instead, urban voters—once including White ethnics and African Americans— are believed to have a "political culture [that] tolerated occasional misbehavior among elected officials, provided the officials worked to meet the material needs of their supporters."[21] According to Steven Taylor, "African Americans have similar expectations of their elected officials, but also forgive errant politicians who have been forceful advocates on behalf of issues that are of great concern to their constituents."[22] This may be true, but only in part. While African Americans look for effective representation from Black political leaders, they are also responsive to the subversive efforts that attempt to undermine their descriptive representation in politics, sports, and business.

This book is also not an analysis of legal guilt or a commentary on the strength of a case brought against Black elected officials. It is not much concerned about whether any of the officials described later in these chapters *did it*. Culpability matters, sure, except that it is weighed against the specter of a racist state action. Still, the reader would benefit from a primer on the technical elements of corruption-related crimes—and the details of specific cases as laid out in a formal, criminal accusation—to understand anticorruption logic and how the instruments of law can be improperly used.

And last, a disclosure: this book is not about Philadelphia. It points to examples of cities in which Black voters are politically incorporated in municipal government, so much so that the Black political leaders there find themselves in curious trouble. Washington, D.C., is prominently featured in one chapter, for example, and Baltimore in the epilogue. In each case, *Marked Men* describes the legal-racial socialization and resulting cognitive process that shapes how Black voters respond to political scandal.

Introduction

Is There Vice in This City?

If I were to ask you which city in the United States is the most corrupt, which would you name? Researcher Thomas J. Gradel and political scientist Dick Simpson answer that "Chicago's city hall is a famous political-corruption scene."[1] Many in the United States think it is Washington, D.C.[2] Others remark it has always been Philadelphia, the founding city of the United States. New Orleans and Detroit are often named, sometimes even Newark, New Jersey, too.[3] What if I asked you how you knew your selected city was corrupt? What would you say? What indicators would you offer as evidence? Imagine you replied with Detroit and used as proof the number of city council members investigated for corruption-related crimes.[4] Perhaps you thought it was New Orleans and cited as support the number of prosecutions in the federal judicial district of which it is a part, the Eastern District of Louisiana. Maybe you agree with Gradel and Simpson that the title belongs to Chicago. The number of convictions secured in that city, or in the Northern District of Illinois, is quite high.

If I asked again, using one of these metrics, would your answer change? Let us suppose it did. You accept Chicago as leader among municipal equals. And you might justify your choice, understandably, by saying these indicators satisfy the legal definitions of corruption. Maybe your answer does not change. Like *Vice*'s Aaron Kase in the prologue, you still *think* the answer is Philadelphia. You conclude the data on federal convictions are unconvincing and of questionable "quality and provenance."[5] You are also not demure about *your opinion* because it is based on what you know about the place. Public opinion then becomes another way of defining corruption. Take Transparency International's Corruption

Perception Index (CPI) as an example since it ranks countries based on the levels of public-sector corruption experts in journalism and business perceive in those places. "A country's score is the perceived level of public sector corruption on a scale of 0–100, where 0 means highly corrupt and 100 means very clean."[6] The CPI for the United States in 2021 was 67.[7]

And while the United States is not rated as corrupt as other countries, many Americans are nonetheless cynical about their politicians and their government. A nontrivial number of them (39.1 percent) think corruption is widespread in government service, for example. Table I.1 summarizes the extent to which U.S. adults think public officials are involved in official malfeasance, including bribery, honest services fraud, misuse of public office, bid rigging, theft of government property, and other state and federal corruption-related crimes. Regardless, fewer than a third think there are "quite a lot" of elected officials (i.e., politicians) taking part in it and about a quarter think the same of government administrators (i.e., bureaucrats). You can see in figure I.1 they also report that "quite a few" in government are crooked, a view that has ebbed and flowed between 1968 and 2012, a period that included the Watergate scandal, which led to President Richard Nixon's resignation in 1974. The number of perceived crooks in government increases around 1984, tracking the Iran-Contra Affair (1985), and again around 2003, following a series of high-profile political scandals in the first decade of the millennium. Most Americans have ideas about what they think are corrupt, though they make distinctions that are not always consistent with the letter of the law. For example, they routinely distinguish between lawbreaking and favoritism, the latter of which, depending on one's socioeconomic background, is acceptable.[8]

But these perceptions are not without problems. Characteristics related to a transgressed official, but unrelated to their alleged misconduct, can influence *what* and *who* we think is corrupt. For example, voters make distinctions between lawbreaking and favoritism, though both may be legally corrupt.[9] And even within these terms, voters do not always discern the appearance of impropriety from conduct that

TABLE I.1. Perceptions of Corruption

	How many politicians in America are involved in corruption? (%)	How many government administrators in America are involved in corruption? (%)
Almost none	1.6	2.4
A few	21.3	24.6
Some	35.0	38.2
Quite a lot	30.3	25.4
Almost all	11.8	9.4

Source: General Social Survey (2016).

contravenes the law, or what some have called legal corruption. These perceptions also vary according to the partisan and racial identity of the accused politician and that of the responding voter. White Americans are less likely to see favoritism as a form of corruption, for instance. And their racial resentment—whether toward Black Americans or toward immigrants—is strongly associated with voter fraud beliefs.[10] There is also evidence that the proportion of Black members of a city's council has a "significant, positive influence on overall perceptions of corruption."[11] That means White urban voters' beliefs about the incidence of political crime increase in relation to Blacks' political incorporation in municipal government. Relatedly, Black politicians have been disproportionately targeted in federal corruption probes at every level of government.[12] For example, political scientists Kenneth Meier and Thomas Holbrook show that states with higher proportions of Black elected officials have a higher rate of corruption convictions. They observe that "while these relationships do not conclusively demonstrate that the Justice Department specifically targets [B]lack public officials for prosecution, they are consistent with that notion."[13]

Which Is the Most Corrupt City?

Potential racial bias in anticorruption activities complicates rankings. Consider the nagging question of the most corrupt city. We might ask instead what it is about the above cities, or the one you imagined in your answer, that has them so troubled. What do they all have in common? The answers seem to depend on the racial composition of the city and its leaders. And public perceptions about who is corrupt plays a vital role in the response. Political scientists Thomas Holbrook and Karen Kaufmann use the Urban Mayor Election Study (UMES) to spotlight that local perceptions of corruption are related to the level of descriptive representation on a city's council. The reader may have noticed that all cities named so far have significant Black populations and histories of electing Black mayors. We can get a sense of this relationship in figure 1.2, reproduced from Holbrook to show the proportion of respondents in the UMES saying there was "a lot" of local corruption in their city.[14] More than 80 percent of Detroit (75 percent Black) residents saw a significant problem with graft there. Miami (16 percent), Cleveland (48.8 percent), Philadelphia (44 percent), and Atlanta (49.7 percent) complete the top five. Chicago and other cities are not included in the sample, making a complete comparison of local perceptions of corruption difficult. And yet a more objective measure such as corruption convictions features familiar cities (figure 1.3). Chicago (30 percent) leads and is followed by Los Angeles (8.1 percent) and New York City (20.1 percent), then Washington, D.C. (45.4 percent), Miami (16 percent), Newark (49.7 percent), Cleveland (48.8 percent), and Philadelphia (44 percent) make the top eight. With some exceptions, the racial pattern holds across the legal and popular definitions of corruption.

We are left to wonder if political scientists Monica C. Schneider and Angela L. Bos are right in their work about stereotypes related to Black politicians. They argue that this specific group of public officials are thought to have "more integrity . . . than [any general, non-raced] politician."[15] There are good reasons to doubt this claim. Rendering Black politicians as distinct from "typical politicians, who are not seen as having much integrity, perhaps due to news media reports of scandals involving politicians' ethics violations," ignores that Black politicians have

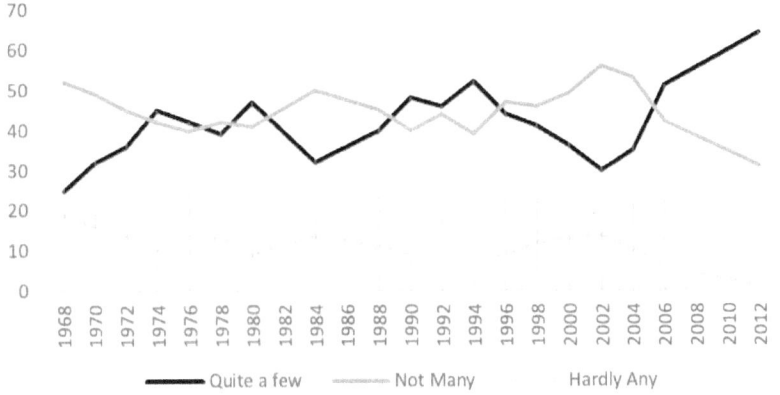

FIGURE I.1. Perceptions of "Crookedness" in Government (American National Election Study, 1958–2012), by Year.
Source: American National Election Study.

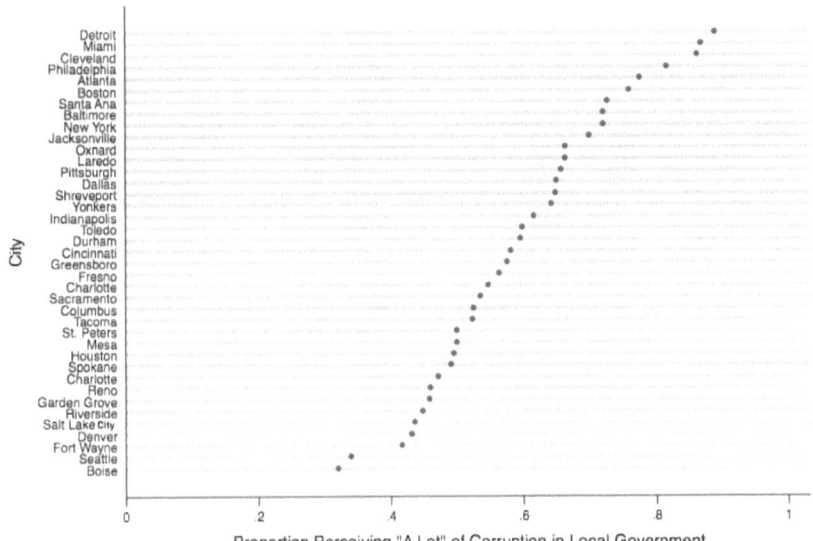

FIGURE I.2. Proportion Perceiving "A Lot" of Corruption in Local Government.
Sources: Holbrook, "Source of Perceptions of Local Political Corruption"; Urban Mayoral Election Study.
Note: N = 6,365, with an average of 159 respondents from each city.

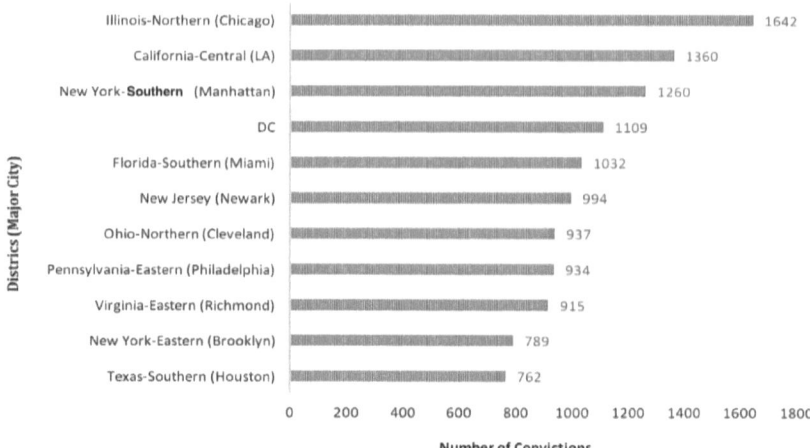

FIGURE I.3. Federal Public Corruption Convictions by the Top Eleven Judicial Districts, 1976–2016.
Source: Transactional Records Access Clearinghouse (TRAC).

long been disproportionately caught up in the federal dragnet and unfairly covered in news media reports.[16] Later I share good examples, including that of Coleman Young, the first African American mayor of Detroit who accused the media and prosecutors of colluding to undermine Black political power in his city. Indeed, it has been the case that problems of the first order (perception) have influenced those of the second order (investigation/prosecution). But if Black politicians have more integrity, it has done little to shield them from charges of impropriety, perceptually or legally.

Scandalize My Name

> I met my brother the other day
> And gave him my right hand
> As soon as ever my back was turned
> He scandalized my name.
> —H. T. Burleigh, "Scandalize My Name"

Most books tell us about causes and consequences of corruption, some describe the anatomy of political scandal, others even share everything. It is important to understand something entirely different. Race is meaningful in how we perceive corruption and certainly impactful in how it is enforced. And yet the racial politics of political scandal is not well understood. African Americans' quest for full citizenship has made them marks to be criminalized, to be the subject of rumor, to have their names scandalized. The political purpose of repression through disqualification is to change, as novelist Toni Morrison put it, "citizens into taxpayers" who are justified in their outrage when public office is abused for private gain. But there was a time when White citizens believed it was their duty to use political violence to deal with allegedly corrupt Black politicians of the post-Reconstruction South, a point to which I return later. Whatever the case, Black politicians have long complained about racist harassment against them by law enforcement and political rivals, only to be accused of playing the race card. Black voters are presumed co-conspirators, the constituents to whom this card is to be dealt.[17] They too are criminalized and scandalized by White-dominated institutions.

We know quite a bit about the scope of discrimination experienced by Black Americans interpersonally, in law and public policy, especially as sponsored by the state. And we know quite a bit about the benefits of Black representation in easing these problems for Black constituents, specifically, in terms of policy responsiveness. We know significantly less about the varied circumstances through which Black voters might support Black politicians. Recall the point I made in the prologue in this regard, notably how Black voters took issue with the FBI bugging the office of Philadelphia's mayor John F. Street. The potential harassment of the Black incumbent was said to have a mobilizing effect as far as it "galvanized [his] Democratic base, particularly his [B]lack base," leading many to conclude "the FBI may have delivered [him to] victory."[18] This book is about why, how, and in what manner this happens. It is about not so much "what the bug did for Street," as the *Philadelphia Inquirer* put it, but about the political psychology of how Black voters respond to the specter of harassment against scandalized Black politicians more generally.

"Forgiveness" of Black Elected Officials

A politician's ability to survive a scandal is influenced by many factors, but a common explanation is that politics is transactional—that is, the benefits gained by constituents make them more tolerant of corruption. But this characterization of tolerance is overstated, especially for Black voters, whose considerations are far more complicated. I advance a theory of racialized suspicion to describe what Black voters experience when Black elected officials are accused of misconduct. I define racialized suspicion and explain why it does more than lead African Americans to simply *forgive* Black elected officials.[19] Instead, this book demonstrates that it generates a protectionist defense on the part of Black voters, or what law professor Katheryn Russell-Brown calls Black protectionism. I present evidence that this rallying effect is dispensed in the form of what social psychologists Abrams, Randsley de Moura, and Travaglino call transgression credits—that is, penalties that are less harsh.[20]

The reader might not be surprised to learn that many politicians, regardless of race or party, survive their scandal and return to public office. Voters do not "always penalize corruption at the ballot box."[21] As a result, some scholars have questioned what "qualities and attitudes law abiding citizens" possess that "have allowed corruption and the underworld to flourish."[22] Others quizzically muse about why voters seldom throw corrupt politicians out! Although previous research shows that scandals reduce electoral support for a beleaguered politician by 5 to 10 percent, there is a good recovery rate in the absence of a conviction or resignation. Some voters remain loyal because of their political benefits, predispositions, and attitudes as well as the conditions of the political-social-economic environment. These factors collide in African

American political life and thought. Black voters are sometimes suspicious of law enforcement action against Black political leaders. Hence, they do not always trust investigations, accusations, or indictments related to alleged misconduct. Indeed, they have little reason to trust a system that has conducted massive surveillance of Black political leaders, students, activists, and clergy under the banner of a counterintelligence program (COINTELPRO). This sometimes illegal monitoring by law enforcement raises reasonable concerns about the integrity of the accusations of wrongdoing they level against African Americans. Thus, their behavior is less about forgiveness or tolerance of malfeasance than an effort to protect Black representation from state actors who may have ulterior motives for their actions.

However, it is important to establish early that Black elected officials are "hardly immune to the lure of illicit gain."[23] Nothing that follows disputes that Black politicians have also engaged in corrupt acts throughout their short political history. Nor do they always have safe harbor among other Black folk. African Americans in the body politic as far back as the Reconstruction era have repudiated evidenced impropriety. So too have other Black elites, including Ralph J. Bunche, Douglas Wilder, and John Lewis. Black protectionism then depends, in part, on whether African Americans *suspect* their government is acting in bad faith when it investigates or prosecutes Black elected officials for alleged crimes. If they believe the state is involved in racist double standards, a problem with which they are familiar, they are more likely to experience suspicious thinking. A common rejoinder is to characterize this *racialized suspicion* as a delusion of persecution or as outright conspiracies. Important to both is an implied exaggeration, an irrationality, in claiming a specific group has been targeted and victimized by an organized perpetrator. The definition of those terms betrays that interpretation regarding African Americans, especially regarding the history of American race relations. This racial group has experienced hostility and ill treatment (i.e., persecution) in the United States because of their race, for example, and much of it was brought about by a secret plan of White-dominated society and their institutions to do something unlawful or harmful (i.e., conspiracy) to Black Americans. The historical record offers repeated accounts.

Other scholars have argued that Blacks' judgments under scandal-legal circumstances are driven by different considerations. Political scientist Claire Adida and colleagues demonstrate that Black respondents react favorably to coethnic and co-minority cues in evaluating a scandalized politician.[24] They contend that higher levels of perceived discrimination against one's in-group lead Black people to respond to explicit coethnic cues (e.g., told that an elected official is Black). The authors do not specify the prejudicial treatment Black voters recall. It could be treatment experienced by the Black body politic, Black elected officials, or both. An explanation by Steven Taylor, another political scientist, suggests political scandals are overlooked in African American communities "when officials are seen to support measures that benefit the community as a whole."[25] Black voters are "public-regarding" in this view, which is an orientation to political culture that emphasizes politics as a means of community benefit. In contrast, White ethnic voters have been once categorized as "private-regarding," wherein politics is an individualistic endeavor. You will read in a later chapter about why this distinction contributes to perceptions that Black politics is corrupt. A final hypothesis proffered by psychologists Paul Skolnick and Jerry I. Shaw is that "Black racism" leads Black (mock) jurors to be more lenient and favorable toward (mock) Black defendants. Labeling this expectation "Black racism" is unfortunate because the authors recognize "Black racism . . . must be understood within this context and the long history of White bias against Black defendants."[26] From this perspective, Blacks' in-group protective judgments of embattled Black persons are seen as anti-White. The difference though has little to do with heightened punishment for Whites but rather is a discount in punishment for Black defendants.

The empirical findings in these scholarly works are consistent; in fact, chapters 2 and 3 exhibit comparable results—Black citizens discount negative penalties for transgressed Black elite. However, they are collectively mum about the political harassment Black elected officials say they have experienced. What happens is agreed, but not for what reason or purpose. For example, Adida and colleagues test their theory by leveraging the ethics scandal of New York City congressman Charles D. Rangel, the once powerful chairman of the U.S. House of Representatives Ways and Means Committee and a founding member of the Congressional Black Caucus (CBC).[27] A panel of the House Ethics Committee found Rangel guilty on eleven counts of violating House ethics rules. Hence, Adida et al. asked respondents in their study how likely they think it is that Rangel "is guilty of the ethics violations for which the House censured him but which he disputes."[28] Setting aside what they found in the data, there is no discussion about members of the CBC raising concerns that Rangel and other "[B]lack lawmakers [were facing] more scrutiny over allegations of ethical or criminal wrongdoing than their [W]hite colleagues." There is also no mention of Rangel's predecessor, Adam Clayton Powell Jr., the first Black congressman from Harlem. "On March 1, 1967, after the special committee recommended several punishments [for alleged misconduct] for Powell, including censure, the House instead voted 307 to 116 to exclude him from the 90th Congress." On the House floor, Powell cautioned his congressional colleagues, "Let he who is without sin cast the first stone. There is no one here who does not have a skeleton in his closet. I know, and I know them by name."[29] In a special election held to fill his own vacancy less than six weeks later, Powell's supporters overwhelmingly elected him back to the House.[30] The exclusion was "ultimately found unconstitutional by the Supreme Court in *Powell v. McCormack*."[31]

Taylor's account inadvertently advances a position that links Black people's political culture to a tolerance of corruption.[32] It is seen as inevitable, essential to their political activity. It tracks with the implicit-exchange theory that posits "that support for politicians suspected of corruption increases when they have a good record."[33] This was certainly the exchange at the height of machine politics of a bygone era and in some places today. Loyalty to the political machine, a coalitional party organization in many big cities, was rewarded with patronage jobs and services. This led voters to "look to politicians for 'help' and 'favors,'" according to Banfield and Wilson.[34] These voters became "far less interested in the efficiency, impartiality, and honesty of local government than in its readiness to confer material benefits of one sort or another upon them." Fans of the HBO series *The Wire* might recall a scene in which Clay Davis, a Black Maryland state senator representing Baltimore, was on trial for money laundering. While testifying on the stand, Senator Davis defends himself with a quick-witted description of how he uses pocket money to address his constituents' needs. "My world is cash and carry," he explains; "you give me twenty thousand . . . I am pulling goodly on that for whatever, whoever comes at me. . . . And excuse me if I didn't ask [that needy constituent] for a receipt." His rousing reply earns him applause from the court gallery and an acquittal.

The scene is comical and absurd but does well in portraying the way a corrupt, self-dealing Black politician is imagined. The example makes clear voters have needs, and if an elected official can make good on meeting them, they will trade public integrity for a political benefit. The logic is intuitive. One can pretend to not know, to not see, in exchange for favor. But Taylor's account understates how much Black citizens are disenfranchised and excluded from the spoils and power of government. To suggest Black voters are simply transactional overlooks that their claims to the government's helpfulness are contested, their representation in that government limited, so they look to Black politicians for help. Even in Taylor's example of Washington, D.C., there is no mention of either Congress's unique power over that majority-Black city's affairs or the constant Republican threats to its home rule charter.

Overall, a theme emerges in the weeds of these stories. Black voters can be protectionist, even of wayward Black politicians, when they suspect a racist threat. And one was said to exist in each of the real-world cases anchoring the empirical findings above. Congressman Rangel and his CBC colleagues claimed they were being harassed by the House

Ethics Committee, while Washington, D.C., mayor Marion Barry Jr. accused federal investigators of entrapment. The conclusion that "Black racism" fuels out-group discrimination on the part of Black Americans misunderstands this context. Experimental studies on racial discrimination tend to focus on interracial judgments, like White prejudice *against* Black targets. It has been argued elsewhere that reverse discrimination is similarly perpetuated by Blacks *against* Whites. But in these studies, in-group favoritism is misinterpreted as out-group derogation. That means Blacks' appraisal of a transgressed White defendant is explained as discriminatory, negative, and punitive. However, in centering an interracial analysis, or Whites as the reference category, the intraracial evaluation at play is ignored. In other words, the observed racial difference is Black evaluators discounting their judgments *for* Black subjects, not augmenting *against* White targets, because of systematic discrimination experienced by Black Americans.

A Racial Politics of Scandal

Each of these studies shows that the response of African Americans is to rally around embattled in-group members, especially Black political leaders. One explanation as to why is best summarized by social psychologists de Sousa and Moriconi: "If citizens do not trust the judicial system, it is hard to conceive that they will trust any indictment of judgment on political corruption coming from an institutional entity that has not enough more prestige to give credit to its decision."[35] Indeed, African Americans are less trusting of the criminal legal system and routinely question its legitimacy.[36] What is more, these misgivings influence political behaviors.[37] For Black Americans, the racial politics of scandal has two parts. First, allegations of impropriety against a Black political leader lead African Americans to process this information with suspicion. Second, this suspicion, prominent within the group, produces discounting judgments that are protective of the scandalized member of the group.

Racialized Suspicion

This may read as mildly conspiratorial, but I call this way of processing information *racialized suspicion*. It is Black Americans' tendency to question whether the government or other White-dominated institutions are involved in untoward behavior designed to embarrass and discredit Black political leaders. With the aid of local media, Black lawmakers have been disproportionately targeted and caught in the federal dragnet. President Richard Nixon routinely used the FBI and Internal Revenue Service to harass political enemies, for example, including members of the CBC. Racialized suspicion reflects neither delusion of persecution nor conspiratorial thinking because the FBI's vast surveillance of Black civil right leaders like Martin Luther King Jr., Malcolm X, and others during COINTELPRO provides a wealth of evidence that there was a secret plan by law enforcement to do something unlawful or harmful to so-called Black radicals or dissidents. We know that Black Americans perceive racial discrimination in the criminal justice system writ large, so it is not difficult to imagine how their concerns might expand to Black political leaders. This does not mean that they do not wrestle with their disavowal of malfeasance; rather, they cannot ignore their understanding of racial double standards enforced by White society that subject Black officials to embarrassing rumors and allegations or to unfair investigations and arrests. Hence, the core argument that follows is that when Black politicians are accused of misconduct, Black Americans process the information with a suspicion that they have been unfairly targeted.

Black Protectionism

Black officials, they surmise, are the subject of law enforcement's watchful eye. In turn, they respond to this perceived state-sanctioned harassment by rallying around their embattled in-group leader and softening the wrath of their evaluations toward them.[38] A rally 'round effect or protectionist response of this kind is not unique to Black Americans. Partisanship, ethnicity, ethnoreligious identity, class, and many other factors have been used to explain why voters discount penalties that we assume *should* be incurred during electoral accountability.[39] While conventional wisdom has held that voters will punish wayward politicians, many are returned to office.[40] The idea that voters punish officials at the ballot box—even when their behavior contravenes the law—is ripe for reconsideration.[41] Few studies have investigated the way race influences Black voters to judge transgressive in-group leaders less harshly than transgressive out-group leaders. I argue that this expression of in-group bias, or what Russell-Brown calls Black protectionism, is motivated by racialized suspicion.[42] If Black people doubt the fairness of the charges brought against an esteemed leader of their group, they are more likely to try to protect the leader.

Harassment of Black Elected Officials

Political scenes in *The Wire* can be seen as a callback to the era of machine-style politics. And while some claim political machines have died out, the "expanding visibility in American cities of Black and Hispanic urban machine, which now face charges of corruption and patronage abuse," suggests it persists.[43] But the power of the machine waned where there was a "growing unwillingness of voters to accept the inducements that it offered."[44] It remained elsewhere because "those who [were] culturally and personally incapacitated in one way or another still value and seek 'favors.'" According to political scientists Edward Banfield and James Q. Wilson, these were the people "least competent to cope with the conditions of modern life," "the poorest of the poor, especially Negro slum dwellers, rooming-housing drifters, criminals, and near criminals."[45] This othering of *who* is captured by the machine's inducements is important to the racialization of corruption. It was not "until many immigrants began to arrive from Europe and settled in American cities," for example, "that the corrupt character of political machines appeared."⁴⁶ It led "many people to suppose that immigrants were substantially responsible for . . . corruption" in municipal government.⁴⁷ And as ethnic immigrants were racialized as White, the characterization and blame was, again, reserved for African Americans.

Even during the Reconstruction era, a period of attempted reunification of the United States following the American Civil War, newly freed Black voters and their politicians were accused of political misdeeds. Historian Eric Foner tell us that "Black participation in Southern public life after 1867 was the most radical development of the Reconstruction years, a massive experiment in interracial democracy without precedent in this or any other country that abolished slavery in the nineteenth century."⁴⁸ The Black community mobilized, and a Black political leadership class emerged. Black officeholders came to occupy political positions at every level of government. In 1870 Mississippi's state legislature selected Hiram Rhodes Revels to serve as the first African American in the U.S. Senate.⁴⁹ But Reconstruction was mired by "political crisis and considerable violence," an experiment many believed had failed. The "charge of corruption did much to discredit" the era, "not simply in the eyes of Southern opponents but in the court of Northern public opinion."⁵⁰ The misuse of public position for private gain was suddenly widespread in several states and "took many forms in the Reconstruction South." "Bribery, either distributed voluntarily by railroads and other enterprises seeking state aid or demanded by local officials," flourished.⁵¹ But it has been revealed, as you will read in the next chapter, that "charges of malfeasance generally arose from hostile sources with a vested interest in exaggerating its scope."⁵² White southerners believed African Americans should have no voice in government nor any authority to rule over them. Take an 1896 speech by Colonel Harry Skinner published in the *Caucasian* newspaper, warning that "the time has not come for the negro to rule and govern the [W]hite people of the state," and that "[they were] not yet qualified for that great work."⁵³

The Case of Black Mayors

"Mayors have a special status in American political mythology."[54] Trailblazing Black mayors, especially, found the mayoralty to be a conduit to Black political power and municipal control.[55] Black political empowerment has been most successful at the municipal level. Black mayors are visible and recognizable in major American cities. And related, cities have been an important site for African Americans political incorporation. That has made local politics a valuable arena to observe racial group conflict,[56] governing performance,[57] and contests for local, racial political power.[58] Last, "[B]lack mayors make an excellent choice simply because there are so many of them."[59] It is cities that have had Black mayors, in fact, that have the biggest challenges with corruption scandals. From a narrative perspective, there are simply more interesting stories to tell about scandals involving local officials for all these reasons. As I suggested earlier, Black mayors and other Black elected officials have not been shy about claiming to have been politically harassed.

Mayor Carl Stokes of Cleveland, Ohio, the first Black mayor of a major American city, recalled how his "own Police Department, all the Cleveland-area papers, . . . the Justice Department, the Internal Revenue Service . . . investigat[ed] [him] because of rumors, allegations and accusations."[60] Tom Bradley, the first Black mayor of Los Angeles, was investigated for alleged financial crimes and professional misconduct by both the city's attorney and later the FBI.[61] However, the California Fair Political Practices Commission declined to prosecute the mayor for violations of ethics laws. The Justice Department likewise ended its probe without an indictment.[62] Newark, New Jersey's, first Black mayor, Kenneth A. Gibson, was not so fortunate after a grand jury returned a 141-count indictment against him that included charges of conspiracy, neglect of office, official misconduct, and other corruption-related crimes.[63] Gibson was later acquitted and beat back "another attempt to discredit Black elected officials."[64] Other first-time Black mayors have been similarly mired in legal jeopardy for alleged misconduct. However, even cities with established Black mayoralties have found themselves in trouble. D.C.'s former mayor Vincent Gray fumed in an op-ed published in the *Washington Post* about how prosecutors ignored the Justice Department's general instruction to guard against "select[ing] the timing of investigative steps or criminal charges for the purpose of affecting any election, or for giving an advantage or disadvantage to any candidate or political party."[65] "My reelection was sabotaged," Gray proclaimed, "and District voters were duped."[66]

I also focus on local government because municipalities were once one of the most important and studied sites of corruption. Now it is often overlooked in political analysis. Previous research, like *Theft of the City: Readings on Corruption in Urban America* and *The Politics of Corruption: Organized Crime in an American City*, and even journalist muckraking like Lincoln Steffens's *The Shame of the Cities* took inventory of the police officer taking a bribe, the ambitious prosecutor, and the council member who had been paid off. Today we take this notion of local corruption for granted, focusing instead on nationalized politics. Yet local officials are

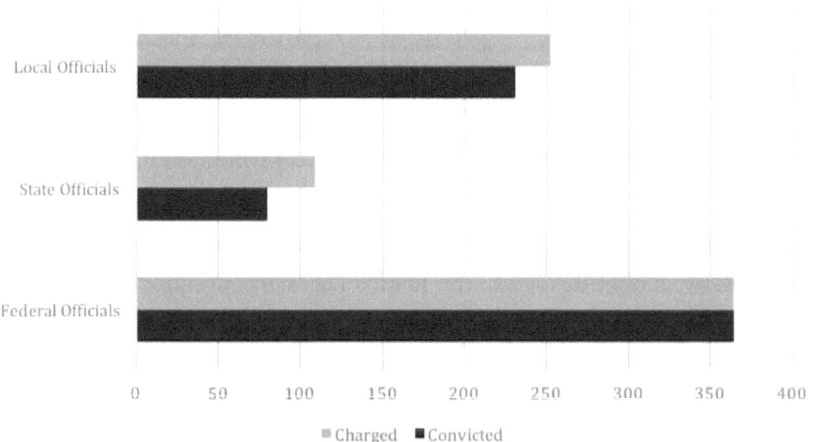

FIGURE I.4. Federal Prosecution of Public Corruption, by Subnational Government, 1970–2000.
Source: Report to Congress on the Activities and Operations of the Public Integrity Section.

the second most likely to be charged or convicted for corruption-related crimes in the United States (figure 1.4). And that makes sense. Stories of misconduct in Chicago are now urban lore. Journalistic endeavors like City Bureau mock it with websites like hasmyaldermanbeenindicted.com. Simply put in your address and learn whether a Chicago alderman has been charged with a crime. The tales of corruption in the fictitious Wincanton, and elsewhere, are memorialized as features of those sites and thus warrant some attention. I add to the roster Black-majority cities like Washington, D.C., and Baltimore and discuss others whose Black elected officials have been implicated.

Why Black Public Opinion

I share the view that the "defining works of White racial attitudes fail to grapple with the complexities of African American political thought and life" and represent a "serious deficiency in the literature on racial politics."[67] New research is finally breaking through to add psychological, emotional, and political texture to the varied Black political experience in the United States. While I do present data on White Americans to test the presence of difference, I do no work to explain White attitudes. This is intentional. The comparative racial case tends to pull attention to what White people think or do in political and racialized environments. What Black American citizens think and do in political and racialized environments is dismissed as obvious, uninteresting, or tangential, if treated at all. As observers muse about the end and future of Black politics, *Marked Men* centers Black public opinion and political psychology to put it under a brighter spotlight because it deserves to be reclaimed and rescued from caricatures about their complicity in corruption and incompetence. In fact, Black voters are especially perceptive about corruption. The data in table 1.2 show that most Black voters believe a police officer accepting bribe to not write a traffic ticket or someone stealing time on the government payroll is extremely corrupt behavior. Other conduct is at least somewhat corrupt.

TABLE I.2. Black Perceptions of Corruption

	M	SD	Extremely Corrupt %
A police officer accepted money not to write a traffic ticket on a speeding driver	4.13	1.12	53
A citizen claimed government benefits to which he or she was not entitled	4.05	1.16	49
A government official gave a contract to a contributor without considering other contractors	4.03	1.17	49
An elected official raised campaign funds while inside his or her government office	3.67	1.29	37
Someone on the government payroll did not work for the pay	4.12	1.18	55
An official recommended an out-of-work friend for a government job	3.25	1.39	27
Voters supported a candidate for office in return for a promise to fix potholes on their streets	3.14	1.43	24
An elected official with many wealthy backers supported a tax cut that largely benefited the rich	3.96	1.24	49

Source: National Black Voter Project (2019).

But there is room for misinterpretation. For example, some might agree with political scientist Ralph J. Bunche's review of Harold Gosnell's *Negro Politicians*. In it he wrote that "to say that the Negro politician was often no better than the average [W]hite politician of Chicago, is to damn him. Certainly it is no praiseworthy achievement for Negroes to supplement the already sordid pages of American municipal politics." Before that he writes that it "is only a left-handed compliment to say . . . that corruption and ballot thievery are as common in [W]hite as in colored neighborhoods" or to "present an implicit apology for petty, grafting, self-seeking Negro politicians by explaining that they merely adopted the 'general patterns of behavior' of the [W]hite politicians." Bunche is not wrong on this count. Rising corruption in public programs increases income inequality and poverty.[68] Both could have a disproportionate effect on African Americans. I do not want to understate the cost of malfeasance in government or its consequences on Black communities. However, Bunche's call for Black leaders to be engaged in a more respectable politics overlooks how little that caution has mattered to a political order set on embarrassing and discrediting them by charging false misdeeds. Still, *Marked Men* should not be read as a defense of wayward Black politicians or contented Black voters. It is an effort to rescue Black political behavior from caricature and to demonstrate that racist double standards do matter to how Black voters understand these circumstances, despite the disapproval of scholars like Bunche.

Defining Corruption and Scandal

I must clarify two important points and provide some definitions. While I use the terms "scandal" and "corruption" interchangeably, the reader should know that "not all scandals are corruption scandals, and not all instances of corruption give rise to scandal."[69] Some misdeeds are personally embarrassing but not illegal. And some behavior is legally prohibited but does not raise much fuss. Nepotism, defined as "the practice among those with power or influence of favoring relatives or friends, especially by giving them jobs," is one example. Other conduct might seem corrupt but is in fact legal, which has been described as the appearance of impropriety, honest graft, and legal corruption. There is considerable academic and legal disagreement about the nature, scope, or meaning of all the related terms. For example, legalistic definitions of public corruption sometimes focus on the conduct of public officials. But that does not always mean those who are elected to office. For example, federal bribery statutes define a "public official" as "a Member of Congress, Delegate, or Resident Commissioner . . . or an officer or employee or person acting for or on behalf of the United States, or any department, agency, or branch of Government . . . in any official function, under or by authority of any such department, agency, or branch of Government, or a juror."

The debate over terms is interesting and wide-ranging but not so relevant here. For the purposes of this book, let it suffice that we are interested in political corruption scandals—illegal actions or events involving a recognized political leader or aspiring leader, elected or appointed. I borrow from Thompson's description of the simplest model of scandal.[70] The basic elements are that "a concealed act of transgression is publicly disclosed or publicly alleged to have occurred, and the public disclosure and/or allegations elicit public expression of disapproval."[71] In our case, these are transgressions of law and are thus crimes. A crime is an offense that may be prosecuted and punished by the state. Public corruption, misuse of public office for private gain, is one such crime.[72] Multiple wrongful acts fill the catalogue of corruption-related crimes. A mayor or city council member taking a bribe, for instance, represents the classic act of corruption by public officials.

Bribery is the "offer or promise to give anything of value to any public official with intent to influence an official act" and is illegal at every level of government. The offense requires there be (1) quid pro quo, one thing (of value) exchanged for another; (2) an official act; and (3) corrupt intent. Illegal gratuities are monies "given or accepted 'for or because of' an official act." If bribery intends to influence, gratuities seek to reward future of past official action.

Elected officials are thought to have a fiduciary duty to the public. When politicians put their decisions up for sale in this way, they deprive constituents of outcomes that are in their best interest and their right to honest services. Hence, public officials can be charged with honest services fraud when they breach that duty.

In later chapters I describe some of these crimes by quoting from indictments, formal documents used to charge people with criminal offenses. You will see in some of those cases that the charges include mail and wire fraud and violations of the Hobbs Act and the Racketeer Influenced and Corrupt Organizations Act (RICO). Most common is mail and wire fraud, schemes to defraud using "the mails or interstate wires in furtherance of that scheme."

Not all unethical or illegal behavior by public officials is public corruption. Adultery can lead to scandals as far as transgressing values and moral codes. But sex scandals do not rise to the level of problem described here. Such behavior, while repugnant to some, is not a crime. Rumor and gossip about personal indiscretions do little to influence racialized suspicion, as I demonstrate in chapter 2. Drug use is decidedly more controversial and satisfies all of Thompson's characteristics of scandal.[73] For example, drug-related activity (1) is a transgression of the law and often done discreetly and (2) is concealed. In the case of Marion Barry, the subject of a later chapter, the (3) public reveal (or disclosure) was followed by (4) public allegations of wrongdoing and (5) strong public disapproval. In chapter 3 we will see how a drug possession scandal influenced racialized suspicion in Washington, D.C. When referring to any of the many corruption- and scandal-related crimes, I switch between words like "graft," "misconduct," "misdeeds," "malfeasance," "impropriety," "wrongdoing," and "transgression" to vary the terminology describing a scandalized politician's behavior.

Plan for the Book

I have explained how perceptions of corruption frame how we think about the political system. In the next chapter I continue with an examination of why race is a fundamental factor that shapes public opinion of corruption with a discussion of how racial violence and political harassment have impacted Black political thought and, more specifically, Black protectionism. Are Black voters suspicious about allegations of misconduct leveled against Black political leaders? What are the consequences of that suspicion, if any, related to Blacks' political judgments about corruption scandals? The rest of this book is devoted to answering these two questions. Chapter 2 is the first attempt to illustrate that there is a racial politics of scandal, consistent with the *theory of racialized suspicion*, using data from a survey experiment. In chapter 3 I test the theory against the real-world backdrop of the highest profile political scandal involving a Black elected official—the 1990 drug arrest of D.C. mayor Marion Barry Jr.—using survey data from the *Washington Post*'s Mayor Barry Pre-trial Poll. By triangulating these data, I can overcome the "overreliance on surveys and observational methods to show a correlation but no follow-up using experiments."[74] Both methodologies generate data that support the notion that African Americans process information about political ethics with a filter of suspicion, and this can influence evaluations of candidates at the ballot box. I conclude with a summary of the findings, comment on their limits, and discuss issues related to Black political leadership, specifically its failure in this context. Last, just as this book opened with a prologue focused on one American city (Philadelphia), it ends with an epilogue that addresses another (Baltimore), with an account of how Black women mayors there have fared in terms of corruption scandals.

1

Perilous Negro Rule

Framing Black Politics as Corrupt

This is a country for White men, and by God, as long as
I am president, it shall be a government for White men.
    —Andrew Johnson

Black political leadership has always been portrayed as precarious. In D. W. Griffith's *The Birth of a Nation*, Black freedmen take power by rigging elections and intimidating White voters, and newly elected Black state legislators are depicted imbibing whisky and eating chicken, with bare feet kicked up on desks in the sacred chambers of a state legislature. Popular depictions of Black presidents on screen are often in the disaster genre, according to communications scholar Phillip Cunningham, while others are in comedies.¹ About thirteen African American men have acted the role of commander in chief across fourteen movies.² In eleven of those films the president is in charge during world-ending natural disasters or terrorist events. Films like *Deep Impact*, *White House Down*, and *Angel Has Fallen* and popular television shows like *24* conjure up images of chaos and ruin under Black leadership.

    Comedic takes on presidential politics are similarly imaginative, most bending to the stereotypes of what White America would expect or fear from a Black executive. Richard Pryor's portrayal of the first Black president on *The Richard Pryor Show* is one example.³ The skit depicts Pryor as the fortieth president of the United States, taking questions in the White House's press briefing room. The back-and-forth with journalists evolves from standard fare to absurd, with hostility building toward the White journalists in the audience. Pryor's response to the White journalists is initially made to sound highbrow but is in fact nonsensical, code switching designed to "sound White."[4] Yet his responses to questions about race and to the Black journalists specifically are more authentic, revealing a president with an unapologetic sense of racial group consciousness. One memorable exchange in the script includes a reporter from the Black magazine *Jet* asking whether Pryor, as president, was considering Huey Newton, cofounder of the Black Panther Party, to be director of the FBI. President Pryor responds with an emphatic yes, noting that Newton, once a target of the agency's vast surveillance program, was the "best qualified" for the post because of his intimate interaction with the institution.

Another Black journalist from *Ebony* magazine rises and greets Pryor with the Arabic greeting "as-salamu alaykum," or "peace be unto you," to which Pryor responds in kind, "Wa 'alaykumu s-salam."[5] The exchange might be interpreted as random, except that its political and racial meaning in the U.S. context is important. For example, it is not only the standard salutation for many Muslims across the world but also a culturally recognizable one in Black communities because it is also the typical greeting of the Nation of Islam (NOI), the Black socioreligious group to which Malcolm X once belonged. Consider that the FBI described the NOI as a Muslim Cult of Islam "born of a chimerical resentment against the supremacy of the White race and nourished on a persistent advocacy of rebellion against its civilization."[6] The FBI was especially worried about its "rebellious tendencies" and sense of racial superiority. "While the majority of Negros in the United States [did] not rush to join the NOI," one FBI file noted, "many seem[ed] to respect it."[7] The exchange portends the comingling of Black institutionalists with elements of Black radical politics and raises Whites' suspicion about the former's sympathies. These concerns came to life more than four decades later when Barack Obama, then-candidate for president of the United States, had to denounce the endorsement of Minister Louis Farrakhan, leader of the NOI, as well as his longtime pastor Jeremiah Wright, whom Republicans accused of espousing anti-American sentiments.

It did not help that many Republicans believed Obama, who became the first Black president of the United States, was Muslim.[8] The rumors and innuendo about Obama's faith and birthplace were so ridiculous that in 2008 the *New Yorker* ran a political cartoon on its front page showing the Illinois state senator dressed like terrorist Osama bin Laden and his wife, Michelle, wearing an afro and military gear, while fist bumping in the Oval Office.[9] The cover sought to satirize the way many White Americans were propagating a politics of fear related to a Black couple in the White House, by invoking images of Islamic extremism and the Black Panther Party, a political organization for Black power founded in 1966. And yet, ironically, Obama could not express the anger or resentment that either of those illustrations implied. "Ever fearful of channeling a [B]lack anger that has long been stereotyped as dangerous and uncontrollable," Obama was careful to avoid reinforcing stereotypes of the angry Black man.[10] So much so that Jordan Peele and Keegan-Michael Key, a sketch comedy duo, mocked this dynamic in a sketch in which a cool, calm, and emotionless Obama, played by Peele, is contrasted against Luther, his anger translator, portrayed by Key, who communicates the anger and frustration that then-President Obama is feeling but cannot express.[11]

Art imitates life. But perhaps not in the way we often might think. The small number of Black elected officials in the United States has meant writers, actors, and comedians have had to imagine the character of a political leader pulled from Black life. And many have imagined public service that is far from exemplary, Black leaders who are incompetent and corrupt. As political scientist Wilbur Rich observes, when "a Black politician is called 'incompetent,' the label has a better chance of sticking than it does with a [W]hite politician" because it is consistent with the White public's stereotypes about Black politicians. Moreover, "when an officeholder is labeled 'incompetent' this characterization has to be documented and sustained by stories of mistakes, misjudgments, and mismanagement."[12] Consider one final example from the comedy genre, as provided by comedian Dave Chappelle's depiction of an African American version of President George W. Bush, or "Black Bush," a combative, profanity-using executive engaged in malfeasance. These fictional takes are harmless in the longer view but underscore how Black elected officials have been cast as menacing and incapable of good governance or effective deeds, effectively marking them as political boogeyman. That these comedic sketches were performed or written by Black creatives should not obscure the fact that they are also representations of the White imagination and concerns about so-called Negro rule.

One aspect of these fictional abstractions hidden in these art forms is the very real ways Black political elite have been subjected to various forms of "Whitelash"—"backlash by White racists against Black civil rights advances"—because of White perceptions about the incompetence of Black people and their propensity toward crime. These portrayals long precede Pryor's, Chappelle's, or Key and Peele's comedic takes, as was evident in southern newspapers during and after Reconstruction when emancipated Blacks began earning political positions. Law professor Terry Smith describes Whitelash as the "reactionary impulse of many White voters toward racial equality movements and societal shifts they perceive as excessive," like Black political incorporation and power. The election and appointment of Black political candidates (i.e., Negro rule) was an especially provocative threat to the believed natural order of racial inequality, which only "Whites should control" in terms of the "pace at which it is dismantled."[13] And for some the Whitelash is ongoing, no longer by way of extralegal violence but through state-sanctioned criminal investigation and prosecution for corruption.

This is an extraordinarily contentious accusation. Black elected officials in the post–civil rights era say that they have long been victimized by political harassment, efforts that, they say, are designed to embarrass and discredit them as Black leaders. Good government reformers and prosecutors reliably disagree, claiming that the evidence is followed only where it leads. But on some level the grievances of Black leaders beset by scandal are not at all meant for their accusers. The real audience is their primary constituents—Black voters—to whom they look for empathy and relief. We should not be surprised that Black elites proffer messages to "invoke racial references because they want to defend themselves against what they see as a racist attack lodged against them" given the historical record of government abuse.[14] Further, because Black citizens are the intended audience, we must consider whether they similarly perceive of the harassment claimed by the Black political elite. So far, however, I have commented on only the latter. African American leaders especially, and thoughtful Black constituents as well, believe that the government and its criminal legal system are uneven, prompting suspicion about allegations of impropriety.

Racial Politics of Scandal

Black Americans face the possibility that a Black public official has engaged in misconduct and the suspicion that the state is racially motivated in their pursuit of the official. I argue here that the Black public responds to this dilemma with racialized suspicion, such that they question whether White-dominated institutions are attempting to embarrass and discredit esteemed members of their racial in-group (i.e., the Black elite). The theoretical perspective I develop in this chapter—racialized suspicion—focuses on how this psychological process influences Black attitudes and behavior. I propose that racialized suspicion is an individual-level factor that can help explain the extent to which the Black public engages in electoral punishment for corruption or in Black protectionism. Consider Thompson's perspective that "political ethics consists of judgments or criteria for making judgments" and that those "criteria should be conceived as a set of factors that citizens consider as deliberate."[15] Racialized suspicion acts as an internal criterion for Black Americans because they worry about whether the government is engaged in untoward behavior to undermine the whole of their community. As James Hilton and colleagues explain, "Suspicious perceivers concern themselves with a different set of questions."[16] Black Americans concern themselves with the question of whether something was done by deceit or trickery to compromise or frame someone Black and important.

What do they do with this suspicion? Does their interpretation of harassment influence their judgment about the consequences for corruption? If Steven Fein and his colleagues are right about the redirecting effects of suspicion, particularly under the circumstances of arbitrarily induced suspicion, the mobilizing effect of racialized suspicion may be most pronounced. One outcome is the Black protectionism described by Katheryn Russell-Brown, in which Black communities rally around esteemed members of the group.[17] These circumstances produce judgments that are less harsh, or what some social psychologists call a transgression credit.[18] This means that Black people discount negative judgments for Black political leaders who stand accused of wrongdoing.

The goal of this chapter then is twofold. First, it takes a historical perspective to identify the factual grounds on which Black leaders have claimed harassment. I focus in brief on two important eras of Black political ascent—the end of Reconstruction and the post–civil rights era. In the racial context, these periods present clear examples of how the Black political elite have become targeted people and marked men. While racist violence defined the method used in one era, charges of lawbreaking have proven to be the primary tool of the other. The objective, however, is to demonstrate how and why suspicion is aroused within the Black body politic. I do this by recounting the harassment concerns expressed by Black officials at every level of government. In addition, while I rely on evidence from other scholars to support the claim of racial disproportionately in corruption-related probes, I illustrate that the federal government's attention to state and local public corruption coincides with the emergence of the Black political class in state and local government by the 1970s. One objection might be that the overlay of this timeline is purely coincidental.

The history of government action against African Americans makes this point unlikely and therefore moot. Further, to be suspicious is to *feel* or *believe* that someone or something is engaging in an unlawful, dishonest, or potentially inappropriate action. Indeed, it is difficult to imagine that the African American public will trust any indictment of judgment on political corruption coming from an institutional agency that is viewed so cynically. That the target of any of these actions may be Black political leaders, ostensibly tasked with advancing the cause of their people but who stand accused of wrongdoing by law enforcement, influences how African Americans process and respond to information about alleged misconduct.

Fearing "Negro Rule"

When Republican Tim Scott of South Carolina was elected in 2014, many observers remarked that he was the first African American to be elected to the U.S. Senate from the South since Reconstruction.[19] But it was Democrat Raphael Warnock of Georgia who "became the first Black Southern senator in 150 years to be elected by African American voters" in 2021.[20] Regardless, we take for granted why there were no Black senators in the South for more than a century. The reason parsimoniously summarized here is that Whites "were appalled when [B]lack men took over positions [they] previously held" before the Civil War—"as alderman, magistrates, deputy sheriffs, police offer, and registers of deeds" during Reconstruction.[21] It was during this turbulent era following the Civil War (1865–77) that "scores of newly-emancipated Black men exercised their right to vote and organized campaigns to run for elected office."[22] Following the adoption of the Reconstruction Amendments—the Thirteenth, Fourteenth, and Fifteenth—the Black community organized rallies, meetings, and petition drives to demand the enforcement of their legal and political rights, particularly the ability to vote. According to historian Eric Foner, "an estimated 2,000 [B]lack men served in some kind of elective office during that era."[23]

"At the same time that African Americans were participating in government in unprecedented numbers, many [W]hite elected leaders worked to undermine and substantially diminish Black political power."[24] In Wilmington, North Carolina, "Democrats maneuvered to undermine the newly won [B]lack voted by elimination the popular election of county commissioners" and gerrymandered the city's Black wards to dilute its power.[25] Toward the end of Reconstruction, "many [W]hite Southerners were calling for 'Redemption'—the return of [W]hite supremacy and the removal of rights for [B]lacks—instead of Reconstruction."[26] And they focused their efforts by using the "well-refined strategy of racist demagoguery perfected by the [W]hite supremacists of previous generations," including the "time-tested tactic of frightening [W]hite votes by warning of the twin menace of [B]lack suffrage and Black beast rapist—or what was called 'Crying nigger.'"[27] Historically, these strategies were employed because "the Black male ha[d] become metaphorical, a way of personifying social and historical forces, of painting a pariah's face on the problems of drugs, disease, and crime."[28]

Twin 1: Black Beast Rapists

Newspapers like the Raleigh-based *News and Observer* played a critical role in spreading this gospel of fear. In 1898, for example, political cartoonist Norman Jennett published a series of illustrations in the paper depicting the terror and menacing circumstances of so-called Negro rule. Jennett's cartoons "reinforced notions of the 'honest White man'" and "propagated stereotypes of African Americans through images of Zip Coon, savage beasts, and parasitic vampires; and questioned the public safety of White women, subsequently raising the threat of miscegenation and rape."[29] In mid-August that year Jennett inked two cartoons depicting Jim Young, a Black politician and head of the Committee on Education at the Blind Institute for White Children in Raleigh, inspecting the living quarters at the school (figures 1.1 and 1.2). One caption reads that "the power conferred upon a negro politician in an institution in which most of the teachers and pupils are White ladies" (figure 1.1). Implicit in Jennett's cartoon is that the political power of Black men is a direct threat to White people, especially White women, whose sanctity, if left unprotected, would be imperiled by these deviant Black men. According to art historian Rachel Marie-Crane Williams, "Jennett always positioned [B]lack office holders as morally, physically, or intellectually inferior" and depicted them "as incompetent buffoons or, worse yet, in the case of Jim Young, as predators or children dressed as soldiers."[30] The documentary *MLK/FBI* includes commentary from historian Donna Murch, who declares that this view of deviance is one of the "core justifications for preventing Black male suffrage" and links the "representation of Black political aspiration" to "sexual threat," the pretext for their "murder, exclusion, discrimination and incarceration."[31]

FIGURE 1.1. Norman Jennett, "Jim Young, the Negro Politician, at Head of the Committee on Education at the Blind Institution for Women and Children at Raleigh." *News and Observer*, August 18, 1898.

FIGURE 1.2. Norman Jennett, "Jim Young, the Negro Politician, Inspecting Apartments in White Blind Institution." *News and Observer*, August 18, 1898.

Twin 2: Menace of Black Suffrage

White citizens were also insulted that Black freedmen could sit in judgment of them. Black people had authority on legal bodies, they complained, and could use their roles as magistrates to interrogate, inspect, and punish honest White men and women. In 1901, one contributor to the *Charlotte-Observer* wrote that Whites in Craven County, North Carolina, "had been thrown from power and low class of [W]hite men and negro politicians put in their stead." What could happen to Whites under this arrangement was a worrisome prospect, because they believed "good [W]hite men were not made to be ruled by . . . incompetent" politicians of the wrong class or race.[32] Resentful and contemptuous of Black political leaders, one contributor to the *Caucasian* believed "it should be emphatically recorded in the mind of every citizen that these negro judges of election constitute part of a jury who sits in judgement on the liberties and rights of the [W]hite voters in every county in which they are appointed. . . . They are judges of the exercise of the highest privilege and right known to the American citizenships," the writer exclaimed. "Their appointment as judges enables them to 'dominate' and dictate the action of [W]hite voters, and to pass judgement on their fitness and qualification as electors and free citizens."[33] And worse, Black officeholders had "shown less capacity for government than any other race of people," according to President Andrew Johnson in one message to Congress. "No independent government of any form has ever been successful in their hands."

In William Dunning's retelling of the Reconstruction era, moreover, "the decade when the Negroes were ushered into political life, from 1867 to 1877, was probably the most corrupt decade in the history of the United States, and of all parts of the United States."[34] Dunning argued that the "exploitation of the poverty, ignorance, credulity, and general childishness of the Blacks was supplemented, on occasion, by deliberate and high-handed fraud. Stuffing of the boxes with illegal ballots, and

FIGURE 1.3. Norman Jennett, "A Warning." *News and Observer*, August 30, 1898.

FIGURE 1.4. Norman Jennett, "The Vampire That Hovers over North Carolina (Negro Rule)." *News and Observer*, September 27, 1898.

manipulation of the figures in making the count, were developed into serious arts," and that "the negroes who rose to prominence and leadership were very frequently of a type which acquired and practiced the tricks and knavery rather than the useful arts of politics."[35] Fears about Black politicians and tales about their indecency and political malfeasance were widespread. Political cartoonist Norman Jennett illustrated this sense of despair in his 1898 image titled "The Vampire That Hovers over North Carolina (Negro Rule)." The graphic includes a Black vampire whose wingspan reads "Negro Rule," while the figure overwhelms a ballot box in monstrous bodily form, its claws grasping White men and women (figure 1.4). According to Foner,

> For many decades, historians viewed Reconstruction as the lowest point in the American experience, a time of corruption and misgovernment presided over by unscrupulous carpetbaggers from the North, ignorant former slaves, and traitorous scalawags ([W]hite Southerners who

supported the new governments in the South). Mythologies about [B]lack officeholders formed a central pillar of this outlook. Their alleged incompetence and venality illustrated the larger "crime" of Reconstruction—placing power in the hands of a race incapable of participating in American democracy.[36]

However, other historians of Reconstruction refute that Black politicians during the era were uniquely corrupt.[37] Richard Bailey points out that while the Reconstruction era is "looked upon variously as a period of Black radical domination and as a period of corruption and debauchery," "in fact, it was neither."[38] Norman P. Andrews suggests that the "charge that the men who were elected to office by the Negroes were always of the most debased and degenerate type is untrue" but that "the charge of corruption laid at the door of the Negro carpetbagger governments is to a large extent true."[39] However, Andrews continues,

> The corruption resulted largely from the work of the interlopers from the North and the "scalawags," using the Negroes to reach their own personal ends. In some of this corruption, however, the Negro was an apt scholar and freely participated. The Negroes were not as a whole prepared for the political privileges which were vouchsafed to them, and they were to a large extent under the wrong sort of leadership. It is equally true, however, that governments were corrupt throughout the United States at this period. The Reconstruction period was one of corruption and if the Negro governments were of a lower order than a few others, they were not far out of accord with the times. The [W]hite people, who assumed control of the government on overthrowing the Reconstruction regime, instituted in several States a rule of corruption surpassing even that of their predecessors.[40]

Pointing out that corruption was widespread across the country and transcending party lines did little to rescue the reputation of Reconstruction as a failed experiment in empowerment. Moreover, "charges of malfeasance generally arose from hostile sources with a vested interest in exaggerating its scope."[41] For example, sociologist W. E. B. Du Bois accused historians of a "deliberate attempt so to change the facts of history that the story will make pleasant reading for Americans.... White historians have ascribed the faults and failures of Reconstruction to Negro ignorance and corruption," he wrote in *Black Reconstruction*. "But the Negro insists that it was Negro loyalty and the Negro vote alone that restored the South to the Union; established the new democracy, both for white and Black, and instituted the public schools."[42]

No matter the truth of the charge, it nonetheless establishes the political function of the "bad nigger" trope. Doing so constructs legitimizing myths—"values, attitudes, beliefs, causal attributions, and ideologies that provide moral and intellectual justification for social practices that either increase, maintain, or decrease levels of social inequality among social groups."[43] Lawrence Levine captures how this works in describing the Black bandit, of African American lore, as "pure force, pure vengeance; explosions of fury and futility." These were men who were "not given any socially redeeming characteristics," he writes, "simply because in them there was no hope of social redemption."[44] This made it easier to visit violence upon them or people like them. Extralegal violence against Blacks in the Reconstruction South was so widespread federal troops had to provide protection, especially at polling places, before they withdrew in 1877, marking the end of Reconstruction. In addition, racial violence was more likely to be carried out against Reconstruction's Black lawmakers in places with higher taxes.[45] The racial violence of November 10, 1898, in Wilmington, North Carolina, was the culminating event that "took place within the context of an ongoing statewide political campaign based on [W]hite supremacy."[46] An armed "overthrow of the legitimately elected municipal government" left many African Americans dead, without property and political standing, as well as against disenfranchised.[47] A "vibrant Wilmington in which African Americans played a vital role in the city's economic and political life" was left devastated by a "riot [that] followed a model of white invasion into [B]lack neighborhoods, loss of [B]lack property, and the deaths of Black citizens plus the creation of a silent African American population."[48]

Surveilling and Subversion

When violence was no longer tenable, methods of oppression were tailored to suit modernizing politics.[49] The primary example for the rest of the chapter is the FBI, which Thomas Emerson describes as the political police. A "substantial proportion of the Bureau's enormous energies and manpower have been devoted to watching over or influencing the political activities of American citizens."[50] According to historian Mark Ellis, "Investigations of Black leaders had begun in 1917, amid rumors that German spies were trying to foment a race war in the south."[51] Among those watched in the pre–civil rights era were Ida B. Wells, W. E. B. Du Bois, A. Philip Randolph, and others considered dissident, subversive, or sympathetic to the communist cause. One of the earliest incidents occurred when J. Edgar Hoover, who would become the FBI's famous autocratic director, set out to destroy Black nationalist leader Marcus Garvey.[52] For example, in 1922, Garvey was charged with mail fraud and convicted one year later after the government alleged a "scheme to defraud" by causing a letter to be mailed to a potential investor in the Black Star Line, "even though the Black Star Line at the time had no ships, was near ruin, and would never obtain any more ships or return to solvency." But "[u]ltimately," writes Justin Hansford, "the unjust trial and conviction of Marcus Garvey was an attempt to silence and kill the powerful voice of an outsider."[53]

The FBI's most serious anti-Black counterintelligence operations came around 1956, with the initiation of the counterintelligence program (COINTELPRO), which was directed to "expose, disrupt, misdirect, discredit, and otherwise neutralize the activities of Black nationalists, hate-type organizations and groupings, their leadership, spokesmen, membership, and supporters," with FBI agents encouraged to "inspire action in instances where circumstances warrant."[54] The FBI relied on a range of detection techniques, including various forms of physical and electronic surveillance, as well as deceit. Much has already been reported about the files kept on Martin Luther King Jr.,[55] for example, though much less has been reported about the FBI's activities related to other Black political and cultural figures.[56] There are too many examples to recount here. Nonetheless, COINTELPRO represents a significant means of marking in the civil rights era because it subjected many Black Americans to surveillance, which was used to investigate and prosecute on the one hand, and to embarrass and discredit on the other.

At an organizational level, the FBI's investigations often included surveillance, the cultivation of informants, and interviewing friends, family, and known associates. That was, in a way, standard operating procedure. What was not were the extralegal methods employed to capture their mark. For example, the FBI established cohorts of racial informants in American cities to report back on activities of Black people in the ghetto, leaked sensitive material to the press about Black leaders, and harassed their targets in a variety of ways, including investigating their friends and family.

Means and Methods

I should address the means and methods by which investigations occur and provide some rationale for why they give the appearance of impropriety. This refers to intelligence collection, that is, an investigative means for uncovering information about misconduct. To do this, law enforcement often relies on three techniques to collect intelligence: (1) communication intelligence (COMINT), (2) human intelligence (HUMINT), and (3) signals intelligence (SIGINT).[57] The first involves intercepting communications like mail that might involve information about the commission of a crime. The second is employing an informant, a person strategically placed within legally murky contexts, to assist federal authorities with their investigations. And the third, SIGINT, covers those bugs or wiretaps placed in offices or on phone lines to listen to the conversations of others. These covert methods have been the source of some controversy because of how they were used to spy on domestic targets.

FBI director J. Edgar Hoover and other field agents used every covert tactic available to surveil and harass Black activists and groups. The problem was so widespread that in 1975 the U.S. Senate established a committee to "conduct an investigation and study of governmental operations with respect to intelligence activities and the extent, if any, to which illegal, improper, or unethical activities were engaged in by any agency of the Federal Government."[58] Overall, the commission found that the "tactics used against Americans often risked and sometimes caused serious emotional, economic, or physical damage." This should be understood in the context and legacy of Hoover's FBI and its expansive surveillance of Black academics, athletes, clergy, and politicians who took critical positions against the government on race issues. If these individuals had a national reputation or were regarded as racial group leaders, the FBI would gather or fabricate information on their "unsavory backgrounds."[59] In other words, COINTELPRO was designed "to expose, disrupt, misdirect, discredit, or otherwise neutralize" Black power groups and their "leadership, spokesmen, members, and supporters."[60]

Even so, methods of surveillance are subject to much debate. Who should be surveilled? On whose authority? For how long? Under what circumstances? Where can one be reasonably or unreasonably subject to this inconspicuous but otherwise intrusive practice? In the context of political corruption, one method—undercover sting operations—is designed quite deliberately to test the honesty of public officials. If the FBI wanted to know whether a city's mayor or councilor was on the take, an undercover agent might offer him a bribe or somehow elicit him to engage in an illegal act. This method is commonplace in investigating corruption-related crimes. Yet it requires deception, some level of coercion that might not have otherwise existed without law enforcement's intervention.

Investigating and Prosecuting Corruption

Marked men are targeted by these methods in the modern political era. But measuring political harassment is difficult to do.[61] The covert function of surveillance is such that targets seldom know intelligence is being collected on them. Additionally, not all investigations lead to a formal accusation or arrest of officials suspected of wrongdoing. Congressman William Lacy Clay, former chair of the Congressional Black Caucus (CBC), lamented in his autobiography for instance that "the most common tactic used to ruin careers . . . was to undertake a series of probes into their political and personal lives."[62] Coleman Young, the first Black mayor of Detroit, complained that despite being under investigation for more than four decades, he had never been indicted for any crime.

Add to this that prosecutors are "the most significant [actors] in the war on state and local government corruption."[63] They brought a "zeal and sense of righteous outrage in their job." Criminal syndicates tried to attack them; others tried to pay them off. But some of the prosecutors were political types, electorally ambitious. The rise of the political prosecutor has made some worry that prosecutors could be tempted to pursue high-profile cases simply to advance their careers.[64] This is a problem in view of legal scholar Arthur Maass's charge that prosecutors succumb to the mentality of the criminal law profession—"to lock up bad people as an expression of public morality more than formulate and implement a public policy related to the integrity of public institutions."[65] Unfortunately, prosecutorial discretion has helped fuel a process of mass incarceration that disproportionately affects Black Americans.

In criminal matters it is difficult to deny the importance of the prosecutor, who leads the investigation, makes charging decisions, recommends bail, helps select the jury, and prosecutes the case. Even Cleveland's first Black mayor Carl Stokes warned others to "mind the great power of a . . . prosecutor."[66] "He can do almost anything," the mayor wrote, "from wiretapping to surveillance to the getting of records. . . . He can get people indicted almost at will. . . . He may not be able to convict you, but he can sure as hell get you indicted." "And even if he can't prove his case, the public stigma of the indictment is enough." These sentiments were echoed by scandalized mayors in other cities like Detroit and Washington, D.C. Nothing had happened in those governments that had not happened long before in another. But those mayors felt the heat; Detroit's Coleman Young mused that the U.S. attorney for Detroit, Leonard Gilman, "salivated at the thought of nailing [his] Black ass."[67] Washington, D.C.'s, former mayor, Vincent Gray, recounted how the prosecutor "brought the kingpin of a political crime operation into court" and "announced that he'd struck a plea deal—and at a news conference, thereafter, suggested that I was a co-conspirator and would soon be indicted."[68] But that indictment would never come, and the case was unceremoniously dropped several months after Gray was defeated in the Democratic primary for mayor.

Local Political Corruption

It is not just these idiosyncratic cases that raise alarms. Other technical legal issues have brought about concerns about the federal authority of

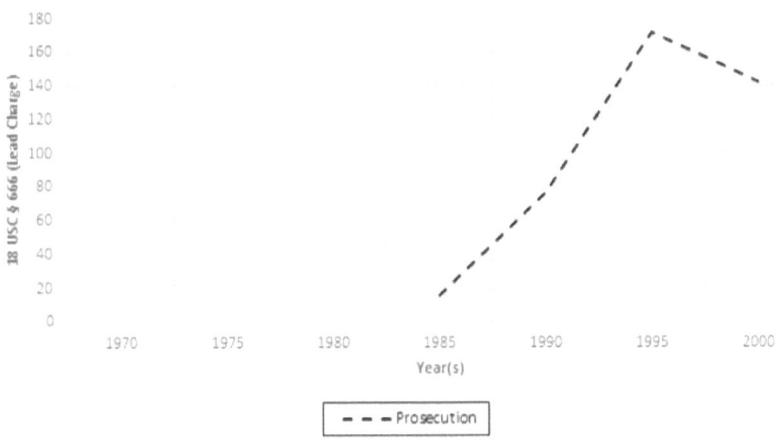

FIGURE 1.5. 18 USC § 666 as Lead Charge in Prosecution, by Year.
Source: Transactional Records Access Clearinghouse (TRAC).

prosecutors as well. Federal prosecutors have no clear statutory authority, some legal scholars argue, to criminalize bribes paid to state or local officials.[69] And what is more curious is that the federal government devoted few resources to combatting state and local public corruption prior to the 1970s.[70] In 1984, however, Congress took actions to make it a crime for state and local officials to embezzle, steal, or obtain by fraud or bribery anything of value from a subnational agency in receipt of federal grant monies worth $10,000 or more.[71] The criminal statute 18 U.S.C. 666 of the U.S. Code includes every American state and many of its cities. For context, federal grants to state and local governments were estimated to be $749 billion in 2019.[72] And importantly, not only have section 666 charges increased since the law was enacted (figure 1.5), but state and local officials are most likely to be charged. And the alleged theft need not be from the exact program the government funds, simply in the jurisdiction in receipt of federal money. These broad sweeps have allowed federal prosecutors to remake case law. Criminal statutes that were once used to prosecute organized crime—for example, the Hobbs Act, Mail and Wire Fraud, and Racketeering Influenced and Corrupt Organizations Act (RICO)—were now the legal tools of anticorruption efforts.

The broad discretion enjoyed by the prosecutor meant that law enforcement could descend upon any local entity in receipt of federal funds.[73] The number of state and local officials prosecuted for public corruption began to rise by the early 1970s. We can observe this upward trend in figure 1.5, with the number of prosecutions of state and local officials over time. Local public officials are second to federal officials in being prosecuted for political malfeasance (figure 1.6).

Race and Local Corruption

What motivated this attention to local corruption in the 1970s? While the answer is unclear, one obvious explanation is that attention to state and local public corruption is correlated with the emergence of a Black political class in state legislatures and city halls. Conduct that was once

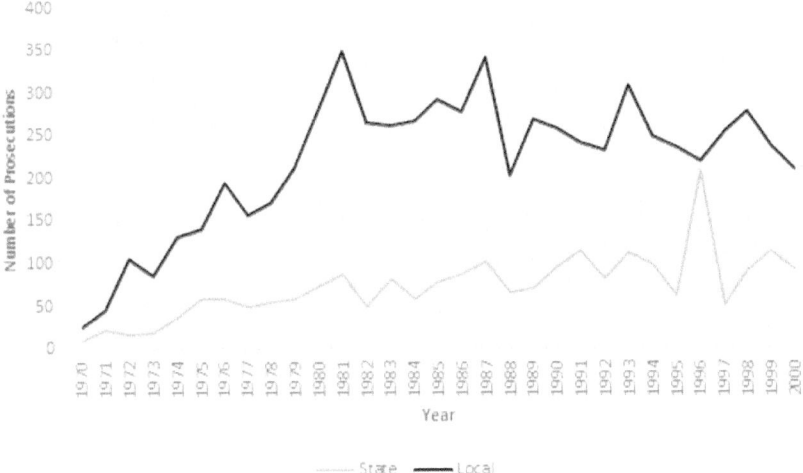

FIGURE 1.6. Federal Prosecution of Public Corruption, by Subnational Government (1970–2000).
Source: Transactional Records Access Clearinghouse (TRAC).

seen as normal, even expected, was now cast as corrupt when Black political leaders took the helm. Consider figure 1.7, which shows the number of Black officials elected to state, local, and educational posts. More than five hundred Blacks were elected to municipal government by the 1970s. That number tripled by 1975. There were only 26 prosecutions of local officials in 1970; the number was 136 by 1975. We can see from that prosecutions of local public officials and the number of Blacks elected to municipal offices track each other. This information is purely descriptive and not evidence of an actual correlation. However, the pattern fits the underlying suspicion posed by the Black political elite—that they were subject to extralegal attention. Political scientists Kenneth Meier and Thomas Holbrook, for example, find evidence of racial (and partisan) targeting regarding the prosecution of corruption public officials during the Carter and Reagan administrations.[74]

For their part, prosecutors at every level deny that race or politics plays any role in their investigative choices.[75] I cannot resolve these competing claims. However, figure 1.8 supports the notion that "Black

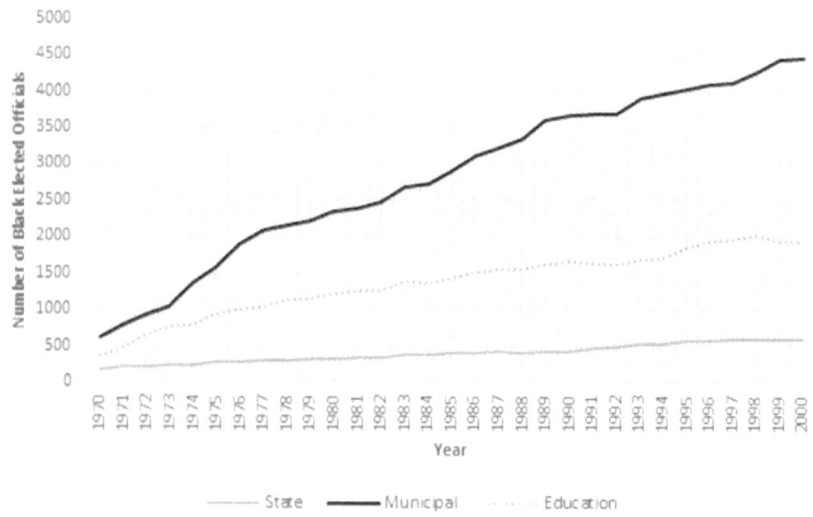

FIGURE 1.7. Black Elected Officials, by Level of Government (1970–2000).
Source: National Roster of Black Elected Officials: A Statistical Summary.

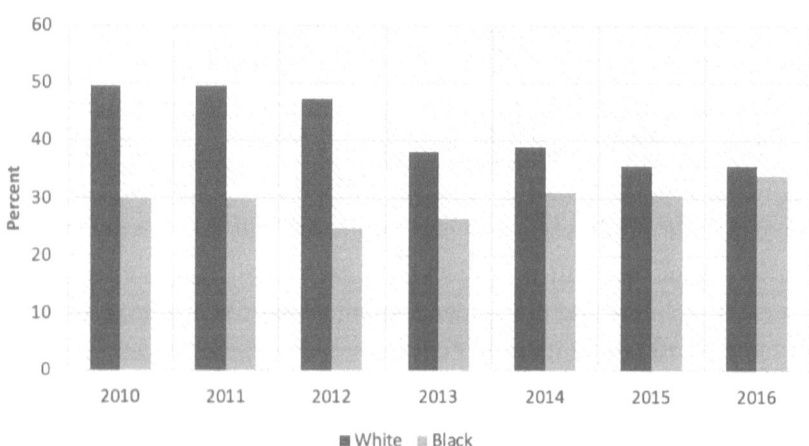

FIGURE 1.8. Bribery Involving Public Officials, by Race (2010–2016).
Source: U.S. Sentencing Commission.

officials are, in fact, being prosecuted more heavily than their representation in the population of elected officials."[76] In the years between 2010 and 2016, prosecutions for bribery included a *disproportionate* number of Black officials. Of course, this is suggestive because federal prosecution of corruption is at a twenty-year low and the data do not include prosecutions in the eighties or nineties, when some Black elected officials believed this behavior was most rampant. According to a 1988 *Washington Post* article by journalist Gwen Ifill, 14 percent of those investigated were African American, although Blacks politicians had accounted for only 3 percent of elected officials at the time.[77]

Dispatches of Discontent

One concern that frames the racial politics of scandal is racist double standards. There is no shortage of examples. Let us consider the observation of Harlem congressman Adam Clayton Powell Jr., who said he was targeted for reprisal for "acting like a White man." He meant by this that he was enjoying the spoils and privileges of being a member of the U.S. House of Representatives, too much like his White colleagues. Another example is that of Bob McDonnell, the White, Republican former governor of Virginia, who had his conviction vacated by the U.S. Supreme Court, while Kwame Kilpatrick, the Black, Democratic former mayor of Detroit, was denied relief for similar offenses that same day. Both had been convicted of corruption-related crimes. Two days after McDonnell's oral arguments, journalist Charles Ellison wondered "if an African-American politician in similar straits would have received the same, open-ear treatment." He wondered about the possibility that such favor would "shift over to corrupt or criminally charged Black politicians." It was unlikely, Ellison suspected. And surely enough, the unsigned order issued on the back of *McDonnell v. United States* two months later confirmed it.

What is important in these examples is that they represent a specific grievance. Black political leaders claim that they are or have been unfairly targeted for extralegal attention and held to a different standard than their White counterparts. The leaders I have discussed so far subscribe to what historian Derek Musgrove calls harassment ideology, a "body of beliefs [that] explain[s] [their] relationship to the White dominated state and news media . . . as being one of repression."[78] When the White power structure sought to make an example of outspoken Black political leaders, they would "use accusations of a criminality as a means of destroying Black political power."[79] As a result, harassment ideology sets "the terms for discussions of state and news media disproportionately investigat[ing] Black elected officials."[80]

A Theory of Racialized Suspicion

Politicians of all races transgress the law or ethics of public office. And political and legal tools are exerted to impose democratic discipline. Articulating a model of racial suspicions should not be understood as an excuse for misconduct; rather, it should be interpreted as what is learned by racially subjugated communities that have been burdened by the state's impropriety toward them. That citizens look at the action of their government and its agents with distrust and suspicion undermines the very legitimacy required for governing. The model of racialized suspicion posits that (1) allegations of wrongdoing against Black political elite make Black Americans suspicious and (2) this racialized suspicion affects electoral punishment for corruption. Figure 1.9 shows the process components involved. Note that the theory of racialized suspicion is a way of processing information. First, the theory does not assume that suspicious thinking depends on an affirmative answer to any of the triggers for Black protectionism (figure 1.9). But to the extent that these questions correspond well enough to actual concerns, they provide useful information about the scale of uncertainty experienced by Black people. "Was he set up?," one might ask. "Did they treat that White guy that way?," queries another. "Are they messing with him, again?" This imagined interrogation

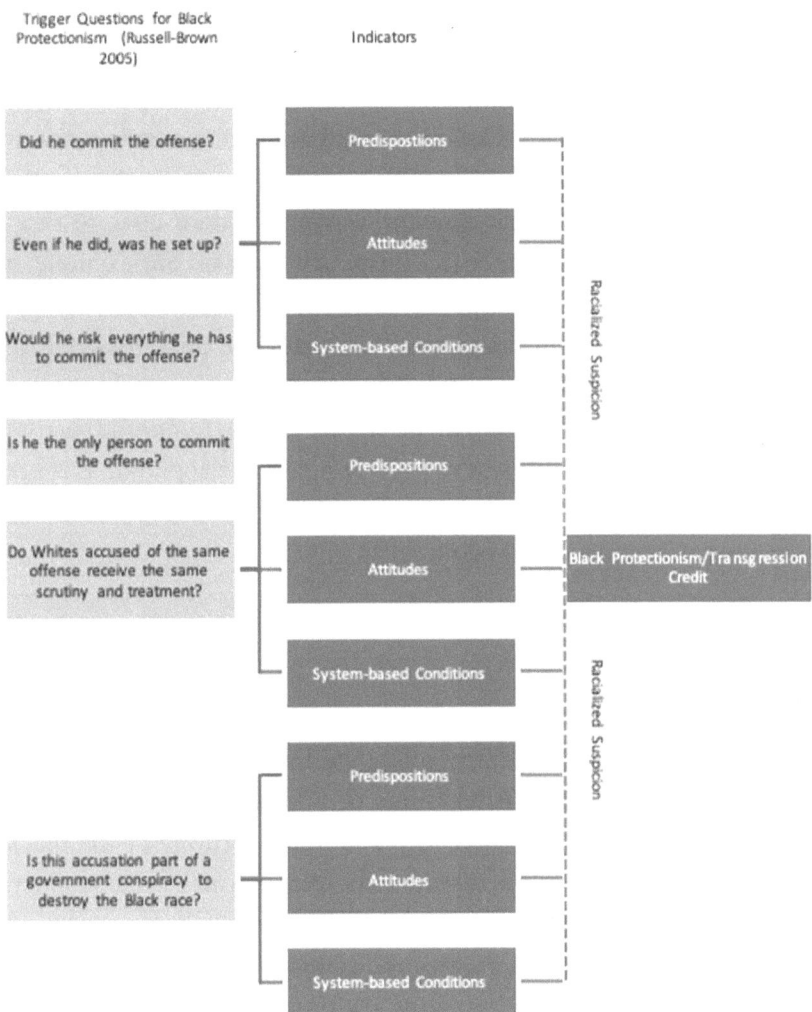

FIGURE 1.9. Theory of Racialized Suspicion.

determines if group-based support will be dispatched. However, Black communities can never be too sure of the answer. They worry that their race puts them at a distinct risk for harassment (predisposition) and distrust the government (attitudes) because it has a history and practice of harm against them (system-based conditions).

I build on the trigger questions defined by Kathryn Russell-Brown, with one of the questions being about targeting, one reflecting concerns about racist double standards, and a third dealing with the possibility of a government conspiracy.[81] In this book, I argue that merely suspecting the answer is yes can activate Black protectionism. Implicit in the triggers is a mistrust of government, leaving the door open to race-based suspicions or race-specific conspiracy theories. For example, it encourages Blacks to assess the legitimacy of an official action against an esteemed member of the group. This evaluation does not occur in isolation. Predispositions, attitudes, and system-based conditions are bundled and determine whether Blacks are willing to punish corrupt politicians at the ballot box or to provide a negative appraisal. It is not that they object to the specific action of, say, fighting corruption but that they cannot be certain it was done fairly.

How Suspicion Works

Any suspicion that an esteemed member of the racial group is being targeted, harassed, or unfairly maligned by Whites is backed by a history of such abuses. Allegations of wrongdoing against Black politicians, as a result, are met with additional scrutiny by the Black public. White-dominated institutions, Black Americans suspect, may be targeting Black political leaders in a discriminatory manner. Ambiguity about what motivates the state actor—that is, that they are racist or that they are pursuing legitimate ends—affects subsequent political judgments. When people are made suspicious of the motives of a social actor, let us say a prosecutor, they are more likely to make negative judgments about the prosecutor and less likely to make dispositional judgments about those affected by that actor's duplicitousness.[82] As a more practical example, Steven Fein and colleagues use an experimental design to illustrate how suspicion can reduce juror bias against defendants.[83] After exposing mock jurors to pretrial information biased against a defendant, for instance, those mock jurors were more likely to vote to deliver a guilty verdict. But when they were made suspicious about the motivations underlying the information's reporting and release, their likelihood of returning a conviction decreased. This was especially true of Black jurors, who were less likely to vote to convict a Black defendant than were White jurors under these conditions.

Paul Skolnick and Jerry Shaw, also psychologists, take a similar approach. However, they misinterpret this judgment as evidence of Black racism.[84] They also find that Black mock jurors judge Black defendants more favorably. But labeling this judgment Black racism presupposes a level of out-group derogation toward Whites that mistakes targets. Black Americans are not so much interested in getting payback on White society as much as they are interested in protecting Black people from racial injury wrought by that society. To be sure, as Skolnick and Shaw write in their closing sentence, verdicts like those involving the famous Black football player O. J. Simpson, who stood accused of double homicide, "must be understood within this context and the long history of White bias against Black defendants."[85] Simpson is Black; the victims were White. This racial perpetrator-victim dyad produces disparate outcomes for Black defendants regarding sentencing and the application of the death penalty. This is partly the result of the racial composition of the juries, most of which are almost all White. This was not the case in the Simpson trial, which had a jury of one Latino, two White Americans, and nine Black Americans. This unlikely jury composition, coupled with this unlikely outcome, raised concern and captured the imagination of many analysts of American legal politics. For example, political scientist James Q. Wilson lamented that the practice of "excusing accountability for some people defined by their group membership" marked "the end of the law."[86]

Neither of these perspectives recognizes the reason suspicion takes root. While Wilson recognizes the "countless indignities" experienced by Black Americans, he believes that the "promise of fair treatment based on individual accountability" is a special kind of recompense supplied by the law.[87] Yet it is precisely Blacks' suspicion that they will not, or cannot, be treated fairly in a racist criminal justice system. Indeed, scholars like Wilson did not account for what scholars like Charles P. Henry understood: "When laws are clearly directed by one race against the other as in slavery, they promote a race-conscious defiance."[88] This resistance is motivated by suspicion that White-dominated institutions are engaged in unfair, illegal, or wrongful action against the community. It is the "double system of justice" about which W. E. B. Du Bois warned.

With suspicions of that double system, the perceiver, in our case Black Americans, "actively entertains different, plausibly rival, hypotheses about another's [the state's] motives."[89] Black Americans would normally scrutinize these explanations during their role as a perceiver of suspicion, but it no doubt matters that their experiences with racial discrimination "are transmitted as a form of collective memory about Blacks' collective experience with race and racism."[90] In other words, they may be predisposed to suspicious thinking about the actions the state takes toward them or members of their racialized communities. The Racial Suspicion model coheres with Russell-Brown's assertion that Blacks pursue a unique line of inquiry "when analyzing an allegation against a well-known Black person."[91] For Whites, any indication of guilt is determinative. There is no need for further inquiry. In contrast, Black people want to know something else: "Is there any indication that the person was set up?" If the answer is yes, the Black community's reaction is protective of their embattled in-group leader. I depart from Russell-Brown's view only insofar as her triggering sequence for Black protectionism continues with more interrogation. I argue that suspicion of a setup would render other inquires moot because revealing the motivations of a state actor (setup) would remove any ambiguities about their action. More than this, suspicion of racially motivated impropriety will inform Blacks' judgments about scandal situations involving Black elected officials.

Black Political Suspicion in Mass Publics

For Blacks to be suspicious, they must believe that a political actor is being deceitful about its true intentions in pursuing a course of action.[92] Consider the perceptions of a group of Black men I encountered canvassing for D.C.'s former mayor Vincent Gray's city council campaign two years after a scandal denied him another term as mayor: There is "no such thing as guilt by association," one said to me. The "whole thing is propaganda." "It doesn't take four years," another interrupted. These men were referring to the fact that the federal probe into Mayor Gray's campaign activities began in 2011, with several aides having pled guilty to different crimes between then and 2014. That year, the U.S. attorney in the District of Columbia offered then-mayor Gray a deal to plead guilty to a single felony count or face a more elaborate formal accusation. "It didn't take that long for Kwame [Brown], Michael Brown, Harry Thomas," Gray's supporter added. "Why stretch it out?" All told, these supporters suspected the government "tried to set [Gray] up." Worse is that their suspicions were affirmed by the policy decision by the federal prosecutor to not charge Gray once he was defeated in the Democratic primary for mayor.

Suspicion was prominent in the minds of these men. "Why did it take so long?" "Why didn't they charge him?" "Was it a setup?" These questions highlight the disruptive and facilitative properties of suspicion. Doubt about one's motivations generates cognitive scrutiny concerning the actor and their action, for example. This often causes shifts in relevant political or social judgments in a manner that is less punitive. In other words, suspicion interrupts how information is normally processed when concerned that a state actor is wrongly motivated in pursuit of their duty. This interpretation is especially likely for Black Americans, who believe that racial discrimination has a deleterious effect on their social and economic outcomes. For example, they are more likely to believe they have "worse jobs, income, and housing than White people"

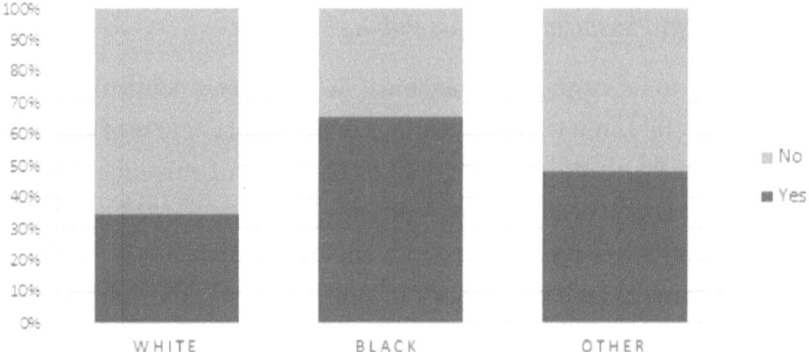

FIGURE 1.10. Differences Due to Discrimination by Race.
Source: General Social Survey 1972–2018 Cumulative Datafile.

and that those outcomes are mostly due to discrimination. Figure 1.10 illustrates this point in showing that 60 percent of Black Americans endorse this view, with close to one-third of Whites saying the same. It is reasonable then that they also suspect racial discrimination is motivating law enforcement.

Sources of Suspicion

The "Black man is the focus of White fear and is made to embody all that appears to threaten social order," writes John Fiske, and "he has to always be watched."[93] It is from the policies and practices manifest in this view that Black Americans have learned to be suspicious of White-dominated institutions. In the next section I describe who and what makes them so in the context of corruption scandals. Recall that suspicion raises questions about the motives of a social-political actor. To understand the seeding of Blacks' suspicions, we must first look at the cast of characters involved. They include the media, in addition to the prosecutor and other law enforcement agents already discussed. None of these individuals need to be dubious to inspire suspicion, nor are all acting in bad faith. Yet Black Americans are socialized by run-ins (direct or vicarious) with racist police officers, the conduct of the ambitious, racist prosecutors, and the stories news media propagate about them. Recognizing their role and their practices is essential to understanding the emergence of racialized suspicion.

Media

News media plays an essential role in the public reveal of private misdeeds. Successful accusations of wrongdoing against political leaders are significantly influenced by the news context.[94] Often, the media is responsible for the public disclosure of private misdeeds and follows it through every state up until its culmination. The role of the press as vehicle for government transparency and accountability cannot be overstated, but the press is hardly passive or neutral regarding mediated scandal. Take as an example Congressman William Lacy Clay's charge that "so called investigative journalists wrote outlandish articles purporting to be factual exposes of criminal activity implicating Black politicians."[95] This tracks with a tendency of the media in its framing of policy issues like crime, most notably the racialization of it, and its profound racial consequences for support for punitive policies. Indeed, we could imagine that crimes like corruption are similarly racialized. Take the members of Congress involved in the 1992 House Banking Scandal as an example. Those members of Congress abused their banking privileges by regularly writing checks for amounts that their accounts did not have adequate monies on deposit to cover. While Democrats and Republicans engulfed in the incident were covered equitably, Black members of Congress received less desirable coverage than their White colleagues.[96]

According to Congressman Clay, moreover, the media was also responsible for reporting and printing "highly suspicious-inducing, inflammatory allegations" against Black political leaders, which "then became the basis for official government investigations by the FBI, the Drug Enforcement Agency (DEA), the Internal Revenue Service (IRS), federal task forces, and postal inspectors."[97] Many of the Black politicians who lamented the racist activities of the prosecutors, or the FBI, also found no friend in the local media. Detroit's Coleman Young reflected this point by suggesting, "The federal government and local media, in a tacit but enthusiastic partnership, moved to take [him] down with an elaborate program of eavesdropping, [and] entrapment."[98] In Washington, D.C., former mayor Vincent Gray lambasted news outlets there for emphasizing "sensational tidbits of 'news' during a scandal involving him," while neglecting their role as skeptics by "reinforc[ing] [the prosecutor's] allegations and direct[ing] readers to reject me" in the upcoming election.

Electoral Consequences for Corruption

Public officials have a duty to protect public trust. If elected, they are expected to represent and advance the interests of their constituents and the will of the people. Ethical lapses do occur, however, with officials routinely violating those expectations. An official using his or her public office for private gain—extortion, bribes, kickbacks—is one such example. Whatever the scheme, government corruption produces waste, abuse, and fraud that cost taxpayers. These schemes deprive the citizen of the honest services of government decision making. Because officials are supposed to be "agent[s] of citizens," their conduct is "judged by different principles, or principles differently interpreted."[99] One assumption is that when officials run afoul of the law or ethics of their office, citizens will draw on the standards of right and wrong to hold those wayward politicians to account.

The literature on political scandal suggests that ethical judgments about malfeasance are far more complicated. Corrupt politicians are punished only marginally at the ballot box. More often, they weather the storm of scandal and return to political life. The reasons voters don't "throw the bums out," as some protest, are varied and many, but all produce judgments that are less harsh toward political transgressors.[100] There are many factors that contribute to the decay of accountability in the scandal environment, including the type of scandal, the embattled incumbent's electoral strength and seniority, attention by the news media, and scandal fatigue.[101] Partisanship, gender, race, and ethnicity also matter to this disbursement of transgression credits. As political scientist Michael Johnston contends, "Many competing issues and personalities can override sentiments about corruption: partisan, ethnic, religious, or other communal loyalties, as well as sheer force of habit, may shape not only the choice of how to vote but perceptions of corruption issues in general."[102]

Research in American politics has only recently begun to explore the role of issues like race as it relates political scandal.[103] What I attempt to describe below is an alternative view of the racial politics of political scandal, one in which the state is an antagonist. I propose racialized suspicion as a relevant indicator for why Black voters may sometimes excuse misbehaving Black politicians. I argue that suspicion introduces alternative criteria by which to judge alleged misconduct by Black political leaders—that is, could these charges be racially motivated? Decentralized law enforcement and disproportionate political harassment—including racial violence—prime Blacks with a racialized policy feedback that suggests these outcomes may affect them most and worse.[104] Law enforcement agencies like state and local police, federal prosecutors, and the FBI routinely satisfy these conditions.

Regarding decentralization, James Q. Wilson describes the "considerations of utility" that motivate law enforcement's discretion in "deciding to arrest, or to intervene in any other way." Although officers claim to fight crime wherever it may be, the decision of whether, where, and how to intervene in situations differs by community. That discretion is born out of great autonomy in law enforcement agencies in general, particularly in the power they wield as bureaucrats with street-level access in a decentralized system. This permits law enforcement agents to engage in conduct that is untoward and corrupt. Much of the early literature on municipal corruption did pay some attention to police malfeasance, from payoffs to outright abuse of citizens. Evidence from racial disparities in traffic stops makes this point clearer.[105] What these interactions teach, in each of their forms, is that Black people have reason to be suspicious and distrustful of law enforcement. This policy feedback has the effect of depressing aspects of their political behavior and policy uptake.[106]

A Note on Racial Paranoia and Conspiracies

I advise caution in concluding that racialized suspicion is simple conspiracism, racial paranoia, or even delusions of persecution. There is a distinction to be made between conspiracy theories that are bogus and those "claims of conspiracy that's true [and aren't] really a conspiracy theory at all."[107] If we accept the more common definition of conspiracy as a "secret plan by a group to do something unlawful or harmful," it is reasonable to conclude that unlawful surveillance of Black domestic targets meets that criterion. Patterned policies and practices like those undertaken by federal law enforcement have cast doubt on the motivations of state actors toward Black people, thus giving rise to racialized suspicion. Black Americans are suspicious of the state, concerned that its pattern of practices—violence, harassment, repression—could be perpetrated against them at any time. Sharon Parsons and colleagues show that an overwhelming majority of African Americans believed that their race was the reason they were harassed by police and that the criminal justice system is not fair toward them.[108] Suspicion is a powerful psychological force. It leads perceivers to consider and question an actor's motives, leading to the normal flow of information being disturbed by increased scrutiny about why an action has occurred.

But it is true that Black Americans do sometimes endorse conspiratorial thinking, especially about U.S. government conduct toward them.[109] Scholars William Simmons and Sharon Parsons add that Black elected officials believed in conspiracy theories just as much as local churchgoers.[110] The spread of these theories therefore finds little resistance in these communities. It is easy to draw unfavorable conclusions from this about the state of African American psychology. Many scholars suggest that conspiracy thinking is rational and motivated by a desire to explain external events. Jennifer Crocker et al. argue that "beliefs in U.S. government conspiracies against Blacks represent a specific type of external attribution for problems facing Blacks as a group"—that is, system blame.[111] In general, these race-relevant conspiracy theories are endorsed because Blacks see government as responsible for Black disadvantage.[112]

None of these perspectives take seriously that the U.S. government has, in fact, been involved in conspiracies against Black people. Part of the problem lies in the conceptual confusion about conspiracies and theories about them. For example, I follow Karen Douglas and colleagues in viewing "conspiracy" as a "secret plot by two or more powerful actors" who "attempt to usurp political or economic power, violate rights, infringe upon established agreements, withhold vital secrets, or alter bedrock institutions."[113] Accordingly, "conspiracies such as the Watergate scandal do happen." I depart from Douglas et al. that when a conspiracy fails "because of the difficulties inherent in executing plans and keeping people quiet, it ceases to be a conspiracy."[114] To be sure, this perspective ignores evidence of widespread surveillance and political harassment by federal law enforcement. Lance deHaven-Smith and Matthew Witt articulate this point more forcefully in writing that "as a concept to designate and stigmatize unreasonable antigovernment allegations, the conspiracy-theory label is problematic, for political conspiracies do, in fact, happen."[115]

Rather than mockery or charging exaggerated paranoia, deHaven-Smith and Witt advocate that "mass suspicions of political criminality in high office" be evaluated on their merits. "The appropriate government response to conspiracy theories is not to try to silence mass suspicions," they argue, "but to establish procedures for ensuring that suspicious events are thoroughly and credibly investigated."[116] To do so—with an eye toward the question of a conspiracy against Black political leaders—would yield volumes of files of intelligence collected on Black political leaders.[117] A reasonable conclusion from this is that suspicious thinking and conspiratorial thinking are not the same. However, they are primed by the same psychological mechanisms—uncertainty, anxiety, and historical context.[118]

Evaluation of Black Suspicion and Protectionism

In the next two chapters I evaluate whether African Americans are in fact suspicious and how those beliefs structure evaluations about scandalized Black elected officials. Explaining Black political judgments in this context requires an account of both transgressed Black elite and the Black mass public. This racialized feedback framework can help us begin to understand how the design and implementation of public policies remake how citizens understand and interpret politics. Given our topic is public corruption, how Black lawmakers react to allegations leveled against them is important to understanding the arousal of suspicion. They are subject to the probes that interest us here and are those whose reputations are put at stake by the possibility of impropriety. Black voters, for their part, are expected to respond to these misdeeds by using the ballot box to punish these politicians for their misdeeds. Like other voters who privilege partisan identity or transactional exchanges, however, Black voters sometimes resist electoral punishment because they are suspicious of any formal accusation of political corruption coming from an institutional entity they believe is motivated by racial malice.

2

Black Suspicion, Black Protection

An Experimental Test

Racial suspicion is one means by which African Americans process information about political scandals involving Black elected officials. Black citizens cannot be sure that federal prosecutors, agents of the FBI, or any other law enforcement officials have no malicious intent in their actions against Black communities or their Black leaders. For some investigations involving a Black political leader, Black citizens are suspicious about the racist motivations of their government. I have defined racialized suspicion as a feeling or belief that White-dominated institutions are guilty of an illegal, dishonest action against Black people. I use the term to describe the racialized reaction experienced by African American voters who report concern that Black political leaders have been unfairly targeted for extralegal attention. In the previous chapter I discussed the various forms of surveillance used against Black civil rights leaders like Martin Luther King Jr. under programs like COINTEPRO and provided examples of the harassment experienced by Black mayors like Cleveland's Carl Stokes, Detroit's Coleman Young, and others. Much of what those mayors said reflects psychologist Rob Brotherton's observation that most suspicion is directed at the government and its various agencies.[1] For example, each mayor complained in one way or another that racist prosecutors, investigators, and journalists were out to "ruin the careers of outspoken Black officeholders."[2]

In this chapter I show that African American citizens are suspicious of the same and that this racialized suspicion facilitates protectionism for Black political leaders. Before I detail the effects of race on suspicious thinking, it may be helpful to briefly situate public corruption.

I am referring to the abuse of public office for private gain. This is broad enough to include a variety of transgressions that can ignite political scandal. But not all scandals are equal, and not all that is considered corrupt or scandalous is a crime.³ Because sex scandals are so common in political life, for example, and because their exposure sometimes leads an embarrassed incumbent to resign, they have an outsized place in our political imagination despite having fewer political and legal consequences.⁴ Throughout this book I assume that Black citizens have greater concern for conduct that invites legal consequences, even though I treat the topic of sex scandals later to demonstrate this point empirically. Specific consequences of financial crimes or abuse of power are more narrowly targeted because they are legally disqualifying. In other words, the purpose of racist political harassment has always been to undermine Black political power by embarrassing and discrediting Black political leaders.

Protection Against Racism

The revelations contained in the report of the Senate Select Committee to Study Governmental Operations with Respect to Intelligence Activities were hardly shocking to African Americans. The federal government had long surveilled "race agitators," including the Reverend Martin Luther King Jr., sociologist W. E. B. Du Bois, and investigative journalist and antilynching crusader Ida B. Wells, and set out to "destroy Black nationalist leader Marcus Garvey under the guise of 'criminal proceedings.'"⁵ When the United States entered World War I in 1917, "the [W]hite press claimed that German agents were spreading anti-war propaganda among [B]lacks, especially in the South," leading the "federal government departments and several local agencies [to maintain] a constant watch on the activities of [B]lack civilians and soldiers and equal rights organizations and publications."⁶ Because of this history, even in the absence of a deep or comprehensive knowledge about it, racialized suspicion is protection against abuses of the state. It is also protection against racist double standards.

An important part of discussions about race and misconduct in the United States concerns whether African Americans are treated differently by the criminal legal system. By most accounts they are, regardless of if their offense was a petty crime, white-collar crime, or political crime. One cannot understand racialized suspicion or Black protectionism without some sense of how racism manages to produce these effects. We know a great deal about White racial resentment and racism and the violence and discrimination it has beget historically and contemporarily. One should not ignore these precedents. Consider the blatant expression by lawyer Charles Hall Davis in the *Virginia Law Register*, in which he argued that although Black and White bootleggers during the Prohibition era were both criminals, the "negro bootlegger [was] the greatest menace we have."[7] As in the Redemption era, this view was motivated by the belief that there were "dangers to the unprotected women and children in the county districts from drunken and lawless men, and particularly from drunken, and lawless negro men, whose passions had been wrought to a frenzy by the liquor sold at the county bar-room."

There will always be a certain lingering question that African Americans ask and has never really gone away: Do "Whites accused of the same offense receive the same scrutiny and treatment?"[8] African Americans believe the answer is no. Blacks are more likely to be stopped by the police, more likely to be arrested and found guilty, more likely to be sentenced longer, and more likely to receive the death penalty.[9] Racial disproportionality in punishment is believed to be the modal experience for Black America, whether among the mass public or among elites. Think back to the speech by Congressman Adam Clayton Powell, who warned, "Let he who is without sin cast the first stone. There is no one here who does not have a skeleton in his closet. I know, and I know them by name."[10] When Powell was accused of impropriety by his House colleagues, he responded he was merely "acting like a White man." Black ambition to inclusion in White systems of power—to have the same rights and privileges of their White compatriots—has been a constant source of White backlash. Accusing Black Americans of any kind of impropriety obscures the fouls accumulated by White Americans, and Black Americans are acutely aware of these double standards because they are reproduced at every touchpoint in American life.

African Americans have taken in these political scenes around them. Their misgivings about the state are passed on in their political socialization, its effects encoded in their political psychology.[11] What do they do with what they know or have seen? I have proposed that racialized suspicion—the feeling or belief that White-dominated institutions are guilty of an illegal, dishonest action against Black people—is one response. Another is to rally around embattled and esteemed members of their in-group—to protect them—when that suspicion is aroused. Some have claimed this occurs when Black political leaders face allegations of impropriety in contemporary politics—they "play the race card" to avoid accountability.[12] The race card is a parlor trick of sorts, or smoke and mirrors as one writer put it, that obscures wrongdoing by cloaking it in charges of racism. This type of racial appeal is referred to as a political account, or explanation of untoward behavior, that is racially styled as a rebuttal or denial. Scholars Charlton McIlwain and Stephen Caliendo call it a racial defense, whereby Black elected officials invoke "racial references because they want to defend themselves against what they see as a racist attack lodged against them."[13] Conservative author Larry Elder, who is also African American, contends that Black leaders "effectively convince their constituents that a racist criminal justice system unfairly went after them."[14] These kinds of racial defenses are believed to be compelling because accusations of racism are understood as a plausible explanation for unfavorable interactions with the state.[15]

However, I have shown elsewhere that African Americans do not need to be told by Black political leaders ensnared in scandal to be suspicious—they often already are.[16] Still, it is helpful to consider the racial defenses the Black political elite have said about their scandals before we go about analyzing Black public opinion of the same. What follows is a brief account of different scandals involving Black politicians. They are drawn primarily from local government, namely, Black mayors who have, in response to legal troubles, countercharged racism. These Black mayors were all elected in or after 1967 and represent Black-majority or -plurality cities. Again, Black mayors occupy a unique political role as executives of a municipality. In the introduction, and discussed further in the next chapter, I suggested that federal law enforcement became more active in its local anticorruption activities at the same time Black mayors were ascendant to city halls across the country. Most of the first big city mayors were scrutinized in this way—Carl Stokes of Cleveland, Coleman Young of Detroit, Kenneth Gibson of Newark, Tom Bradley of Los Angeles, Richard Arrington of Birmingham, Alabama. I include their case details and a few others here to illustrate this point.

Bill Campbell, Atlanta, Georgia

In 2004 the federal government indicted former Atlanta mayor Bill Campbell on charges that he "conducted the City's affairs through a pattern of racketeering activity."[17] A five-year investigation of municipal corruption during his tenure alleged that the then-mayor accepted thousands of dollars in cash, campaign contributions, and other things of value in exchange for city contracts. For example, one count in the indictment accused the mayor of soliciting and accepting corrupt payments ($25,000) from a computer contractor to provide Y2K services for the city. Another charge alleged that Campbell solicited campaign contributions from a club owner seeking a liquor license and that the mayor accepted payments for personal benefits from the Water Filter Company while the company received a municipal contract. Campbell denied the allegations. He was quoted in the *New York Times* proclaiming, "They're lies from beginning to end. . . . The only thing that's correct in this indictment is the spelling of my name."[18] He added that the federal probe was racially motivated. "The F.B.I. has never been a friend of the African American community," he said, "and they're not a friend now."[19] Campbell would be found guilty and sentenced to thirty months in prison.

Coleman Young, Detroit, Michigan

Coleman Young, the first Black mayor of Detroit, was once described in the *Washington Post* as a "provocative politician, blunt and casually profane."[20] The local media, meanwhile, took "delight in referring to [him] as the flag-bearing racist of Detroit." Indeed, a series of public corruption scandals, namely, those called Vista and Magnum, fueled a hostile exchange between Mayor Young, federal prosecutors, and the city's local press. In the Vista case, the government investigated kickbacks in the city's Water and Sewage Department. "The Federal government and local media, in a tacit but enthusiastic partnership," Young wrote, "moved to take me down with an elaborate program of eavesdropping, entrapment, innuendo, and collusion."[21] Young lamented that he had been the subject of federal surveillance and scrutiny for four decades but was never once indicted for criminal wrongdoing. For Coleman, "there [were] strong vestiges of racism" in Detroit and elsewhere that motivated these inquiries into his conduct. For example, communication scholar Lee Becker and colleagues were commissioned by the mayor to examine how Detroit's local press covered scandals involving then-mayor Young. Becker and his colleagues published their findings in the *Detroit Free Press*, concluding that the stories about Coleman's alleged misconduct were in fact racist.[22] Several journalists as well as the editor took exception to this characterization.

Richard Arrington Jr., Birmingham, Alabama

Arrington was elected the first African American mayor of Birmingham in the late 1970s. Early in his tenure the mayor alleged that he had long been the "target of investigations and harassment by the FBI," DOJ (Department of Justice), and IRS—covering "virtually every aspect" of his business, financial, and political dealings.[23] These law enforcement efforts used a variety of intelligence gathering techniques, including "electronic devices, video monitoring, concealed body microphones, audiotapes, 35-milimeter photographs, and visual surveillance by agents." Arrington, who had been investigated more than a dozen times over the years, became a "leading voice among those asserting that Black elected officials were singled out."[24] In fact, the mayor even invited local and national organizations to take up the issue of "the selective prosecution and harassment of [B]lack leadership."[25] He said he was "convinced that Black elected officials who constitute less than 2 percent of [the] nation's elected officials [were] being disproportionately" targeted.[26] In 1992, Mayor Arrington was found in contempt of the court and sentenced to ten months in jail after refusing to cooperate with an investigation by turning over appointment logs related to a probe into whether he had received kickbacks from an architect who had done contract work in the city.

Sharpe James, Newark, New Jersey

James was longtime mayor (1986–2006) of Newark and a state senator in New Jersey. In 2007 the former mayor was indicted on thirty-three counts of corruption-related crimes. The government alleged that he "knowingly and willfully did devise and intend to devise a scheme and artifice to defraud the City of Newark of money and property by means of materially false and fraudulent pretenses, representations and promises."[27] Part of the charges stemmed from the use of two city-owned credit cards held by the mayor, one issued to pay for business-related expenses incurred by his security detail, with which he was accused of making improper purchases. The government alleged that in another scheme to defraud James misused "his official positions as Mayor of Newark and State Senator to improperly favor [a close associate and] obtain more than $500,000 in money and [city-owned] property."[28] The mayor was found guilty on fraud and conspiracy charges and sentenced to twenty-seven months in prison. James accused then-U.S. attorney Chris Christie of using him as a step for his gubernatorial race.

Kwame Kilpatrick, Detroit, Michigan

In Detroit, an embattled Kilpatrick took the defensive and ran a full-page advertisement in the historically Black newspaper the *Michigan Chronicle* with the headline "Lynching Is Still Legal in America."[29] The ad drew on the brutal imagery of American racial violence and characterized Detroit's media as a racist lynch mob looking to defame and hang the city's Black mayor for false crimes.[30] At the time, Kilpatrick was running for a second mayoral term and facing spiraling political scandals. He initially denied being responsible for the ad but a subpoena of one of his political strategists showed the mayor paid for the placement. The first of the mayor's many legal troubles began in 2003 with the "rumored, but never proven, wild party taking place at Manoogian Mansion, the Detroit mayor's home" in which an exotic dancer was shot in her car.[31] Then came a lawsuit from a former police officer who claimed the mayor retaliated by reassigning him for investigating the shooting, followed by the disclosure of text messages that revealed Kilpatrick was having an extramarital affair with his chief of staff. All this and more transpired before the DOJ indicted the former mayor on thirty counts, including RICO conspiracy, bribery, extortion, mail/wire fraud, and other corruption-related crimes.[32] Kilpatrick was found guilty of twenty-four of those counts and sentenced to twenty-eight years in federal prison, a sentence many called too harsh despite offering little sympathy to the mayor.[33]

These cases are far from exhaustive of racial defenses. In 1984, under the headline "Barry's Racial Defense Wins Some Backers," two staff writers for the *Washington Post* wrote that Marion Barry Jr. was using "racial arguments to rally support in 70 percent black Washington."[34] Barry's primary goal, they wrote, was to "shift the public debate to the conduct of the Joseph E. diGenova, the [W]hite U.S. Attorney for the district appointed by President Reagan." They continued that "Barry's supporters have grumbled for weeks that diGenova has sought to discredit a [B]lack mayor's administration by leaking uncorroborated evidence linking Barry to Johnson during the year-and-a-half that she admitted to selling drugs." And by their reporting, "the maneuver [racial defense] seem[ed] to be working." We will return to the example of Mayor Barry in the next chapter.

Non-mayoral Example: Alcee L. Hastings

A less well-known example is Alcee L. Hastings of Florida, the state's first African American federal judge and the first and only African American to ever be impeached. In 1981, then-judge Hastings was charged with conspiracy, obstruction of justice, and bribery in return for "reducing the sentences of two mob-connected felons convicted in Hastings' court." Although Hastings had been acquitted in 1983, a special committee of the Eleventh Circuit Court of Appeals launched a further investigation into whether Hastings lied under oath and tampered with evidence in the process. Concluding that he had, the judicial panel referred the matter to the House of Representatives and recommended Hastings be impeached and removed from office. Hastings lamented that these efforts were part of a "witch hunt" by southern judges who were motivated by institutional racism.[35] On August 3, 1988, the House voted 413 to 3 to approve seventeen articles of impeachment, leaving it to the U.S. Senate to decide on Hastings's removal a year later. On the Senate floor, Representative John Conyers of Detroit, also African American and who represented the House subcommittee that led the investigation, warned that "there have been a lot of problems in our judicial system in which race has been involved. This is not one of them or I would be the first person in the Congress to tell you so." In response, Judge Hastings testified that "race is not my defense, was not my defense, and when you decide this case do not decide it because an African-American is standing here."[36] In October 1989 the Senate ordered Hastings removed from the bench.

A Racial Politics of Scandal

Ironically, four years later Hastings would go on to win a congressional seat representing Florida, a seat he held until 2021. And Representative

Conyers's wife Monica, then a Detroit City Council member, would plead guilty to bribery in 2009. Even more paradoxical is that in 2017 Congressman Conyers, then the dean of the House of Representatives (i.e., the longest serving member), resigned from Congress amid allegations of sexual harassment, sparking accusations of racist double standards by members of the Congressional Black Caucus.[37] Putting aside whether racism sufficiently explains the harassment experienced by Black elected officials, a separate question is how voters respond to the specter thereof. In a letter to the editor of the *Washington Post*, for instance, William M. Kunstler wrote that Hastings "deserved far better than . . . cavalier dismissal of racism as a factor in the impeachment process against him."[38] And while White voters in Birmingham were less comfortable with Arrington's charge of racism—an issue that had once defined the politics of that city—one Black city council member remarked that he would "have all the support he needs to run the city from the jail cell if he has to."[39]

Certainly, many have objected to characterizing investigations in racial, or racist, terms. So much so that Frank Donaldson, the U.S. attorney for the Northern District of Alabama, then head prosecutor in Arrington's case, protested by filing civil suit against the mayor for slander.[40] When Lee Becker and his colleagues reported that newspapers like the *Detroit Free Press* "contained some clear instances of racist language" regarding the scandal involving Mayor Coleman Young, a column in the opinion section said that when the report's authors "got to the subject of racism . . . they fell into a swamp and never got themselves out."[41] In another column the paper's executive editor, David Lawrence Jr., responded that the "report is at times neither careful nor precise in its repeated use of the words 'racist' and 'racism'" and that "it serves no one's interest, nor truth, to use those words without making sure everyone understand how they are intended."[42] Even Douglas Wilder, the first Black governor of any state, admonished Black lawmakers while he was lieutenant governor of Virginia by saying "there are no '[B]lack' public officials under criminal investigation or '[W]hite' public officials under investigation . . . a public official is a public official . . . a guilty criminal is a guilty criminal." When he was lieutenant governor Wilder declared, "You must refuse to serve as a patsy for any public official who finds that they are in trouble with the legal authorities."[43]

However, it is objectionable and perhaps dismissive to cast any Black voter as a patsy—a person who is easily taken advantage of—*if* they are independently suspicious of the harassment these Black figures lament. The next section takes up this issue empirically to determine if Black citizens share the harassment ideology of Black political elite by expressing racialized suspicion. If so, then we must consider what they do with their suspicion. For example, the second part of the experiment tests whether suspicion increases the likelihood of Black protection of Black political leaders.

Data and Methods

The empirical goal of this chapter is to examine the interaction of race and political scandal. I do this by drawing on data from a novel survey experiment, a method that has become increasingly common in the study of public corruption and political scandal.[44] Such experiments have provided insight related to transgression credits; how the character of embattled politicians is evaluated;[45] which news sources reporting on allegations are seen as credible;[46] the effectiveness of the political accounts used to explain away allegations of misconduct;[47] how hypocritical politicians beset by moral scandal are judged by voters;[48] how scandal information affects policy recall;[49] and punitive judgments for transgressed leaders.[50] The strength of the experimental approach is in the level of control that can be exercised as well as the ability to manipulate one or more variables of interests, or what we call treatments, to determine their causal effect on an outcome.[51] In this chapter, for example, I vary (1) the race of an elected official and (2) the type of scandal to test their effect on (1) racialized suspicion and (2) the disbursement of a transgression credit in relevant political judgments.

TABLE 2.1. Experimental Conditions

	Type of Scandal	
Race of Mayor	Financial	Sex
Black Mayor	Using $25,000 municipal credit card for nongovernment business	Having an extramarital affair with a staffer
White Mayor	Using $25,000 municipal credit card for nongovernment business	Having an extramarital affair with a staffer

The experiment was designed to vary the race of a city mayor (Black or White) and the type of scandal (financial or sex) in which *he* was alleged to be involved. Participants were randomly assigned to one of the four conditions (table 2.1). One benefit of this design over some others is that I use fictitious political figures to avoid the challenges associated with extraneously relevant biographical characteristics.[52] By doing this, the analysis can more fully extract the effects of race on suspicion and see if or how they are aroused across two distinct types of political scandal. For example, participants were exposed to a fictitious news story in which a city's mayor, depicted as Black or White (i.e., race factor: Black/White), was accused of engaging in either financial misconduct or marital infidelity (i.e., scandal factor: financial/sex). One common criticism of this experimental approach is that it artificiality "precludes any generalization to a real-life situation."[53] However, I have taken care to maximize experimental realism by modeling real-world scandals as stories in a reputable print news outlet (see the appendix).

To test these claims, I draw on data from a sample of 715 voting-eligible Black and White Americans. I measure suspicion by asking participants whether they believed the hypothetical mayor, Daniel Highton, was unfairly targeted for investigation. Table 2.1 provides partial wording of the vignette used in the experimental treatment (see the appendix). Participants were randomly assigned to one of the four conditions in which they were asked to read a fictious *New York Times* article about a mayor involved in a political scandal. We can see in that instance that one condition alleges that the mayor, who is married, had an inappropriate relationship with a female aide. In the other the mayor was accused of inappropriately claiming $25,000 of government funds for his personal use—a crime. This treatment closely mirrors similar conduct alleged against former mayors Sharpe James and Kwame Kilpatrick, both of whom were convicted of financial crimes. As political scientists Donald R. Kinder and Thomas R. Palfrey advise, "By randomly assigning subjects to treatments, the experimenter . . . can be confident that any observed differences must be due to differences in the treatments."[54] To be sure, I included a manipulation check that asked respondents to judge the seriousness of each offense. Figure 2.1 shows that both were judged as serious, but as expected the financial scandal was judged as significantly more serious.[55]

An Empirical Test of Racialized Suspicion

What influence does race have on suspicion? Recall the answer embedded in the theoretical proposition offered in the previous chapter—that

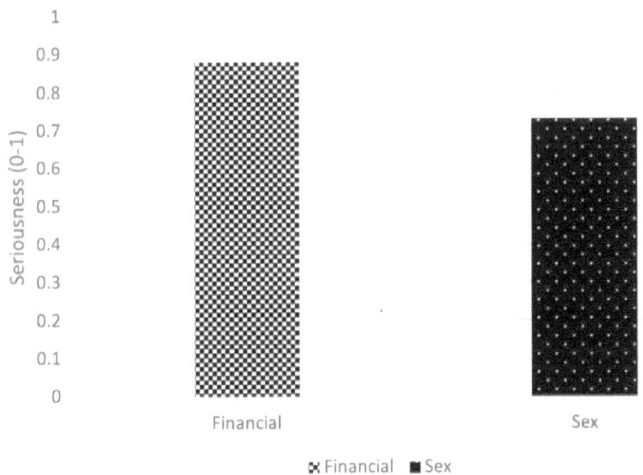

FIGURE 2.1. Mean Seriousness, by Type of Scandal (95 Percent CIs).
Source: Mayor Experiment.

African Americans are more likely to engage in suspicious thinking when they believe a Black elected official has been unfairly targeted to be embarrassed or discredited. Using the experimental approach described above, I can isolate the causal effects on race and scandal type on this outcome, or what I have called *racialized suspicion*. I measure suspicion by asking respondents the extent to which they believe the (fictitious) embattled mayor was unfairly targeted for investigation. Evidence of suspicion should reveal a concern that the government or law enforcement is unfairly targeting Black elected officials. Agents are potentially guilty, in the mind of Black voters, of an illegal, dishonest, or inappropriate action. The claim of racialized suspicion is that doubt, or suspicion, about this conduct being systematic and discriminatory against a Black politician sets the terms for their political judgments. Hence, if African American respondents report more suspicion in the condition with the Black mayor than with the White mayor, then there is evidence of racialized suspicion.[56] I determine this by subjecting the measure to a three-way analysis of variance having two levels for race of mayor (Black, White) and two levels for type of scandal (sex, financial) by the race of the participant (Black, White).

Are Black Voters Suspicious?

Figure 2.2 reveals an interaction effect between the three factors ($p < .05$). Note the left panel represents the mean difference in expression of suspicion by White participants in the study, and the panel on the right represents the same for Black participants. Also note that the point estimates displayed represent the difference in suspicion related to the Black and White mayor, by each racial group and by each scandal type. A zero on the x-axis indicates no difference in the suspicion expressed by respondents, while positive differences indicate suspicion related to the Black mayor. Again, I hypothesized that Black respondents exposed to the story about the Black mayor accused of financial impropriety would be more likely to express racialized suspicion. The main

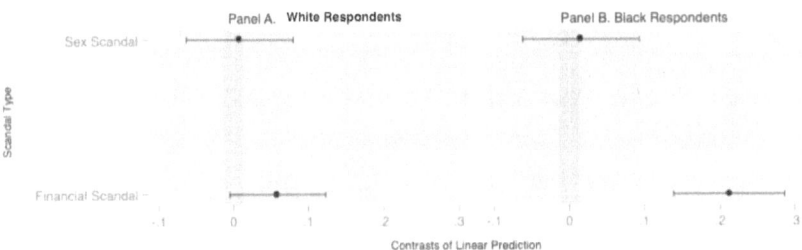

FIGURE 2.2. Mean Difference in Suspicion, by Race and Scandal.
Source: Mayor Experiment.

finding at the bottom right corner of the figure 2.2 confirms this expectation. When the fictitious mayor was accused of a financial misdeed, Black respondents were significantly more likely (20 points) to believe he was unfairly targeted when the mayor was Black compared to when the mayor was White. There was no effect for White respondents—that is, scandal allegations against the White mayor did not make them differentially suspicious.

It is important to note, moreover, that the sex scandal had no effect for either group of respondents. Another way to understand this finding is to discern between incidents that are illegal, those that contravene the law, and those that violate moral norms. Although sex scandals receive considerable media attention, they mostly involve noncriminal, private indiscretions like extramarital affairs that do not rise to the same level of seriousness as lawbreaking.[57] This noneffect is not surprising. Political scientists have demonstrated elsewhere that voters can and do make distinctions about types of conduct.[58] Racialized suspicion is similarly discerning. Sex scandals are less likely to arouse Black suspicion because that conduct is usually consensual and holds few *legal* consequences.[59] In other words, Black suspicion can be concluded to be a response to criminal, legal, and political harassment. And apart from politicians who solicit prostitution, which is a crime in every U.S. jurisdiction except Nevada, or sex with a minor, which is considered statutory rape in some states, or sexual harassment, private trysts do not seem to weigh heavily on the mind of Black voters.

Are Black Voters Protectionists?

Having established that African Americans are in fact suspicious about allegations of political corruption, let us now consider how this way of thinking influences political judgment. I expand the analysis to include outcomes that help us assess Black protectionism, specifically by looking for transgression credits in reputational judgments, the assignment of blame and punishment, and vote intention.[60] A candidate's character or reputation is measured as a composite score of perceptions of honesty, morality, and trustworthiness.[61] Accountability is measured in two ways, the first by asking a question about the extent to which the candidate should be punished for their alleged misdeed; the second is whether, or to what extent, the respondent would consider voting for the fictitious candidate. Unlike above, I do not analyze the data related to the sex scandal since we did not observe suspicion related to that conduct. What Black elected officials do in their private lives, while tantalizing or full of intrigue, does not generate the same kind of suspicion or concern among Black respondents, and so I omit it here. Similarly, the analyses that follow focus only on the Black mayor involved in a financial scandal and restrict the examination to Black respondents.

The reader is reminded that the story in the experimental treatment involved an African American incumbent mayor, Daniel Highton, accused of "using over $25,000 of the city's expense account for personal, non-government business" (see the appendix). The treatment recalls the financial misconduct of embattled former Detroit mayor Kwame Kilpatrick, who "allegedly charged at least $210,000 on his city-issued credit card."[62] Although few were sympathetic to Kilpatrick's misconduct, a point to which I return in the concluding chapter, Black protectionism for the fictious Mayor Highton should materialize as a discounted (negative) or augmented (positive) evaluation depending on the outcome measure. In the case of assigning blame, which has a negative valence, a transgression credit is evinced when respondents assign less blame. If racialized suspicion matters, as I have argued, then it should reduce or discount that appraisal. In contrast, evidence of a transgression credit for a variable with positive valence, like reputation, should produce positive evaluations. The relationships between racialized suspicion and these variables are depicted graphically in figures 2.3 and 2.4.

Appraisal of Blame and Character

Figure 2.3 presents the marginal effects of perceived attribution as a function of whether Black respondents think the mayor was targeted. The left panel displays the effect of racialized suspicion on respondents' judgment of who is to blame, while the right panel shows how it relates to their appraisal of the candidate's character. As expected, we see that this scrutiny reduced negative attributions for the Black political mayor in both cases. As Black respondents' suspicion that their racial in-group leader was unfairly targeted increased, they became less likely to blame him for the alleged misdeed ($p = .002$). In the absence of their suspicion, however, blame was quite high ($M = 0.75$). This finding is consistent with previous research as far as that when suspicion casts doubt about an actor's motivations, who is to blame becomes an important organizing question for how one responds to alleged misconduct.

Although respondents may not blame the mayor for the alleged misconduct, they still may not think very highly of him. The right panel of figure 2.3 examines this possibility. The data show that suspicion has a positive and significant relationship regarding reputational traits.[63] For example, racialized suspicion led Black respondents to evaluate the mayor's character more favorably ($p = .000$). This finding may appear counterintuitive. Running afoul of public ethics, in a business that requires the public's trust, can quickly bring good reputations into immediate disrepute.[64] One compelling explanation about why this has happened with Black respondents is again provided by Katheryn Russell-Brown: Black protectionism works to protect Black political leaders against character assaults by White society.[65] If this is true, then it makes sense to see a transgression credit materialize as an augmented judgment

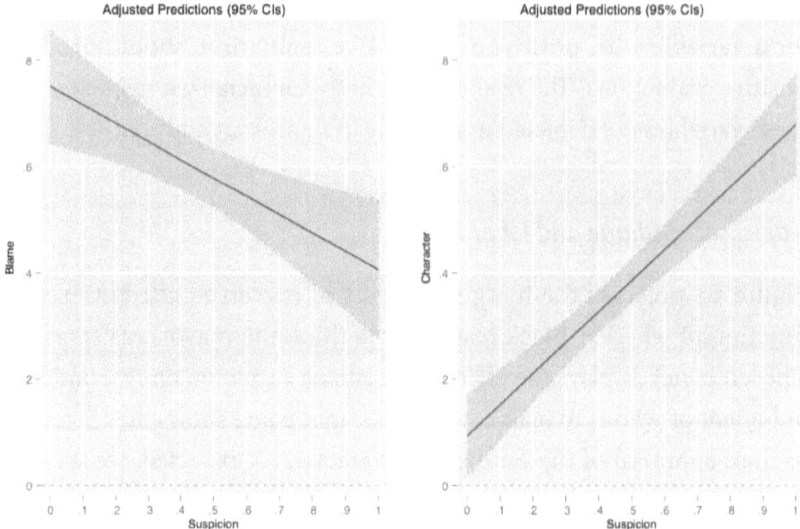

FIGURE 2.3. Effect of Suspicion on Blame and Character.
Source: Mayor Experiment.

about the character traits of the transgressed leader in the experiment; indeed, figure 2.3 supports this interpretation. By augmenting Highton's reputation, respondents have attempted to counteract the concerning perception that the mayor is deviant, incompetent, or unethical.

Punishment and Vote Intention

What has been observed regarding how blame is assigned and character appraised previews the direction of more consequential judgments. In general, transgression credits aim to minimize negative outcomes for transgressed leaders. In the legal arena, for instance, social psychologist Steven Fein and colleagues show that suspicion on the part of mock jurors reduced the guilty verdicts rendered for Black defendants, especially among African American jurors.[66] I test whether this effect is replicated in the political context. Similarly, for instance, I expect that racialized suspicion will lead to discounted negative judgments in terms of punishment and vote choice. Figure 2.4 displays the electoral consequences of corruption as a function of whether the respondent thinks the mayor was targeted. The left panel (A) shows the effect of suspicion on the extent to which Black respondents believed the embattled mayor should be punished, and the right panel (B) shows the degree to which they would commit to voting for him.

Let us begin with the punishment assigned to the mayor by respondents. The variable ranges from "none at all" to "maximum possible" on a ten-point scale. Outside of elections, maximum punishment typically includes being fully prosecuted with the possible outcome of imprisonment. For example, Detroit's Kwame Kilpatrick was convicted and sentenced to twenty-eight years in federal prison for corruption-related crimes.[67] Although voters get to make such judgments only in the criminal legal system as jurors, how punitive they are is nonetheless helpful in foreshadowing the anticipated consequences of public corruption. How judgments of punishment change as a function of the suspicion harbored by African Americans is exhibited in figure 2.4. The

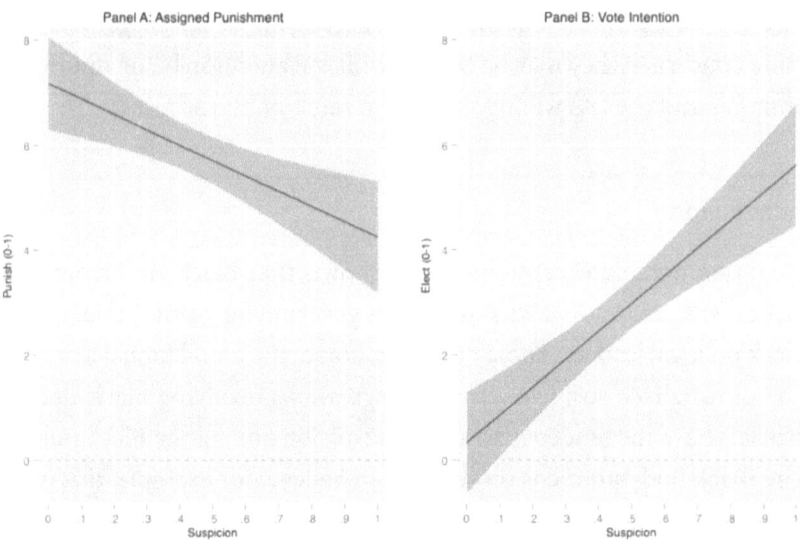

FIGURE 2.4. Effect of Suspicion on Punishment and Vote Intention.
Source: Mayor Experiment.

left panel (A) demonstrates a negative relationship—respondents were less punitive toward the beleaguered Black mayor as they grew more suspicious about his scandal ($p > .05$). Consistent with the expectation of racialized suspicion, Black protectionism evolves out of a concern about unfair treatment.

The same is true regarding electoral outcomes. The right panel (B) of figure 2.4 provides some insight to the common query in the scandal and corruption literature: why don't voters punish transgressed officials at the ballot box? Of the factors presented elsewhere, racialized suspicion is the most relevant among Black Americans. If Black citizens are suspicious of the criminal legal system, "it is hard to conceive that they will sanction the accused when the accusing institutions do not have the rapport, history, or creditability of acting fairly."[68] Thus, the evidence in panel B demonstrates that suspicion has a positive, significant relationship with respondents' vote intention. When respondents were suspicious of the allegations, they were more likely to report that they would vote for the fictitious scandalized mayor. These data establish that a buffer against escalating penalties exists. The logic is simple: the more unsure Black voters are about the underlying reason for the allegations, the more concerned they may be about extralegal attention being untoward or unfair and the less willing they are to sanction the accused.

Conclusion

With one notable exception, I have shown that Black Americans do express suspicion about what motivates government agents in pursuit of Black political leaders. These data corroborate the foundational assumption of racialized suspicion, that transgressions involving Black elected officials have the tendency to arouse suspicion among the Black public. The Black body politic is more likely to believe, for example, that allegations of Black wrongdoing are part of a concerted effort by the state to discredit or embarrass Black leaders. Moreover, because Blacks were not suspicious in the sex scandal condition, one interpretation is that racialized suspicion is concerned with conduct that might contravene the law, that which is a crime. That view is most consistent with academic and practical concerns about the variety of consequences found in how racially subjugated communities are policed.[69] That suspicion is aroused in response to allegations of wrongdoing is insightful. It demonstrates for us that it is one of the criteria that inform Blacks' political ethics. What Black communities may have learned from their interaction with racist systems and street-level bureaucrats, whether direct or vicarious, is that they should be skeptical of state action against them.

Concerns about what motivates law enforcement actions against Black people take root not because of prosecutorial delusions or racial paranoia but because of the plausible, recorded, and actual methods used to selectively prosecute and harass Black people. It is not all surprising when Black political leaders complain that they too are victims of state-sanctioned harassment by the very government they have been elected to serve. According to Mary Warner, author of *The Dilemma of Black Politics: A Report on Harassment of Black Elected Officials*, "Harassment of Black officials is in large part about vested economic interest. . . . It is about the threat posed to the existing power configuration when people got jobs who never got jobs before, got promotions when they never got promotions before."[70] This is especially true in Black politically empowered cities, where political trust and efficacy, participation, and satisfaction are in greater supply among Black urban voters.[71] When Black political leaders of these Black politically empowered cities are subject to state-sanctioned racial injury, it confirms for Blacks the level of malevolence, racism, and duplicitousness of White-dominated institutions.

If racial paranoia offered a better explanation or delusions of persecution defined Blacks' schematic understanding of these interactions, then judgments that are in-group favoring would emerge regardless of the type of misconduct. Instead, we see from the data from the survey experiment that Blacks are discerning about the type of conduct that arouses their suspicion. Those who are suspicious, or engage in suspicious thinking, interrupt information processing in favor of scrutinizing *why* there are allegations against an esteemed member of the group. But how does this relate to Black political judgments? I argued that racialized suspicion materializes into what Abrams, Randsley de Moura, and Travaglino call a transgression credit, a protective-type judgment that is discounted and less harsh in the context of wrongdoing.[72] I interpret transgression credits as evidence of Black protection. Indeed, the evidence presented above shows that racialized suspicion influences transgression credits in each of the outcomes observed. In other words, the more suspicious Black people are, the less punitive they are in their evaluations.

While the data presented here support the hypotheses related to racialized suspicion, the artificiality issue remains a concern as far as a generalization can be made to the real world. In the next chapter I address this challenge by testing the effects of race and suspicion using public opinion data to look for these effects beyond a survey experiment. To do this I introduce Washington, D.C., for an analysis of one case, notably the 1990 drug arrest of that city's mayor, Marion S. Barry Jr. Triangulating data in this way will bolster confidence in my claims about the specter of state-sanctioned harassment and how it leads African Americans to protect esteemed members of the racial in-group when they are beset by scandal.[73]

3

"Bitch Set Me Up"

The Suspecting Harassment of Marion Barry

"I'll be goddamn." "Got a setup." "Goddamn, a setup."
"Shit!" "I'll be goddamn."
—Marion Barry Jr.

Jokes abound when it comes to the 1990 drug arrest of Washington, D.C.'s, then-mayor, Marion Barry Jr.[1] "He'll get the hookers off the streets—and into the hotel rooms," cracked David Letterman on his show in August 1990. Nearly twenty years later, *Tonight Show* host Jay Leno quipped that there "was so much white powder in D.C." following a 2009 snowstorm "people thought Marion Barry was mayor again." Even sketch-comedy shows like *In Living Color* and *Saturday Night Live* joined in depicting the mayor as uniquely deviant. The most memorable roast came in the 1996 HBO special *Bring the Pain*, starring comedian Chris Rock and filmed in Washington, D.C.[2] The fifty-eight-minute comedy special was so well received that Rock received two Emmy Awards. In one bit about the former mayor, Rock asked, "How the hell Marion Barry get his job back? . . . How the hell Marion Barry get his job back," he repeated. "Smoke crack [and] got his job back. How the hell that happen?" How could any political candidate be "so bad," Rock mused, "they [could lose] to a crackhead?"

The source of Rock's bewilderment was Barry's successful reelection to D.C.'s municipal government, only a few years after being arrested and convicted in a criminal court. It was specifically about Barry's successful bid for D.C.'s city council in 1992 and for mayor in 1994. The *New York Times* reported on the 1994 victory with the headline "From Disgrace to

'Amazing Grace'";[3] the *Washington Post*'s headline read, "Barry Comes Roaring Back in D.C."[4] Richard L. Berke wrote in the *New York Times* that it was a remarkable "comeback that was as stunning as his fall from office."[5] Over the years, as Jeff Smith writes in *Politico*, "most [W]hite voters, in Washington, D.C. (District of Columbia) and nationally, often winced and wondered how on earth Marion Barry kept getting re-elected."[6] In the 1994 Democratic primary for mayor, for example, the then-councilman drew 47 percent of the vote in a seven-way race that included D.C.'s incumbent mayor, Sharon Pratt, the first African American woman to be the city's leader. And despite the occasional reference to F. Scott Fitzgerald's apocryphal claim that there are no second acts in American lives, many like Barry have enjoyed encores. Yet the question of his postconviction electoral success has never been answered well.

In this chapter I explore the question posed by Rock and Smith, as summarized by political scientists Robert C. Smith and Richard Seltzer: "Why did the city's African American majority return a convicted drug user to its highest office?"[7] I agree and demonstrate here that part of the answer is in their observation that "many [Black Washingtonians] saw [Barry's] arrest as a 'setup,' a conspiracy by powerful [W]hite men to bring down a powerful and effective Black leader."[8] Applying the theory of racialized suspicion, I use local survey data to illustrate these circumstances in the sole case of Washington, D.C., and its embattled former mayor.

Mayor for Life

On the northeast corner of the John A. Wilson Building, home to the Executive Office of the Mayor and the Council of the District of Columbia, stands an eight-foot bronze tribute to the city's second and fourth mayor and longtime city councilor, Marion S. Barry Jr. Titled "MAYOR FOR LIFE," an appellation given to him by *Washington City Paper*'s Ken Cumming and one embraced by many in the city as well as the name of Barry's autobiography, the plaque on the statue reads, "His fervor for justice, fairness, and equality led him to become a champion of the people."[9] When the former mayor died in 2014, the *Washington Post* called him the "most influential and savvy local politician of his generation," with "personal and public lives ... fraught with high drama and irony."[10] An activist in the South, involved in the civil rights movement, Barry was selected to be the first chairperson of the Student Nonviolent Coordinating Committee (SNCC) in 1960. "Determined to take the struggle up north," writes historian Howard Gillette Jr., "Barry moved to Washington, D.C., to set up a SNCC office in June 1965."[11] It is important to note that this was at a time when D.C., "the nation's capital, with a [B]lack population of 54 percent ... did not have voting representation in the U.S. House of Representatives and the U.S. Senate and was unable to vote for the U.S. president or elect its own mayor, City Council, or school board."[12]

Congress enacted the District of Columbia Home Rule Act in 1973, finally enabling residents to choose the city's legislative and executive branches.[13] Before then, the district's school board was the only elected office and held its first election in 1971, one of the first electoral victories for Barry. He served as that body's president until 1974, when he won a seat on the D.C. city council, where he served intermittently for five terms.[14] In 1978, with the endorsement of the *Washington Post*, Barry would then run and win the city's mayoralty, which he held until 1990. By many accounts, the mayor's first term was successful, earning him another endorsement from the *Post* in 1982: "We think Marion Barry should be renominated for mayor—and reelected. He has earned the right to a second term in office."[15] And indeed he won the seat handedly, with 58 percent of the vote. By 1984, however, the mayor's fortunes began to change "as alcohol, drug, and legal problems surfaced for Barry as well as his inner circle."[16] In particular, he was compelled to testify before a federal grand jury regarding allegations relating to buying and using cocaine.[17] Rumors and open secrets about the mayor's drug use dogged him at the end of the 1980s and hit a fever pitch in the new decade.

Anatomy of a Setup

In January 1990 the government collected video evidence, "flickering images of a black-and-white" Mayor Barry, "lighting crack cocaine and inhaling deeply from a crack pipe" in room 727 of the Vista International Hotel.[18] Steve Daley wrote in the *Chicago Tribune* that "the 90-minute videotape was the central element in the government's prosecution of Washington's three-term mayor." It was also the source of "acrimonious debate" among journalists and the public. Much of the dispute concerned whether the undercover sting operation used to arrest Barry was an act of entrapment—that is, tricking him into committing a crime to secure his prosecution. There had been rumors about the mayor's alleged drug addiction as well as related scandals. In 1989 a friend of the mayor, Charles Lewis, testified in court that he had sold crack cocaine to the mayor on "more than one occasion."[19] Barry denied the allegations and was never formally charged with a crime. But just after the new year in 1990, Barry was lured to a downtown hotel by Rasheeda Moore, the married mayor's former girlfriend turned FBI informant; there he was surveilled by federal and local law enforcement and then arrested.

The transcripts from the wiretap that night present a mayor apprehensive and suspicious about visiting Moore inside her hotel room. At one point Barry is heard telling Moore he would "come by in a little jif and [they could] meet downstairs and have a drink and talk." Moore asked why Barry wouldn't "just come upstairs?" The mayor replied, "I don't want to do that," revealing later he did not "like to go in hotel rooms."[20] When the mayor arrived he telephoned Moore's room, 727, and asked if she was "ready to come downstairs." She replied that she had just ordered room service, to which the mayor responded, confused and frustrated, "Why you go and do that? I told you I was comin' over here."[21] After a while, the mayor relented and went upstairs to the room. While there Barry made sexual advances toward Moore. "Can we make love before you leave, before you leave town?" Barry asked. "It would be a good idea, just for old times' sake. You know, catch up." However,

Moore rebuffed his efforts. Barry is later heard on tape eluding to drugs in asking if Moore's "friend mess around?" "So, what, you want to do something?," Moore asked about the drugs. "Not tonight, naw," the mayor answered. Not long after, a woman named Wanda, Moore's drug connection, calls to ask if she could come to the room. Unbeknownst to Barry, Wanda was an undercover agent who delivered narcotics to the room, for which Barry paid Moore.

For a period after the purchase Barry feinted knowledge about what to do. "How does this work?" he asked while holding a pipe under the light. "I, I don't know how this works . . . I never done this before," Barry says. "That's what we used to do all the time. What are you talking about?" Moore replies. "I'm new," Barry says. "We never done this before, give me a break." Barry then says to Moore in what seems like a test of loyalty, "You do it." "No," Moore says. "I'm not doing nothing." "No, no, nope, nope," Barry protests. "I thought you bought this because you wanted to take a hit," Moore says, calling the mayor a "Chicken" when he hesitates.[22] "Aw, naw, you do it," Barry says. "It's all right here . . . are you going to do it?" Finally, accepting the decline, Barry raises the pipe up and inhales. After two hits on the so-called crack pipe, the mayor says, "Let's go downstairs. . . . Let's go downstairs and meet your friend." As the mayor heads for the door, police detectives and FBI agents burst into the room. "Police!" yells one officer. "FBI! FBI! You're under arrest!" yells another. "We're special agents from the FBI and Metropolitan Police Internal Affairs Unit," says FBI agent Ronald Stern. "You are under arrest for possession and use of illegal narcotics."

"That was a good setup, wasn't it," the mayor mutters. "That was a setup, goddamn it. It was a fucking setup," Barry laments in deep irritation. "Goddamn, I shouldn't have come up here," Barry says. The mayor continues to repeat in various iterations his dismay at being set up:[23]

"That was a good setup, wasn't it," the mayor asks rhetorically.
"That was a setup, goddamn it. It was a fucking setup."
"Goddamn, I shouldn't have come up here."

"I'll be goddamn."
"Got a setup."
"Goddamn, a setup."
"Shit!"
"I'll be goddamn."
"Bitch set me up, I'll be goddamn," Barry protests.
"Set me up like that."

It is difficult to describe a sting operation as anything other than a setup—placing federal audio and visual equipment in a room to which the mayor was invited, for the purposes of collecting details about his visit, plus federal and local authorities waiting to burst inside the door and arrest the mayor. According to law professor Bruce Hay, in fact, "the defining feature of a sting operation is that through covert means, the authorities create or facilitate the very offense of which the defendant is convicted."[24] The whole incident threw the city's media and political establishments into a tailspin, leaving the Black press wrestling with how to cover the mayor's transgression and the White media's racist coverage of him.[25] According to the *Washington Post*'s Paul Ruffin, some Black newspapers were reporting Barry's side by focusing on the "purported racism of the prosecution and the white press," while "virtually ignoring the significance of Barry's behavior."[26] "[W]hile many [B]lack reporters accept the contention that the [W]hite media are often biased," he continued, "many find it much hard to swallow another assertion: that the proper role of the [B]lack press—and by implication all [B]lack reporters—is to protect [B]lack leaders rather than criticize them, particularly when they are under attack by [W]hites."

Taking a protective posture in support of the mayor proved to be less of a dilemma for some Black voters in the city, many of whom viewed the infamous tape and "could see for themselves that Barry was more interested in sex than drugs" and that "Moore clearly used her considerable sex appeal to entice the mayor to smoke crack cocaine, lending credence to Barry's claim that he had been entrapped."[27] Black

Washingtonians therefore believed something else was afoot. To be sure, Smith and Seltzer find in their research that "the arrest, trial, conviction, and subsequent reelection of Marion Barry display[ed] the largest cleavage between the races, differences so great as to constitute a canon—a grand canyon of the racial divide."[28] In August that year a jury convicted Barry of only one of fourteen charges against him—a misdemeanor for drug possession that earned him a six-month sentence in prison.

The Nine Lives of Marion Barry

Marion Barry was routinely involved in political scandals throughout his political career, earning a documentary about his life the title *The Nine Lives of Marion Barry*—a call back to the ancient proverb that some cats survive despite their encounters with death or disaster. He first won a term on the city council in Ward 8 and then a fourth term as mayor and many more as a city councilor after being released from prison. In that first council race Barry captured more than 69 percent of the Democratic primary vote—a three-to-one margin against the incumbent—despite the labels of "convict" and "crack head" cast about. By 1994 Councilman Barry would best the incumbent and first woman mayor of D.C., Sharon Pratt, and was returned to the mayoralty. There had long been a sense among some in the city that "Barry was on his way to reelection . . . because black Washington voters could not bring themselves to cut loose this sad figure."[29] However, the puzzle of Barry's nine lives links up with much deeper reflexes about Black political leadership and hides a contempt for Black voters, or some exasperation about the latter's political choices. Barry is hardly the only officeholder to win an election after a scandal, and Black voters are not at all unique in their support for an embattled candidate. Indeed, an entire body of research is devoted to the varieties of why voters excuse alleged impropriety.[30]

There is context worth repeating about D.C. and Barry's 1990 arrest. For example, de Sousa and Moriconi posit that "individuals have a tendency or inclination to react in a certain way to certain situations according to a given set of individual features and values shaping their personality and understanding of the world that surrounds them."[31] The features of the situation are easily summarized in three parts: First, Mayor Barry had been set up by law enforcement in the Vista Hotel at a time when Black lawmakers across the country complained they were being harassed politically. Second, after Barry's arrest and political revival, Republicans in Congress threatened D.C.'s home rule charter because some of them believed the city to be "scandalously corrupt and hopelessly incompetent."[32] Threats to the autonomy of a majority-Black city that already had only limited authority had long been understood as an attempt by the White power structure to regain control from Black politicians. Third, Mayor Barry's personal challenges with drug abuse were no different from the addiction problems facing many of D.C.'s Black residents at that time. In fact, when Black Washingtonians were asked about the principal factor in their decision to support Barry immediately after his arrest, they "mentioned concern about the city's drug and crime problem . . . while [citing] Barry's personal conduct and corruption were less important."[33]

There is no doubt some will find this reasoning ironic.[34] Yet it is consistent with our assumptions about representative government, that leaders should understand the concerns of their constituents. In many ways Barry had similar struggles with substance abuse as some of his constituents. It is also important to recognize that Black folks were not ignorant to or deniers of the alleged drug use—for example, many residents believed Barry had in fact used drugs before he was arrested.[35] Nor were they excusing his abuse of narcotics. Instead, many Black citizens objected to the circumstances and spectacle and thus evaluated them based on their understanding of the racist world that surrounded them. What this means is that some Black citizens became suspicious, leading their attention to be shifted away from the alleged misconduct to the person making the allegation (e.g., prosecutor). Indeed, it made them want to know *why they set the mayor up like that.*

Racial Politics of Scandal

The task of this chapter is to assess the extent to which racialized suspicion, or the underlying belief of a "setup," may help explain the disbursement of a transgression credit in evaluating Marion Barry. The mayor's arrest provides a great case against which to test the theory of racialized suspicion because the circumstances allow us to augment the findings from the previous chapter to demonstrate that African Americans are more likely to believe that Black elected officials are targeted for harassment and that this racialized suspicion leads Blacks "to protect and defend members of their own racial group."[36] Empirically, this means that if African Americans expressed suspicion, those Black elected officials besieged by allegations of impropriety should be judged less harshly across attitude and behavioral measures. This a transgression credit, an operationalization of Black protectionism, whereby perceptual attitudes or actual behavior evaluations are more favorable than punitive for Black political leaders under siege. In the next section we examine whether Black Washingtonians were in fact suspicious and whether that suspicion translated into Black protectionism.

Data and Methods

The empirical goal of this chapter is to determine whether African Americans engage racialized suspicion and its influence on candidate evaluations and other political judgments. The analysis relies on survey data collected by the *Washington Post* in 1987 and 1990, respectively. These datasets are helpful because each survey includes measures that approximate in several ways what I have called racialized suspicion. Also, the years of the survey capture not only the turbulent tenure of Washington, D.C.'s, fourth mayor but a time when there were rising concerns that Black elected officials were being targeted for political harassment.

The ABC News / Washington Post *Poll*

By the late 1980s several news outlets began reporting concerns that there was a double standard in who was investigated for public corruption. In 1988 journalist Gwen Ifill wrote in the *Washington Post* that whether this was true "depended on how you read the numbers." She concluded the "raw data shows that Blacks are, in fact, being prosecuted far more heavily than their representation in the population of elected officials." Black elected officials "only ma[d]e up 3 percent of the nation's elected officials." However, in weaving between the competing narratives of federal prosecutors and the accused Black officeholders, she seemed less sure that meant prosecutors were racist.[37] One year prior, in September 1987, the *Washington Post* asked the question differently to a nationally representative sample of Americans: Is there some effort underway to discredit or embarrass Black political leaders?[38] (See the appendix for question wording.) Respondents were asked which of two views was closer to their own, that (1) investigations were based on factual evidence that the Black leader may have committed a crime or that (2) investigations were attempts by Whites to discredit or embarrass Black leaders. The second response option here is operationalized as racialized suspicion in the analysis that follows.

The Mayor Barry Poll

On Friday, January 19, 1990, after Mayor Barry was arrested, the *Washington Post* ran the following headline: "Barry Arrested on Cocaine Charges in Undercover FBI, Police Operation." Other newspapers across the world began reporting that D.C.'s elected executive had been detained by the FBI and his own local police. An official statement from the Office of the United States Attorney for the District Columbia said that the "undercover operation was part of an ongoing public corruption probe." Before the month was over, the *Post*'s polling outfit conducted a survey of adult D.C. residents, known as the pretrial

Mayor Barry Poll, asking "if they had read or heard anything about the arrest, if they thought Barry should resign, if federal investigators would have tried harder or not so hard to arrest Barry had he been white, and if they thought Barry was indeed using drugs on the night in question."[39] This second survey allows for the best test of the theoretical proposition of racialized suspicion in a real-world setting for several reasons. First, obviously, Barry's arrest remains a well-known reference of a Black elected official involved in a political scandal. Second, Washington, D.C., was then a majority-Black city, which means that a representative sample should permit us to make inferences about Black public opinion there. Third, the data were collected before news of the now-infamous tape of Barry allegedly smoking crack cocaine became widespread. This is valuable in uncovering the theoretical value of suspicion because it captures Black public opinion *before* residents realized the nature of the undercover sting operation involving the mayor. Finally, the survey includes variables that can be used as proxies for generalized and racialized suspicion. For example, the question asking whether law enforcement would have tried as hard to get Barry had he been White is an example of the racialized suspicion.

An Empirical Test of Racialized Suspicion

Table 3.1 displays the extent of suspicious thinking across both datasets without regard to race. On the question of political harassment of Black political leaders in the 1987 survey, 56 percent of respondents believed there was an effort to discredit or embarrass a Black political leader. About 44 percent said allegations against Black political leaders were based on factual evidence. On the question of whether Mayor Barry was harassed, specifically, 46 percent of D.C. residents said the mayor had only himself to blame, 16 percent said law enforcement was out to get him, and 38 percent said both were to blame. Nine percent believed federal investigators would have tried harder to arrest the mayor if he were White, compared to 35 percent saying they would have tried less

TABLE 3.1. Summary Statistics for Outcome Variables
ABC / *Washington Post* Poll, 1987

	%
As you may know, a number of black political leaders have been investigated in recent years by the state or federal prosecutors. Some people say most of these investigations are attempts by whites to discredit or embarrass black leaders. Other people disagree and say most of these investigations are based on real evidence that the black leader may have committed a crime. Which of these two views is closer to your own, or don't you know enough about the issue to say?	
Discredit Blacks	56
Real evidence	44
Washington Post / Mayor Barry Pre-trial Poll, 1990	
Now I'm going to read to you two statements people are making about the Barry incident. And I want you to tell me which one comes closest to the way you feel. Do you believe that . . .	
Law enforcement officials were out to get Marion Barry any way they could?	16
Barry has only himself to blame?	46
Or do both statements equally express your thinking about this incident?	38
Do you think federal investigators would have tried harder or not as hard to arrest the mayor if he were White, or do you think they would have tried as hard to arrest him?	
Tried harder	9
Tried less hard	35
Tried about as hard	56

hard and almost half reporting law enforcement would have tried just as hard. These three measures provide initial evidence of suspicion related to Black elected officials.

Still, we want to know whether race is a significant factor in the expression of suspicion. A logistic regression was applied to these data to make this determination. In the ABC News / *Washington Post* Poll, an effort to discredit another exemplifies the kind of ulterior motive that riggers suspicion; therefore I coded "discredit" as 1 to indicate that a person is suspicious and "real evidence" as 0 to indicate that a person is not suspicious. Likewise, in the Mayor Barry Poll, reporting that law enforcement was "out to get" (i.e., general suspicion) or would not have tried as hard to arrest (i.e., racialized suspicion) Marion Barry was also coded as suspicion. The generalized suspicion measure is decidedly nonracial, while the second taps into Blacks' anxiety about racial double standards. Further, each model includes standard controls like other socioeconomic variables.[40] After we have determined whether Black Americans are suspicious, the analysis turns to whether that way of thinking leads to Black protectionism in the form of transgression credit. For example, the outcome variable probes respondents on if the mayor should resign, coded 1 for yes and 0 for no, and includes a trial heat question about which candidate a voter would select in the city's upcoming Democratic primary, which included the incumbent mayor.

Are Black Voters Suspicious?

Are African Americans especially suspicious of law enforcement actions against Black political leaders? One answer from the ABC News / *Washington Post* Poll is illustrated graphically in figure 3.1. The data display the probability of being suspicious horizontally on the x-axis, as a function of the factors listed vertically (y-axis). In general, we observe that Black respondents were more likely to suspect law enforcement action was designed to embarrass and discredit Black political leaders. A one-unit change in the race variable from White to Black increased the probability of suspicion by 29 percent ($p < .05$) (see the appendix). This first analysis confirms that there are in fact racial differences in suspicious thinking. Except for party identification, the remaining variables are in the opposite direction, indicating a reduced incidence of suspicion. Only political ideology is significant, with conservatives being less likely to report suspicion. So even before we consider the case of Marion Barry, the first survey provides evidence of racialized suspicion concerning Black elected officials more broadly.

Next, consider the evidence presented in figure 3.2 to discern if race matters to the likelihood of being generally and racially suspicious on the question of Marion Barry's drug arrest ($p < .05$ for both) (see model in appendix). The left panel in figure 3.2 shows the effect of race on the probability of engaging in generalized suspicion, that is, believing that law enforcement was out to get Barry any way they could. The right

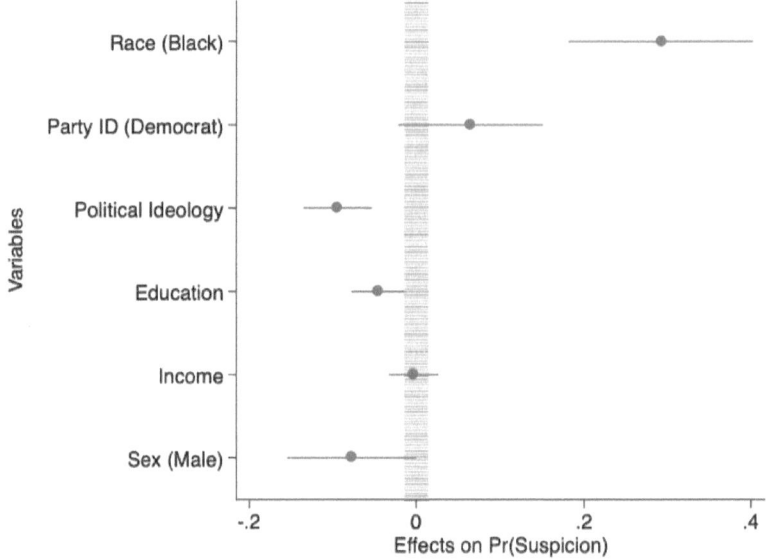

FIGURE 3.1. Racialized Suspicion about Political Harassment (95 Percent CIs). Source: ABC News / *Washington Post* Poll Series, 1987.

panel in figure 3.2 shows the effect of race on the probability of engaging in racialized suspicion or believing that a White mayor would not have been pursued by law enforcement with the same kind of vigor. In general we can see in both graphic representations in figure 3.2 that African Americans, in each case, were associated with an increase in suspicious thinking. Again, this is consistent with the theory of racialized suspicion. The following section discusses the effects of being Black in greater detail.

Generalized Suspicion

What are the effects of race on generalized suspicion? It is generalized only because the content of the question wording is race-neutral, in contrast with the previous analyses and the one that is to follow. Racialized suspicion posits that a relationship exists, for instance, and that it is marked by racial differences in suspicion. A generalized notion of suspicion about harassment is ostensibly unrelated to race. The question wording notwithstanding, any racial differences in suspicious thinking that emerge are no less relevant to racialized suspicion. For example, the focus on a single transgressor, here Marion Barry, permits a more careful consideration of racialized suspicion in a case of wrongdoing. No longer were there just rumors, allegations, or gossip of the mayor's drug use; the FBI and D.C.'s local police arrested the mayor during the commission of that very crime. Yet local Black voters had some doubt about what motivated the arrest.

A logistic regression analysis confirms this notion. Race has a significant effect on the expression of general suspicion. Black Americans reported a suspicion that prosecutors and corrupt police officers they believed were "out to get" Barry. Being Black increased the likelihood of

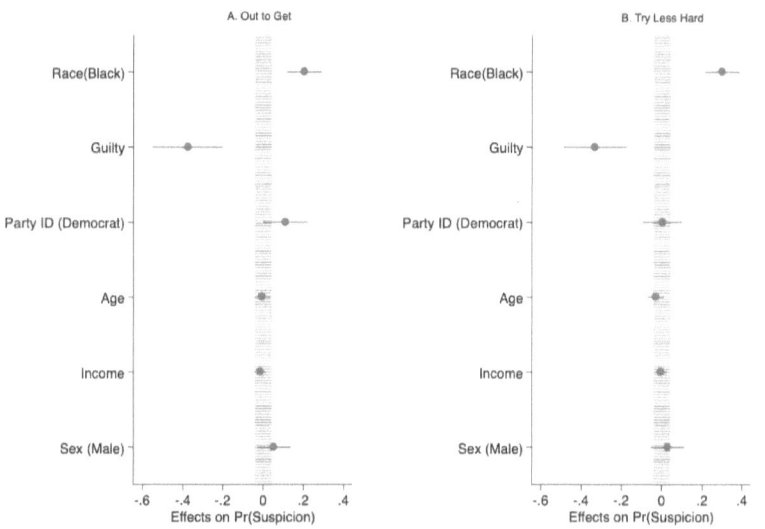

FIGURE 3.2. Racialized Suspicion about Political Harassment of Mayor Barry (95 Percent CIs).
Source: Mayor Barry Poll.

suspicious thinking by 21 percent ($p < .05$) (model in the appendix). This is presented graphically in the left panel of figure 3.2, which shows that Black people are, again, more likely to be suspicious than their White counterparts. This result is revealing because it is captured by the survey prior to the revelation of the now infamous video of the setup. In the immediate aftermath, the sting operation at the center of the arrest, however, raised questions from Black residents, Black journalists, and the local NAACP about whether the mayor had been set up.

If Blacks express generalized suspicion, then what might we expect the effects of race to be on the racialized terms of suspicion? If the findings from the last two sections are any indicator, then we should conclude that being Black affects suspicious thinking. Consider the core lesson in Jamila Michener's racialized policy feedback framework, whereby disproportionality and decentralization act as guides to determine whether to account for race in policy feedback analysis.[41] On the first count, we know from the previous chapter that Black elected officials are subject to extralegal attention.[42] On the second count, we also know from the previous chapter that prosecutors have broad discretion in their pursuit of public corruption cases. You might recall from our discussion of Black protectionism in the previous chapter that Russell-Brown argues one of the questions that triggers this group-based response is whether "Whites accused of the same offense receive the same scrutiny and treatment."[43]

Our second measure of suspicion gets to this issue more directly by engaging with a counterfactual question: Would Mayor Barry have been arrested if he were White? Because the principle of disproportionality often defines the concern about law enforcement actions in racially subjugated communities, including Black elected officials, it is likely that Blacks will register racialized suspicion in part because of the double standards they have come to expect in the enforcement of laws. Accordingly, we see in the right panel of figure 3.2 that being Black increases the likelihood of believing that law enforcement would *not* have tried as hard if Barry had been White by 30 percent. This finding suggest that Blacks were more likely to believe, as Barry did, that his arrest was part of a "racist plot."[44]

Should Mayor Barry Resign?

Let us begin this analysis by testing the role of suspicion on a less formal sanction: telling a politician to resign. To demand the mayor tinder his resignation is a critical rebuke, a de facto punishment that requires the transgressor to self-sanction. Vacating the office under these conditions is preferred by constituents to avoid further scrutiny or embarrassment, to ensure that residents are represented without compromising distractions. Because of this, calls for Barry's resignation came from every corner of the city, including 57 percent of residents, and even trusted advisors were concerned his staying in office would "exacerbate racial tensions."[45] One editorial concluded that "aside from whatever legal resolution may come of the formal charges against him, Mr. Barry should resign."[46] In a letter to the editor a year earlier, one writer concluded, "It's time for D.C.'s citizens to give action to their words in a meaningful way by demanding the resignation of the chief executive whose daily presence mocks every effort currently under way to rid Washington of the drug scourge and the violence it has brought."[47] While the U.S. Department of Justice maintains that resignations are an "appropriate and desirable object in plea negotiations with public officials charged with federal offenses," a public official must be convinced surrendering their office is appropriate.[48]

Mayor Barry was not persuaded. He refused a plea bargain and refused to resign from office.[49] And while that decision was "irrelevant to the prosecution of [the] case," according to a statement issued by a spokesperson for the prosecuting attorney, pressure from that office for Barry to resign was viewed as an affront to Black political power. These perceptions were made worse by a nagging concern that law enforcement engaged in an "embarrassingly abundant measure of federal artfulness and contrivance, not to say a troublesome element of a trap," to arrest the city's mayor.[50] Having established that Black Washingtonians were suspicious about the circumstances of the mayor's legal problems, we should next want to know whether it influenced their calls for him to resign from office. If suspicion reduces the likelihood of Black voters

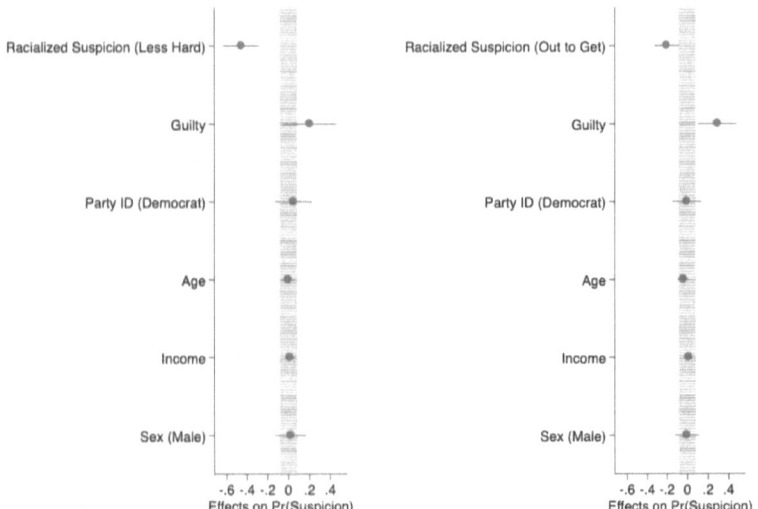

FIGURE 3.3. Effect of Suspicion on Calls for Resignation for African Americans. Source: Mayor Barry Poll.

asking the mayor to step down, this will provide initial evidence of Black protectionism in the form of a transgression credit.

We can look at figure 3.3 for an effect. Both panels show Black Washingtonians engaged in suspicious thinking were less inclined to call for the mayor to step down. Respondents who believed law enforcement was out to get Barry were 46 percent less likely to say the mayor should resign. The right panel exhibits the same pattern. Black Washingtonians were 20 percent less inclined to call for the mayor to step down when they expressed suspicion about a racist double standard. These findings suggest that suspicious thinking triggers Black protectionism in this case by calming calls for resignation.

Who Would You Vote for if the Election Were Today?

Perhaps the most significant question in this period was whether Mayor Barry would run for reelection after his legal troubles. The mayor, "reeling from his arrest on a federal drug charge, ha[d] been strongly urged by top political aides to abandon his reelection bid" because of the "futility [of doing so] in a city plagued by drug abuse and drug-related homicides."[51] In June, six months later, Barry declared he would not run again. In a radio broadcast by Howard University television and radio stations, the mayor offered this report: "What good does it do to win the battle, if in the process I lose my soul? And in my heart I believe it is time for me to serve you, and God, in other ways. Therefore, tonight I am announcing that Marion Barry will not be a candidate for reelection for my fourth term."[52] Barry removed himself from the roster of candidates that would have appeared on the ballot for the Democratic primary the following September, and therefore it is difficult to determine what kind of political support he would have otherwise garnered in the wake of his scandal. However, there is some evidence that 25 percent of voters continued to support him, leading some to believe he could "resurrect his mayoral bid."[53]

Accordingly, we can understand electoral consequences in many ways. First, the idealized expression of democratic accountability is loss of votes—that is, when voters withhold their support or cast ballots against misbehaving politicians. After all, the ballot is the most powerful instrument available to evaluate political performance. It allows the public to deliver the most righteous strike to the hand of grifters and delinquents, or those who simply fail to deliver on their campaign promises. Conventional wisdom has it that voters will cast out from office any who are corrupt and all who are corrupting. In the case of Marion Barry, however, we have already seen that a quarter of voters were willing to overlook his transgression and return him to the mayoralty. In this context, it is useful to think about and understand why in view of the question at the top of the chapter: How did Marion Barry get reelected? Or less generous, how did an official arrested for past drug abuse while in office regain political power?

The most public and cynical answer is reduced to racial voting. There is another parallel explanation provided by racialized suspicion.

However, limitations in local level survey data make it difficult to test this claim when Barry reentered local politics in 1992 and 1994. Data availability remains a significant challenge with studying local elections.[54] I overcame this limitation by drawing on a trial heat question regarding D.C.'s Democratic primary in the pretrial poll. The item asked respondents which candidate they would choose for mayor if the election were held that day. Among the options were Sharon Pratt, John Ray, and David Clarke, with branching possibilities for respondents who answered Jesse Jackson. The response options were recoded 1 to indicate preference for Barry and 0 for all other candidates, then subjected to logistic regression analysis.

Again, we want to know whether suspicion had any influence on Black political judgment. The data reveal, first, that generalized suspicion on the part of African American respondents significantly increased preference for Barry. Specifically, we observe in figure 3.4 that a one-unit change from no suspicion to suspicion—suspicion that law enforcement was out to get Barry any way they could—surges support for the embattled mayor by 43 percent. Likewise, the race-specific measure of suspicion—suspicion that law enforcement would have tried less hard had Barry been a White mayor—boosted electoral intentions of Black Washingtonians for Barry by 19 percent. In both cases, and consistent with the totality of the findings in this and the last chapter, figure 3.4 confirms the effect of suspicion on Blacks' vote intention. Thus, the answer revealed by these data suggests that suspicion may have been a nontrivial, if not potent, factor explaining Barry's second and third political acts after his 1990 arrest.

These racialized dynamics are not without boundaries. For example, they do not necessarily overcome the constraints of local institutional and electoral arrangements. Although Barry decided not to seek a fourth term as the city's mayor, after his conviction on a misdemeanor drug possession charge but before he was sentenced, the former mayor went "after a less lofty [at-large] seat on the City Council" as an independent.[55] "He had been defeated for the first time in

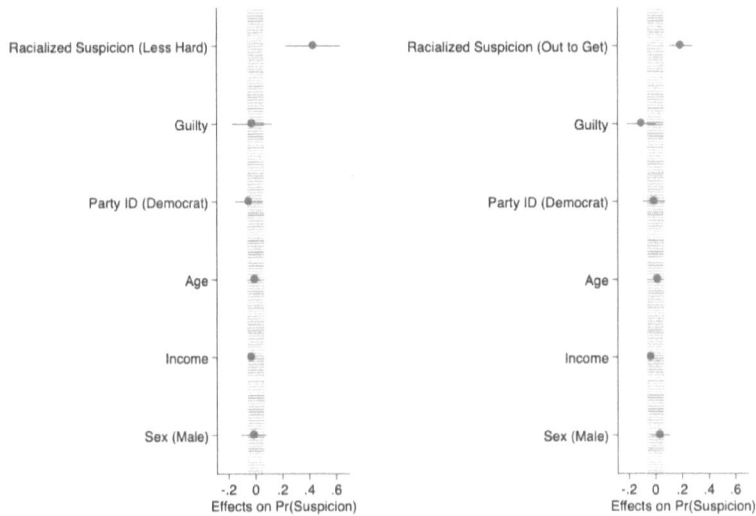

FIGURE 3.4. Effect of Suspicion on Vote Intention.
Source: Mayor Barry Poll.

his political career, reported the *Washington Post*, "not in a bid for an unprecedented fourth term in office, but in a desperate campaign for one of two at-large seats on the D.C. Council."[56] His loss was treated as a personal and political repudiation, a notion Barry rejected. A reasonable question to follow the results above, then, is why suspicion did not rescue Barry in this instance but may have done so in later elections. The criminal case, as well as the circumstances surrounding the election, point to two possible explanations: U.S. district judge Thomas Penfield Jackson waited "until just 11 days before the general election to sentence Barry." The prospect of the former mayor going to jail loomed large, making it unlikely he would be able to fulfill any elected term. This insight would prove prescient in that Barry would begin his prison term a year later, on October 27, 1991.[57] Finally, Barry campaigned for an at-large council seat, unaffiliated with a political party, in a city where Democrats hold governing power, a short time after announcing he would not run for mayor.[58] And while his legal problems were unchanged, his political circumstances had shifted. These colliding challenges were unlikely to be overcome by suspicion. Even so, I do not contend that racialized suspicion delivers a scandalized official to victory. Instead, I maintain and show empirically that it helps buffer misbehaving politicians from the full scope of negative political judgments.

Conclusion

These racialized dynamics help us understand more accurately how and why suspicion spurs Black protectionism. To summarize, Black people suspect these agents of the state are lying to them or *lying on* those they identify as esteemed members of their racial in-group. These are Black political elites, sometimes others, who come under fire by White-dominated institutions. The foundational concern underlying racialized suspicion, or the core of its scrutiny, is that White power structures are seeking to embarrass or discredit effectual Black political leaders like Marion Barry, whom Black voters must protect. The logic assumes, necessarily, that these Black leaders hold a position of status or influence and could be what J. Edgar Hoover called a "Messiah," someone "who could unify, and electrify, the militant Black nationalist movement."[59] Black political leaders did not need to cleanly satisfy these conditions of insurgency; even those invested in a community nationalism that "advance[d] strong [B]lack community control and autonomy within the American political system" were seen as a threat.[60] It was a young Marion Barry, then the director of the SNCC, who, after all, announced the formation of the "Free D.C. Movement" in "February 1966," with the objective "to organize Black people for Black power" and to fight for home rule.[61]

Clearly, the limited formal authority granted to Washington, D.C., and the oversight powers Congress holds over it have important implications for Black political power. In 1978, for example, journalist

Lillian Wiggins, then writing for the *Washington Afro-American*, described what she called "The Master Plan."[62] By her account, there was an effort underway by White power brokers to reclaim domain over the majority-Black D.C.[63] Residents were "constantly reminded," she claimed, "that Black folks in Washington, D.C. [were] bad." But "if we assume that both Blacks in the District and the District itself is bad," she added, "then why is there so much movement back to the District? Why is there so much elevation in the price of housing . . . so much new construction?" Wiggins believed the "new game" in D.C. included the *Washington Post* and "other nameless and faceless power brokers." They would "continuously [point] out D.C.'s ills, hoping that Blacks [would] become discouraged and run out of the city."[64] They accused Blacks of wrongdoing, moreover, and engaged in campaigns to "divide and water down Black influence in Washington."[65]

It was easy then to dismiss Wiggins's 1978 suspicions as an absurd conspiracy theory; they were certainly described as such.[66] But today's D.C. has undergone a transformation that bears a striking resemblance to the one Wiggins foretold. She wrote in the *Afro American* for example that Black flight out of the city would mean that Whites would "become the recipients of their houses."[67] Indeed, Washington, D.C., had experienced the most intense gentrification of any other city in the United States by 2019. Neighborhood change meant new construction, increased rent burden, and the direct displacement of the city's longtime Black residents by more affluent Whites. In other words, gentrification meant that Whites had taken over the housing stock previously occupied by Black residents. Furthermore, these migration patterns have tipped the demographic balance such that the city's majority-Black status hangs in the balance, raising questions about the future of Black mayoral leadership in that city.[68] This was the foretold outcome of "The Plan"—the seizure of municipal power by White power brokers, which would be accomplished in part by issuing criminal charges to bring the Black politicians into ill repute.

With this backdrop, it is not surprising that Black Washingtonians were suspicious that a well-regarded official with a rich and storied history of community nationalism and commitment found himself under siege or that Black voters would disburse transgression credits in the form of Black protectionism for their mayor for life.

Conclusion

Black Power Failure: Toward a Critical Black Protectionism

Our errors always cost us more.
  —Ta-Nehisi Coates

Black people's thinking about what could happen to them or Black leaders—elected, religious, intellectual, or radical—is informed by what has already happened to them before. Far from the paranoid style of American politics lay the slain bodies of popular Black figures, combatants for the cause of their people's liberation, all felled by bullets: Martin Luther King Jr., Malcolm X, Medgar Evers, and Fred Hampton, to name a few. Where death was not accomplished, freedom and reputation could be compromised instead. The surveillance and prosecution of Black political figures, for example, was widespread and led to their disproportionate capture in the federal anticorruption dragnet. What was less clear was the extent to which Black people suspected government actions toward their leaders were untoward and whether that suspicion conditioned how they responded. In this book I adopt the context of corruption scandals and argue that Black Americans are often suspicious about the legitimacy of criminal accusation (and the law enforcement action) and protective of accused Black officeholders.

Summarizing the Racial Politics of Scandal

The focusing questions of this book are in two parts. The first considers to what extent African Americans engage in suspicious thinking. I developed a theory of racialized suspicion to explain that African

Americans experience disruptions in their information processing when law enforcement level allegations of lawbreaking against a Black elected official. Suspicions about the ulterior motives of a state actor, like a prosecutor or police officer, mean that African Americans will scrutinize their actions more. They are more likely to believe, moreover, that Black leaders are being targeted or harassed. Racialized suspicion shifts the evaluation from the accused to the accuser. The second question ponders what Black voters, once suspicious, do if they believe law enforcement is engaged to discredit or embarrass Black elected officials. The theory of racialized suspicion proposes that suspicion facilitates discounted judgments. Where there is evidence of transgression credits, there is an example of what Katheryn Russell-Brown calls Black protectionism.[1]

What Have We Learned?

In short, we wanted to know whether Black voters were suspicious thinkers and whether scandal incidents encouraged them to dispense transgression credits. The answer on both counts is yes. Many African Americans are aware of fragments of what the state can do to them—what has been done to them before—throughout the history of the nation. Some recognize the state's reputation for meddling, threats to Black political power, and the criminalization of their communities. The suspicion aroused from these concerns led them to take a protective, discounting posture in defense of esteemed members of their in-group who stand accused of wrongdoing.

Suspicious Thinkers

On the first question, I showed four empirical examples in which African Americans are more likely than their White counterparts to express racialized suspicion. In chapter 2 I drew on data from a survey experiment and presented evidence that Black respondents were especially likely to believe a Black incumbent was unfairly targeted relative to a White incumbent. This was conditional on the type of scandal in which the official was alleged to be involved. The prominent effects were for the Black official accused of a financial crime. In contrast, sex scandals did little to trigger suspicion. Chapter 3 examined suspicion using the 1987 ABC News / *Washington Post* Poll and the 1990 *Washington Post / Mayor Barry Poll*, which included three relevant questions used to measure suspicion. The first asked if respondents believed there was an effort underway to undermine or embarrass Black leaders. The second item, from the Mayor Barry Poll, suggested that law enforcement was "out to get" the mayor, while the third suggested law enforcement would not have tried as hard if the mayor were White. Despite their different constructions, each measure captured doubt about the evenhandedness of investigations related to Black officials and served as an indicator of racialized suspicion. Regardless of the measure, African Americans were significantly more likely to express suspicion in each case.

Transgression Credits as Black Protectionism

Racialized suspicion influenced Black people's political judgments about embattled incumbents. On the second question, I show the presence of suspicion reduces the negative penalties for scandalized Black politicians. From the Scandalized Mayor Experiment to the Mayor Barry Poll, each highlighted how suspicion leads to the discounting of negative appraisals and the augmenting of positive assessments. Chapter 2 showed that suspicious Black respondents in the experiment reported more favorable evaluations of the candidate's character traits, assigned less blame to them, and said they would consider voting for them in a future election. In chapter 3, with the Mayor Barry Poll, Black residents engaged in suspicious thinking were less likely to call for Marion Barry to resign and more likely to say they would vote for him in the primary. In general, the data reveal that suspicion generated transgression credits for the imperiled mayors. These results suggest that doubt about the motivations of law enforcement results in varying levels of Black protectionism. Black Americans, unsure about the integrity of the state, specifically related to public integrity, redirect their scrutiny away from the accused. In return, their judgments of the officeholder are less harsh.

Limits on Suspicion and Protection

Peter Digeser raises an important question about forgiveness and politics: Is it ever appropriate for citizens to forgive wrongs done to them by their government?[2] Forgiveness, as a political concept, sometimes gets in the way of justice. Certainly, it could be argued here that group-based protectionism is "letting transgressors off the hook by releasing [them] from the punishment . . . that is owed."[3] That debt is settled in two ways—political or legal—and one takes precedent over the other. No voter, no matter how sympathetic or suspicious they may be, can restore to power an official that is remanded to prison or forbidden from holding public office because of past misdeeds. As a political matter, though, the electorate has the first right to forgive—and often does. For African Americans, I have argued, forgiveness as transgression credits is about not necessarily the harm inflicted by scandalized Black politicians but the perceived injury served by White-dominated society against Black people and their leaders.

However, it is also not clear that all Black officials benefit the same from the disruption of suspicion or if suspicion and protectionism are enduring effects. In the epilogue I address the claim that Black women have not benefited from the collective cloak of Black protectionism. Black law enforcement, whether prosecutors or police, may also not arouse the same kinds of concern. Few Black Americans seemed to mobilize to defend Philadelphia's former district attorney, R. Seth Williams, when he was indicted, resigned, and was sentenced to prison for corruption-related crimes. This may have been the case for two relevant reasons. First, Black prosecutors and police officers are agents of the state, often tasked with carrying out assaults on Black communities. For example, many were quick to dismiss claims of racism in the Vincent Gray and O. J. Simpson cases because the prosecutors were also Black. But so too were the informants used during COINTELPRO. Second and related, as explained by political scientist Julian Wamble, African Americans prefer to support officials who have a commitment and record of action that serves the racial group's interest.[4] In the case of Williams, the district attorney, the conflicting commitment is well articulated by Solomon Jones, a local African American writer and radio host, who wrote in WHYY,

> I'm angry because Seth Williams pursued charges against five [B]lack public officials who accepted, but did not report, small gifts from . . . a lobbyist who turned out to be a government informant. Williams pursued and won convictions against those officials, knowing all the while that he'd collected $175,000 in unreported gifts from two wealthy businessmen. I'm angry because when his own misdeeds became public, Williams repeatedly told me in radio interviews that he wanted the black community to forgive him. He assured my listeners that what he had done was not the same thing he prosecuted others for doing.[5]

There are also claims we are witnessing the end of Black politics.[6] After sixty-plus years of Black political power, a growing view is that the Black political class is ineffectual, neoliberal, and too far captured by White interests.[7] It has been argued that decades of Black political leaderships, including the first Black president, have done too little to materially and significantly advance Black interests in a way that justifies strict racial voting for the sake of descriptive representation. Younger generations of Black Americans seem especially cynical of old-school Black politicians and contemptuous of the old style of Black politics that "regularly fail to rise to the challenges that confront young people."[8] And a more critical Black protectionism that is not bound by the in-group traditions of race politics is starting to take root.[9]

Moreover, patterns of corrupt abuse that undermine community commitments lead voters to question the quality of their representation.

This is exacerbated by already low satisfaction with local government services in cities with high levels of Black political incorporation.[10] And while Black mayors may have inherited "hollow prizes"—"cities depleted of the resources needed to significantly improve the quality of the lives of the city's residents"[11]—widespread corruption compounds and further imperils urban voters. This may explain the paucity of sympathy for Kwame Kilpatrick, the former mayor of Detroit. In 2013 the Motor City filed the biggest municipal bankruptcy in U.S. history. And many believed Kilpatrick put that "city through a corruption scandal so vast that prosecutors say it helped accelerate" its march toward financial ruin.[12] Although there is disagreement about who is to blame—and Kilpatrick insists it was not his fault—his conduct may have been unforgiveable because the consequences were not abstract pocketbook issues but unpaid pensions of city workers and disruptions to municipal service delivery through the whole of the majority-Black city. And yet many observers nonetheless believed his prison sentence—twenty-eight years—was too harsh.

Twice as Good

It is often said that Black Americans must be twice as good at all things to get half of what White Americans receive. This is the racialized wisdom underlying Ralph J. Bunche's review of *Negro Politicians*. You read earlier that Bunche observed that the book's author, Harold Gosnell, offered only a "left-handed compliment" in writing that "corruption and ballot thievery [were] as common in [W]hite as in colored neighborhoods." According to Bunche, "it [was] no praiseworthy achievement for Negroes to supplement the already sordid pages of American municipal politics" by contributing to maladministration.[13] It did not matter to him that Gosnell was responding to the "impression . . . that bribery and election corruption [were] prevalent in the sections inhabited largely by Negroes," and the complaint "common for [White] candidates to say that they lost in the 'Black Belt' because they did not spend money there."

Like in the Reconstruction-era charges of Black political misdeeds, the fact is corruption was widespread and not at all unique to Black elected officials. For example, Gosnell found that evidence of "recounts, special investigations, and the records of prosecutions" showed that Black and White politicians were no different in their graft.[14]

Both views represent a dilemma in Black politics. Quite apart from celebrating unethical behavior, it would be wrong to walk away from the summarized conclusion that Black Americans believe Black politicians should have an equal go at ethical lapses, to waste, defraud, or abuse taxpayer resources. Instead, Mary R. Warner, author of *The Dilemma of Black Politics*, captures well the underlying concern during a panel discussion on racial harassment: "It is important to assert both our integrity and imperfections; they are not mutually exclusive. Certainly, all elected officials should be held accountable—that is a given—but Black elected officials should not be required to be perfect, and neither should Black elected officials be held to a double standard of performance."

At the same time, observers like journalist Chuck Stone believe that "no matter how stained his hands, how sullied his reputation, or how unpopular his manners, if the Black politician has played power politics with the same efficiency as White politicians, he [would] soon be accepted by Black people as the most important power brokers in society."[15] And because they were among the newcomers to whom part of "the traditional forms of machine politics [had] been directly bequeathed,"[16] Black candidates and Black voters wanted in on the city's system of patronage.[17] However, there is some evidence, and even Bunche suggests, that the patronage for Black urban voters was menial. Regardless, Blacks in places like Philadelphia were suspicious of municipal reforms targeting such spoils, with W. E. B. Du Bois arguing that they saw the reforms as efforts to "eliminate their participation in political life and from the best chances of earning a living." But times have changed, and the spoils of local government do not trickle down the same. When politicians steal or abuse their office, the gain is most often their own. And while such misbehavior is costly to all taxpayers, the most vulnerable suffer when public programs are misused by officials. Waste, fraud, and abuse are inefficient and undermine the capacity of government to deliver honest services to those who need them most.

And lest the ghost of Ralph Bunche accuse the preceding chapters of being an "implicit apology for petty, grafting, self-seeking [Black] politicians by explaining that they merely adopted the 'general patterns of behavior' of the [W]hite politicians," I want to take serious that "to say that the [Black] politician was often no better than the average [W]hite politician" was "to damn him."[18] Certainly, the errors of Black political leaders always cost them more. This book does not excuse malfeasance or betrayal of the political ethics of public office. A critical Black protectionism, as posited by Katheryn Russell-Brown, with which I agree, urges greater discernment and consistency so as "not [to] give a pass to the Black person under scrutiny, the victim, or the government" but to acknowledge "wrongdoing and calls for sanctions where appropriate."[19] Without it, James Q. Wilson's warning that the "end of law" is found at the other end of "excusing accountability" may well be true.[20]

However, the point of this book is to reframe what Wilson and others overstate in the way they believe the law supplied "a promise of fair treatment based on individual accountability," a special kind of remedy to the indignities suffered by African Americans.[21] This book offers an alternative explanation for why African Americans do not take this view. Suspicious of the double standard regarding public integrity—such that politicians are unfairly targeted and disproportionately prosecuted—African Americans rally around to protect embattled in-group leaders. We have already seen the ways in which race is intertwined with the public's imagination of who is corrupt and how those manifest in terms of law enforcement. The government has a long-standing reputation for discriminating in the application of the law that makes it the subject of Blacks' suspicion. But racialized suspicion and Black protectionism may now be in shorter supply. Not much of a fuss has been made of recent scandals involving figures like Buffalo, New York's, mayor Byron W. Brown or the former mayor of Tallahassee, Florida, Andrew Gillum.

Closing

Public integrity is an exercise in government virtue. It claims to demand behavior that reflects the high moral standards of public service. Those who enter government are duty-bound, taking an oath—solemnly swearing—to support and defend the Constitution of the United States against all enemies, foreign and domestic. This duty cannot be faithfully discharged if decisions are put up for sale by those entrusted with them. Politicians on the take deprive citizens of the honest services of their government. When and where this conduct is practiced, watchdogs of good government, in civil society, the media, and law enforcement, raise flags on what they believe may signal official misconduct in office. However, we routinely overestimate the extent to which the public rises up and demands accountability at the ballot box by casting out those wayward politicians. While some incumbents do lose some electoral support, many are returned to office despite tales of impropriety. Why? The reasons are varied—some straightforward, others more complicated. The factors are economic, psychological, institutional, and identity based. Circumstances, moreover, determine what matters, how, why, and to whom. In this account, racialized suspicion begets Black protectionism, a civil rights strategy and effort to counteract disparate racial treatment that sometimes leads African Americans to mobilize around beleaguered officials.[22]

Epilogue

This book has provided evidence for what I have called racialized suspicion and its effect on Black protectionism. As is evident from the title, *Marked Men*, I have focused exclusively on Black political psychology and behavior regarding the alleged misconduct of Black male elected officials. This is a reasonable orientation given that men are more likely to hold political power. But the growing prominence of women in elected office, especially Black women, raises important questions about whether the protective dynamic described herein is equally applied to women in public life. Katheryn Russell-Brown, whose work is foundational here, maintains that that while "only a handful of Black women have been eligible for Black protectionism . . . none have received it." In this epilogue I agree that this "raises question of whether Black protectionism is available to Black women or solely the province of Black men."

There are now more Black women in elected office than ever before. This was also true at the time Russell-Brown argued this point. At the time of this writing, meanwhile, a South Asian Black woman, Kamala Harris, serves as the first female vice president of the United States. The Center for American Women and Politics estimates that there were 24 Black women serving in the U.S. House of Representatives in 2021, 354 Black women serving in state legislatures, including 82 members of state senates and 272 members of state houses, and 8 Black women serving as mayors of some of the most populated cities. Black women's ascent into the halls of power in American politics has been slow and steady. The double burdens of racism and sexism have contributed mightily to their exclusion. Yet in the second decade of the millennium Black women have "achieved a historic milestone" that has also been accompanied by increased scrutiny related to their conduct in office. In chapter 2

I briefly mentioned the bribery allegations that rocked Monica Conyers of Detroit. Shortly after I arrived in Philadelphia, the state representative for my district, Michelle Brownlee, resigned after pleading guilty to corruption charges after she was caught up in a sting operation.[1] More recently, Rochester, New York's, first Black woman mayor, Lovely Warren, resigned from office after being indicted for two campaign finance violations and gun charges.[2]

Women Politicians, Corruption, and Scandal

Research on women elected officials demonstrates that they not only are less likely to be involved in corruption scandals but are associated with lower perceptions of corruption.[3] When they do transgress moral or legal boundaries, the evidence about how voters respond is more mixed. For example, a "politician's sex is important in determining which types of scandals are most egregious."[4] Female politicians are less likely to be punished for sex scandals—i.e., counterstereotypical scandals—and receive higher scores regarding their character.[5] But those evaluations depend on political ideology and sexism. Conservatives are more punitive toward women politicians involved in sex scandals, for instance, as are those who hold sexist attitudes toward women.[6] On balance, though, women in politics do not seem to be overly or differentially penalized for their misdeeds.[7]

What is not yet clear is how race and gender at the intersections matter to these evaluations.[8] For example, we know that Black women are most likely to support Black women candidates.[9] But we do not know whether, or to what extent, Black women politicians are beneficiaries of Black protectionism. Unfortunately, I do not have data to sufficiently answer that question here.[10] Yet if we look fifty-three miles north of Washington, D.C., to Baltimore, Maryland, we may find hints at a partial answer. The so-called Charm City is unique in that it has had three Black women serve as mayor in rough succession between 2007 to 2019. And despite their unprecedented reign, the tenures of two of them—as well as of one state's attorney—were effectively ended by indictments.

Sheila Dixon

Sheila Dixon was an elected member of the Baltimore City Council from 1988 to 2007 and spent almost eight years as president of that body. In 2007 she was elected mayor of Baltimore, the first Black woman to ever hold that office. Two years after becoming the city's chief executive, law enforcement raided the mayor's home and Dixon was indicted on seven criminal counts, including theft, fraudulent misappropriation, and misconduct in office. The criminal complaint filed by the State of Maryland alleged that Dixon, "in violation and perversion of her duties as Mayor to uphold, enforce and obey the laws of the City of Baltimore and the State of Maryland, commit[ed] malfeasance by corruptly stealing and converting to her own" various gift cards intended for needy families.[11] A jury convicted the mayor on "one count of embezzlement for stealing gift cards meant for poor residents, but it acquitted her of three other charges, including the most serious felony theft charge."[12] Dixon received four years of probation and community service and agreed to step down as mayor as part of a plea deal that allowed her to avoid jail time.[13]

A Baltimore Girl

Political scientists agree that whatever the impropriety or indiscretion, politicians beset by scandal are often returned to office.[14] Incriminating information against them reduces their electoral margins, but it is seldom enough to oust an incumbent. But what are the prospects for an official who leaves office in disgrace? That was the question that framed Baltimore's 2016 Democratic primary for mayor. It was widely speculated that Sheila Dixon would enter the race as a candidate after vacating

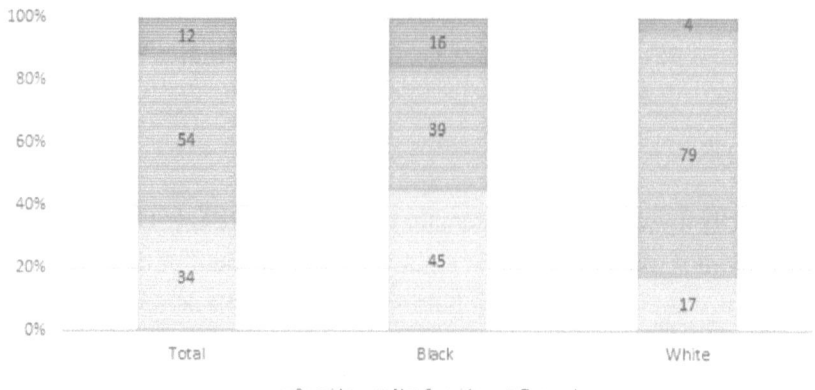

FIGURE E.1. Baltimore Mayoral Likely Voter Poll, 2011.
Source: *Baltimore Sun* / Opinion Works.

it because of scandal. Long before then, in 2011, the *Baltimore Sun* asked voters to "look ahead to 2015, [and] if Sheila Dixon were to be a candidate for mayor again," would they consider supporting her, or not. Approximately 34 percent of residents indicated they would consider supporting the formerly disgraced mayor. And 45 percent of African Americans in the city said the same, compared to only 17 percent of White residents (see figure E.1). In the mind of Faraji Muhammad, cohost of *The Larry Young Morning Show*, the White residents of Baltimore did not trust Dixon and never "truly forgave her."[15] However, the *Sun* polls consistently showed that Dixon could attract voters if she ran again—and so she did.[16]

Dixon announced she would challenge the incumbent mayor, Stephanie Rawlings-Blake. However, Rawlings-Blake shocked supporters when she ultimately decided not to seek reelection after Baltimore erupted into chaos after Freddie Gray, a Black man, died in police custody and the city rioted.[17] At first glance, those early *Sun* polls seemed like prophecy as Dixon emerged as an early frontrunner in the race, eclipsing her closest rival, Catherine Pugh, by eleven points.[18] As the race warmed up and Dixon sought forgiveness and a second chance, one political action committee (PAC) was quick to remind voters of her past impropriety.[19] In one punishing video ad by Clean Slate Baltimore PAC, titled a "A Baltimore Christmas Story," Dixon was depicted as the "Grinch Who Stole Christmas" with a child narrator recounting her theft and ending by asking, "Does she really think we won't remember?" In another instance, the PAC circulated a flier with side-by-side images of Pugh and Dixon, the latter posed in a mugshot, a tactic Dixon called "downright dirty."[20]

Election Day

On Election Day, April 26, 2016, I traveled to Baltimore from Philadelphia to observe the city's primary for mayor. It was hot and sunny as well as curiously quiet at ten o'clock that morning given that it was a primary day. Maryland voters had to choose among a menu of Democrats for high- and low-level offices. The sounds of the local Black talk radio station filled the car. As I entered the city, the station's music programming was interrupted with a report of vandalism from a mob of angry campaign workers that had formed outside the headquarters of mayoral candidate Senator Catherine Pugh.[21] Despite the news, I continued to visit polling places, intermittently checking the Dixon campaign's Twitter account to see if I could catch the candidate between locations. I settled at a local elementary school but learned that I had just missed the former mayor. Still, I stayed and talked to canvassers, quietly fascinated by a mobile billboard truck plastered with "Sheila Dixon for Mayor" that circled the block; the driver generously slowed down upon realizing I was trying to snap a photograph of the moving campaign poster.

John 8:7

I asked one African American woman, Ms. P., what she thought about Dixon. She responded that the former mayor was a "Baltimore girl," which I took to mean "one of them," while Pugh, in contrast, was not. When I asked Ms. P. her opinion about the circumstances surrounding

Dixon's resignation years earlier, she surprised me by quoting biblical scripture, John 8:7: "Let he without sin be the first to cast the stone." There were no innocents, and only she who was pure could cast judgment. Although Ms. P. was canvassing for a candidate for a different office and would not say whether she was supporting Dixon, the half smile that framed her face seemed to betray her. After a while, Dixon returned to the site. A news crew assembled around to interview her. At the same time, she kept glancing at me and my notebook, assuming, I think, that I was a reporter looking for a quote. I hesitantly approached her, asked for a sticker, and told her I had been in touch with her campaign manager about interviewing her for my research. She was either indifferent or familiar—either way, it was a no-go. I hung around her car as she talked to voters and eventually struck up a conversation with her driver, a former police officer, with whom I was sharing in the misery of perspiration under the beating sun. He was friendly and loquacious, enough so, I thought, that I also asked him what he thought about Dixon's transgressions years prior. And without pause he too recited the same scripture as Ms. P., chapter and verse.

There was a remarkable regard for the former mayor. It turned out that many attributed Dixon's troubles to "the fact that the state prosecutor's office is all [W]hite guys who don't practice in the city."[22] "Many Dixon supporters view her court case like this," wrote Luke Broadwater for the *Baltimore Sun*: "A successful Black woman rose too high and was railroaded by a Republican-appointed prosecutor. She was subjected to the indignity of having her home raided and her reputation tarnished."[23] He recounted versions of this to me on the phone. To be sure, when Dixon was convicted, the *New York Times* wrote that "some residents viewed the trial as politically or racially motivated. . . . If you ask an African-American out on the street, they tell you right away that Sheila Dixon is innocent," said one Baltimore resident. "But if you ask a White person out on the street, they say she's guilty."[24]

At the end of that Election Day, Dixon, once the frontrunner, lost her bid for a second chance by a slim margin (figure E.2). With 34.8 percent

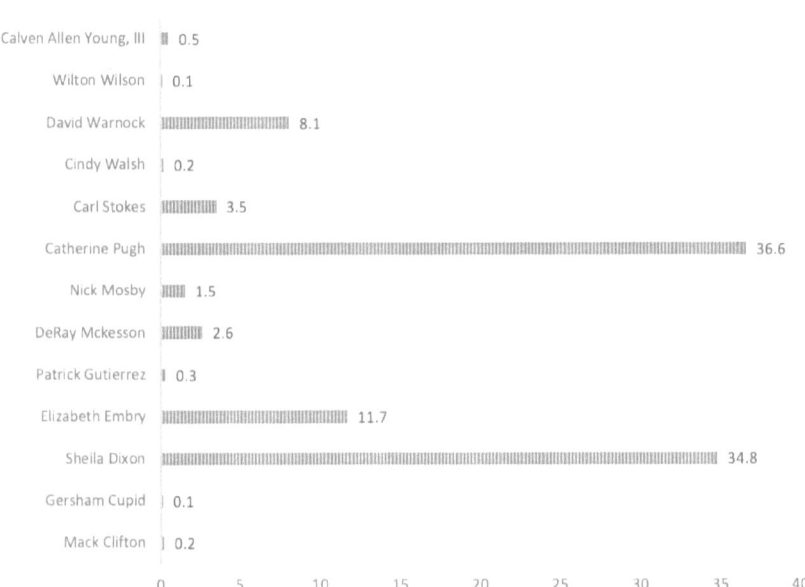

FIGURE E.2. Democratic Primary for Mayor, Baltimore, Maryland, 2016. Source: Baltimore City Board of Elections.

of the vote, Dixon lost by less than two points to Catherine Pugh, who would become Baltimore's third Black woman to serve in the mayoralty. Dixon ran again in 2020 and was again only narrowly defeated. As of this writing in 2023, she has announced her candidacy for the mayoralty once more.

Catherine Pugh

Catherine Pugh served as a senator in the Maryland State Senate from 2007 until 2016. In addition, she was the "sole proprietor of Healthy Holly, LLC ("Healthy Holly"), a business she established in 2011 to produce and sell children's books she had written and illustrated."[25] Three years into her mayoral term, Pugh would also be engulfed in a scandal of her own "over lucrative book deals for Healthy Holly."[26] According to a federal indictment, the books "were marketed and sold directly to non-profit organizations and foundations, many of whom did business or attempted to do business with Maryland state government and Baltimore City." Pugh approached leaders of these organizations about purchasing these books "on the condition that the purchase be on behalf of, and for distribution to, school children in the Baltimore City Public Schools (BCPS)."[27] In one instance, a nonprofit health care organization agreed to the purchase and donation; the books were printed and stored in a BCPS facility. However, the U.S. government alleged that Pugh "did knowingly devise and intend to devise a scheme . . . to defraud purchasers of Healthy Holly books and to obtain money and property from such purchases as means of materially false pretenses. . . . that is, the defendant promised to print and deliver books . . . when, in truth and fact, [she] had no intent to provide the books." Instead, Pugh later used "the books for her own personal use" by removing the donated books from BCPS and giving them away at various political events unbeknownst to the nonprofit or the school. Pugh would later resign the mayoralty and be convicted and sentenced to three years in an Alabama prison.[28]

It is difficult to miss the irony of Pugh's downfall. Pugh, a former state senator, overcame a strong field of Democrats, including former mayor Sheila Dixon, who resigned office in 2010 also because of a corruption scandal. And as I described above, a "political action committee backing Pugh [was] circulating a flier with a photo of Dixon doctored to look like a police mug shot."[29] Perhaps Pugh's undoing is surprising only in considering that Dixon, despite her sullied political history, was the candidate she needed to beat in the primary. And yet Pugh's downfall was an extraordinarily odd ordeal: the mayor hid away from the press, claiming she had pneumonia, and as scrutiny mounted Pugh resigned from office via her lawyer. Comparatively, there is less to say about Mayor Pugh's case in terms of racialized suspicion; few residents or voters seem to have responded the same way they did to Dixon's misdeeds.

One incident, though, clarifies the underlying premise. A 2019 public relations controversy involving WJZ-TV news anchor Mary

Bubala is illustrative. Bubala asked a guest if the resignation of Baltimore mayor Catherine Pugh was "a signal that a different kind of leadership [was] needed to move Baltimore City forward." The city had had "three female, African-American mayors in a row," she said, before concluding, "two resigned, though." The "different kind of leadership" to which Bubala referred carried racial and gendered overtones, which were understood to mean White and male leaders were needed to run the city. WJZ-TV promptly fired Bubala for the question. Whatever the newscaster's intentions, the issue illustrates the latent casting of Black politics as corrupt and incompetent, while White politics, in contrast, is presumed to be the default of good governance. Yet this misunderstands the history of municipal corruption, which existed in colonial cities and before Blacks become a freed people in the United States. But the notion that Black leadership is somehow worse lingers. It sets the conditions under which racialized suspicion can flourish.

Marilyn Mosby

In 2016, amid racial turmoil following the police killing of Freddie Gray—another powerful Black woman, Marilyn Mosby, a young, elected prosecutor for Baltimore, "leaped onto the national stage—as heroine and lightning rod."[30] When Mosby filed charges against the officers responsible for Gray's detention death, she developed a prominent national profile.[31] It is worth noting that Mosby's husband, Nick Mosby, a member of the Baltimore City Council, was also a candidate in the 2016 primary for mayor against Dixon and Pugh. In 2022, a "federal grand jury ... returned an indictment charging Marilyn J. Mosby [with] federal charges of perjury and making false mortgage applications, relating to the purchases of two vacation homes in Florida."[32] The U.S. government alleged that Mosby lied about financial hardship during the coronavirus pandemic to claim eligibility to draw down from the city's Deferred Compensation Plan and that she made false statements related to her mortgage application.[33] The two-term incumbent prosecutor lost her Democratic primary in July 2022, several months after the indictment. She was convicted of two counts of perjury in November 2023.

Are Marked Women Protected?

One would anticipate that the principles of racialized suspicion and Black protectionism would adapt to cover newly emergent Black political leaders, regardless of gender. The case of Sheila Dixon is the only one of those I have discussed that is compelling in hinting at that potential in Baltimore. If the function of racialized suspicion is to question ulterior motives of White attacks on Black elected officials, it seems apparent that the rise of Black women to political office would recalibrate Black protectionism to cover the other racial subgroup. As more women rise to political power, examples of alleged misconduct or harassment may be more available for analysis. Although these examples can be readily described, the research infrastructure necessary to capture local Black public opinion needs to be in place to more effectively answer the extent to which Black women's troubles raise suspicion and spur protection. Fortunately, more Black women are rising to political power in local, state, and federal government. Unfortunately, if the pattern of racialized political harassment continues, we will see increased trouble for those officials in the future.

ACKNOWLEDGMENTS

I must convince myself that the gods have been favorable to me in this endeavor. But there are days when I have serious doubts. Friends and colleagues who shared news stories about the legal troubles experienced by Black political leaders, always with the note, "Did you see this?!," sustained and encouraged my efforts. I am grateful to them for their interest and gentle nudges. I also appreciate my many neighbors—encountered on the street or in our local restaurants (2637Brew), bars (Sarah's, now Otto's Taproom), and coffee shops (Lucky Goat Coffeehouse)—who have repeatedly and sincerely asked me over the years, "How's the book?" I would always smile sheepishly, head bowed, and mumble that it was "coming along." However, that answer never felt quite true and, in many ways, exacerbated my uncertainty about whether it ever would be finished. And yet, here it is.

David Riverbank, Calvin Thrall, and Bria Wilson provided outstanding research assistance over the years. I owe a special debt to Leanne Powner, who suffered through many bad and incomplete drafts as my developmental editor. I admit to not knowing what I was doing for most of this long haul, but Leanne and others helped me find a way forward. Without their insight and engagement, this work would remain an ugly draft. Still, any errors that remain are mine alone.

I have been unusually fortunate to work with supportive colleagues at Temple University. If you ever want to know why I wrote this book, Vin Arceneaux and Robin Kolodny are to blame. They were waymakers whose good counsel and support pushed me to consider alternatives when my attempts to publish in refereed journals were not successful in my early years on the tenure track. I also very much appreciate Robin Kolodny, who, as chair of the department, was unrelenting in checking on my progress and in being a cheerleader whose support never wavered. Not far behind Robin, often lurking in the administrative shadows of the dean's office, was Sandra Suarez, whose generosity has not gone unnoticed. Others in my department have been similarly encouraging and helpful in this process. I am grateful to be on a team with people who want me to win.

I have also benefitted enormously from the goodwill and interest of other colleagues. Marc Meredith invited me to Penn to present versions of this work at the American Politics Workshop my first semester in town. Other invitations to present at Rutgers, Northwestern, Georgetown, and Princeton soon followed. Many thanks to Melanye Price, Al Tillery, Michael Bailey, and Vin Arceneaux for those opportunities to share early parts of this work. But it was Ilene Kalish, editor at New York University Press, with whom I had an hour-plus-long conversation at APSA in San Francisco, who restored my fleeting confidence in this project. I am delighted this book has been published by this press. It was the first choice, the only choice, and always the right choice. Melanye Price and Heath Fogg-Davis are both owed a credit too, for they separately recommended NYU and spoke glowingly of their experience working with Ilene. One or both made the initial introduction. My hat is also tipped to Christina Greer and Matt Wray, who went out of their way to share draft book proposals to get me started; and to Davin Phoenix and LaFleur Stephens-Dougan, who did their best to hold me accountable in an early book writing group.

I feel fortunate to have good friends and a solid community of conspirators. Those who hang around me provide strong support. Especially undefeated are those friends who make and take phone calls. Thank you Lindsey, Monet, Nyasha, Sahar, Andrea, Daria, Brea, Marcus, Grant, Maurice, Ousmane, Chris, Ali, David, and Bennett for your patience and fellowship. I also want to shout out LaFleur and Helen, Christian, Duiji, Mr. Martin, RL, Jamie and Bamidele, Mayor John F. Street, and so many others who have, along the way, made the long haul worthwhile. I owe my gratitude to those who took notice and those who took good care.

None of this would have come about without earlier investments in my academic career by Kathleen McGraw and Ismail White and the guidance of Wendy Smooth and Tom Nelson. I am also grateful for the encouragement of my family, who never quite understood this undertaking but were no less supportive.

This book is dedicated to my dear friend Gwendolyn, a brilliant, whimsical scholar, who suddenly passed in December 2021. I wish I were half as smart, witty, and magical as she.

APPENDIX

DATA AND METHODS IN CHAPTER 2

For these analyses, 715 voting-eligible Black (44 percent) and White (56 percent) Americans were randomly assigned one of the four conditions show below. Each treatment was depicted as a news article in the *New York Times* since scandals are mediated events and newspapers are viewed as reliable sources for such reporting.[1] The experiment varied the race of the transgressed elected official by digitally altering an artificial headshot to look either African American or White. A manipulation check indicated that a high proportion of respondents reported the correct race in each condition; others were dropped from the analysis. The treatment also included a fictitious story about one of two scandal types, a financial crime or sexual infidelity, both of which were being investigated. I was primarily interested in the effect of race and scandal type on the production of racialized suspicion and the effect of that suspicion on political judgments. I measured suspicion by asking respondents if they thought that Mayor Highton was unfairly targeted and determined it to be racialized if African American respondents were more likely to report this belief in the presence of the Black mayor than the White mayor. Accordingly, racialized suspicion is the first dependent variable in chapter 2's analysis. I also measure the presence of Black protection by identifying a transgression credit—that is, judgments that are less harsh—in reputational judgments, the assignment of blame and punishment, and vote intention. A candidate's character or reputation is measured as a composite score of perceptions of honest, morality, and trustworthiness (a = .92). All variables ranged from 1 to 10 and were rescaled to range from 0 to 1.

Experimental Conditions

The wording of the experimental condition and instrument used in the treatment follow. Brackets indicate the factors varied: "Daniel Highton, mayor of the City of Aurora, has been implicated in a yearlong investigation concerning misuse of government funds, according to official reports from the Committee on Government and Political Conduct. Based on an investigation, the evidence is said to conclude that Mayor Highton (pictured below) [Black/White], [used over $25,000 of the city's expense account for personal, non-government business / who is married, had been engaged in a sexual relationship with a female aid]. According to sources close to the mayor's office, Highton became the target of an investigation after an anonymous tip to authorities."

Question Wording
1. How serious are the accusations facing Mayor Highton? 1 = Not serious, 10 = Very serious
2. How honest is Mayor Highton? 1 = Not at all honest, 10 = Very honest
3. How moral is Mayor Highton? 1 = Not at all moral, 10 = Very moral
4. How trustworthy is Mayor Highton? 1 = Not at all trustworthy, 10 = Very trustworthy
5. How blameworthy is Mayor Highton? 1 = Not at all blameworthy, 10 = Very much worthy of blame
6. How responsible is Mayor Highton? 1 = Not at all responsible, 10 = Totally responsible
7. Do you think that Mayor Highton was unfairly targeted? 1 = No, not at all, 10 = Yes, absolutely
8. What kind of punishment should be given to Mayor Highton? 1 = None at all, 10 = The maximum possible
9. Would you vote for Mayor Highton if he runs in the future? 1 = Definitely not, 10 = Definitely yes

Analytic Approach

A three-way between-subjects analysis of variance was performed to compare the effect of the respondent's race, the race of the mayor, and scandal type on suspicion. All main effects were statistically significant at the .05 level. There was also a significant interaction effect between the three factors, $F(1, 707) = 3.99$, $p > .0460$. I explore the three-way interaction by applying contrasts and testing the effects of race of mayor across the levels of respondent's race and scandal type. For example, the effect of the Black mayor versus the White mayor for Black respondents in the financial scandal condition is significant, $F(1, 707) = 31.89$, $p = .0000$. As a result, I restricted the remaining analyses to African Americans in the condition in which the Black mayor was accused of a financial misdeed. Table A.1 presents the coefficients that define figures 2.3 and 2.4.

DATA AND METHODS FOR CHAPTER 3

The ABC News / Washington Post *Poll*

"This data collection is part of a continuing series of monthly surveys that evaluate the Reagan presidency and solicit opinions on a variety of political and social issues. Topics covered include an evaluation of the United States Supreme Court and the nomination of Robert Bork, 1988 presidential candidates and characteristics that would influence the vote

TABLE A.1. Effects of Racialized Suspicion on Transgression Credits / Black Protectionism

	Blame	Character	Punish	Vote Intention
Suspicion	−0.344***	0.585***	−0.293***	0.529***
	(0.107)	(0.0786)	(0.0875)	(0.097)
Constant	0.751***	0.0937**	0.717***	0.0335
	(0.0542)	(0.0398)	(0.0443)	(0.0491)
N	95	95	95	95

Note: Standard errors in parentheses.
*p < .10. **p < .05. ***p < .01.

of the respondent, the incidents involving Senator Joe Biden, and the candidacy of Jesse Jackson. Demographic characteristics of respondents also were recorded." Households were selected by random-digit dialing. Within each household, the respondent selected was the adult living in the household who last had a birthday, was at home at the time of the interview, and was a resident of the district.[2]

VARIABLES

Racialized Suspicion

The ABC News / *Washington Post* Poll constructed a survey item that began by reminding readers that a "number of Black political leaders have been investigated in recent years by the state or federal prosecutors," then asking participants which of the two responses most closely reflected their belief—was it an effort to "discredit" Black politicians, or did it reflect "real evidence"? An effort to discredit another is a clear example of an ulterior motive; therefore, I code "discredit" as 1 to indicate that a person is suspicious, while coding "real evidence" as 0 to indicate that a person is not suspicious. Most participants (56 percent) in this response set believed the investigations were the result of real evidence, while 44 percent were suspicious.

Question Wording: Discredit Blacks / Real Issue

"As you may know, a number of black political leaders have been investigated in recent years by the state or federal prosecutors. Some people say most of these investigations are attempts by whites to discredit or embarrass black leaders. Other people disagree and say most of these investigations are based on real evidence that the black leader may have committed a crime. Which of these two views is closer to your own, or don't you know enough about the issue to say?"

STATISTICAL CONTROLS

Typical demographic control variables, where available, were included in the model. These included party affiliation, income, race, and sex.

Party affiliation was recoded to include three categories: Democrat, Republican, and Independent. Respondent race was recoded to include only Black and White respondents.

Party Affiliation
"Generally speaking, do you usually think of yourself as: Republican; Democrat; Independent, or What; DK/No opinion; NA/Refused."

Education
"What was the last grade of school you completed?" 8th grade of less; Some high school; Graduate high school; Some college; Graduate college; Post-graduate; DK/No opinion; NA/Refused

Political Views
"Would you say your views in most political matters are very liberal, liberal, moderate, conservative, or very conservative—or don't you think of yourself in those terms?" Very liberal; Liberal; Moderate; Conservative; Very conservative; Don't think in terms; DK/No opinion; NA/Refused

Race
"Are you of Hispanic origin or background?" [IF YES, ASK:] "Are you White Hispanic or Black Hispanic?" [IF NO, ASK:] "Are you white, black, or some other race?"

Income
"If you added together the yearly incomes, before taxes, of all the members of your household for last year, 1986, would the total be: [READ LIST]."

Respondent's Sex
1. Male
2. Female

A logistic regression was performed *to examine the predictors of whether respondents believed investigations were efforts to* discredit or embarrass Black leaders. The item is operationalized as a measure of

TABLE A.2. Effect of Race on Suspicion (ABC News / *Washington Post* Poll 1987)

	Discredit and Embarrass		
	b	OR	ME
Race (Black)	1.301***	3.67	0.291***
	(4.88)	(0.980)	(5.15)
Party ID (Dem)	0.300	1.134	0.064
	(1.49)	(0.271)	(1.46)
Ideology	−0.446***	0.640	−0.093***
	(−4.23)	(0.067)	(−4.49)
Education	−0.218**	0.804	−0.045**
	(−2.73)	(0.064)	(−2.80)
Income	−0.0160	0.984	−0.003
	(−0.22)	(0.070)	(−2.80)
Sex (male)	−0.362	0.696	−0.077
	(−1.96)	(0.128)	(−1.95)
Constant	1.796	6.025	
	(3.59)	(3.01)	
N	571	571	571

Note: Standard errors in parentheses.
*p < .10. **p < .05. ***p < .01.

racialized suspicion. The outcome variables are coded as 0 or 1, where 1 indicates that racialized suspicion is present. The primary predictor variable of interest is race, such that African American respondents were more likely to be suspicious, as reported in table A.2 and displayed in figure 3.1.

Washington Post *Mayor Barry Poll, January 1990*
"This survey was conducted following the arrest of District of Columbia mayor Marion Barry on drug charges. Respondents were asked if they had read or heard anything about the arrest, if they thought Barry should resign, if federal investigators would have tried harder or not

so hard to arrest Barry had he been white, and if they thought Barry was indeed using drugs on the night in question. Respondents were also asked for whom they would vote if the mayoral primary were held that day, toward which candidate they were leaning, whether they would vote for Jesse Jackson if he were a candidate, and whether they would vote for Jesse Jackson or Maurice Turner if the mayoral election were held that day. Background information on respondents includes political alignment, registered voter status, age, race, sex, and income."[3]

VARIABLES

Racialized Suspicion

The dependent variable is measured two ways—(1) *the extent that respondents agree* that federal investigators would not have tried not as hard to arrest the mayor if he were White (less hard); and (2) law enforcement officials were out to get Marion Barry any way they could (out to get). Each response is recoded to equal 1 to indicate affirmative racialized suspicion, 0 otherwise. The question wording for each survey item is as follows:

Did Barry's Race Influence Federal Investigators?

"Do you think federal investigators would have tried harder or not as hard to arrest the mayor if he were White, or do you think they would have tried as hard to arrest him?"

Respondent's Opinion on Barry Incident

"Now I'm going to read to you two statements people are making about the Barry incident. And I want you to tell me which one comes closest to the way you feel. Generally speaking, do you believe that [READ LETTER BEFORE EACH STATEMENT] A. Law enforcement officials were out to get Marion Barry any way they could. [OR DO YOU THINK] B. Barry has only himself to blame. OR do both statements equally express your thinking about this incident?"

TRANSGRESSION CREDIT / BLACK PROTECTIONISM

The dependent variable is measured two ways—(1) an opinion on whether the mayor to resign; and (2) vote intention, for whom the respondent would vote, if the Democratic primary were held today (trial heat question). A transgression credit is observed when the outcome of either variable is less punitive or more favorable to the incumbent mayor. For example, a reduced likelihood to call for the mayor to resign is evidence of a transgression credit. Each response is recoded to equal 1 to indicate a favorable outcome for the mayor, 0 otherwise. The question wording for each survey item is as follows:

Should Barry Immediately Resign?
"Barry was arrested Thursday night for possession of cocaine. Do you think Marion Barry should resign as mayor immediately, or not?"

Respondent's Preference for Mayor Candidate at Poll Time
"As you may know, District voters will elect a mayor this year. Suppose the Democratic primary were held today and the candidates were: Marion Barry, John Ray, Sharon Pratt Dixon, David Clarke, or Charlene Drew Jarvis. For whom would you vote?"

The dependent variable is measured two ways—(1) *the extent that respondents agree* federal investigators would not have tried not as hard to arrest the mayor if he were White; and (2) law enforcement officials were out to get Marion Barry any way they could. Each response is recoded to equal 1 to indicate affirmative racialized suspicion, 0 otherwise. The question wording for each survey item is as follows:

Guilt
The independent variable is measured by asking if respondent believed Barry was using drugs on the night of his arrest and included as a control variable. Each response is recoded to equal 1 to indicate affirmative, 0 otherwise. The question wording for each survey item is as follows:

Does Respondent Believe Barry Was Using Drugs?
"Just your best guess: do you think Barry was, or was not using drugs in that hotel room Thursday night?"

STATISTICAL CONTROLS

Typical demographic control variables, where available, were included in the model. These included party affiliation, income, race, and sex. No variable for education was available. Party Affiliation was recoded to include three categories: Democrat, Republican, and Independent. Respondent race was recoded to include only Black and White respondents.

Respondent's Party Affiliation
"Generally speaking, do you usually think of yourself as: A Democrat, A Republican, An Independent, A Statehood Party Member, Something Else."

Household Income for Previous Year (1989)
"If you added together the yearly incomes, before taxes, of all the members of your household for last year, 1989, would the total be: [READ LIST]."

Respondent's Race
"Are you of Hispanic origin or background?" [IF YES, ASK:] "Are you White Hispanic, or Black Hispanic?" [IF NO, ASK:] "Are you White, Black, or some other race?"

Respondent's Sex
Male or female
A logistic regression was performed *to examine the predictors of whether Barry's race influenced federal investigators (less hard) and* law enforcement officials were out to get Marion Barry any way they could (out to get). Each item is operationalized as a measure of racialized suspicion. Outcome variables are coded as 0 or 1, where 1 indicates

TABLE A.3. Effect of Race on Suspicion

	Out to Get			Less Hard		
	b	OR	ME	b	OR	ME
Race (Black)	2.198***	9.00***	0.205***	1.666***	5.29***	0.300***
	(0.642)	(5.77)	(0.0437)	(0.291)	(1.53)	(0.0445)
Guilty	−2.367***	0.093***	−0.375***	−1.610***	0.199***	−0.332***
	(0.500)	(0.046)	(0.0892)	(0.388)	(0.077)	(0.0789)
Party ID (Dem)	1.021*	2.77**	0.112**	0.0149	1.01	0.00273
	(0.526)	(1.46)	(0.0567)	(0.271)	(0.274)	(0.0496)
Age	−0.0420	0.958	−0.00459	−0.168	0.845	−0.0308
	(0.183)	(0.175)	(0.0201)	(0.115)	(0.096)	(0.0208)
Income	−0.135	0.873	−0.0148	−0.00972	0.990	−0.00178
	(0.132)	(0.115)	(0.0143)	(0.0837)	(0.082)	(0.0153)
Sex (male)	0.502	1.65	0.0549	0.152	1.16	0.0279
	(0.395)	(0.653)	(0.0430)	(0.233)	(0.271)	(0.0426)
Constant	−1.554	0.211		−0.133	0.875	
	(1.119)	(0.236)		(0.655)	(0.573)	
N	260	260	260	418	418	418

Note: Standard errors in parentheses.
*$p < .10$. **$p < .05$. ***$p < .01$.

that the outcome of interest is present. The primary predictor variable of interest is race, such that African American respondents were more likely to be suspicious, as reported in table A.3 and displayed in figure 3.2.

MODEL

A logistic regression was performed with a *subpopulation of African American respondents to examine the predictors of* whether the mayor should resign. The question wording for each variable is included above. Outcome variables are coded as 0 or 1, where 1 indicates that the outcome of interest is present. Two predictor variables approximating

TABLE A.4. Effect of Suspicion (Out to Get) on Calls for Resignation

	Resignation		
Variable	b	OR	ME
Suspicion (out to get)	−2.037***	0.130	−0.458***
	(0.442)	(0.057)	(0.0887)
Guilty	0.983*	2.67	0.204
	(0.591)	(1.58)	(0.132)
Party ID (Dem)	0.279	1.32	0.0502
	(0.489)	(0.646)	(0.0886)
Age	−0.0330	0.967	−0.00595
	(0.176)	(0.170)	(0.0317)
Income	0.0763	1.07	0.0137
	(0.129)	(0.139)	(0.0229)
Sex (male)	0.109	1.11	0.0196
	(0.410)	(0.456)	(0.0740)
Constant	−0.298	0.741	
	(0.996)	(0.739)	
N	356	356	256

Note: Standard errors in parentheses.
*p < .10. **p < .05. ***p < .01.

racialized suspicion were entered separately into these models and estimated the effects reported in tables A.4 and A.5. For ease of interpretation, figure 3.3 displays the marginal effects.

A logistic regression was performed with a *subpopulation of African American respondents to examine the predictors of* whether vote intention in a municipal primary election in which Barry would have been a candidate for mayor. The question wording for each variable is included below. Outcome variables are coded as 0 or 1, where 1 indicates that the outcome of interest is present. Two predictor variables approximating racialized suspicion were entered separately into these models and estimated the effects reported in tables A.6 and A.7 and displayed in figure 3.4.

TABLE A.5. Effect of Suspicion (Less Hard) on Calls for Resignation

Variable	Resignation		
	b	OR	ME
Suspicion (less hard)	−0.905***	0.404***	−0.203***
	(0.280)	(0.113)	(0.0621)
Guilty	1.266***	3.54	0.291***
	(0.414)	(1.46)	(0.0940)
Party ID (Dem)	−0.0150	0.985	−0.00312
	(0.348)	(0.342)	(0.0723)
Age	−0.185	0.830	−0.0385
	(0.134)	(0.111)	(0.0278)
Income	0.0478	1.04	0.00995
	(0.0987)	(0.103)	(0.0204)
Sex (male)	−0.0169	0.983	−0.00352
	(0.287)	(0.281)	(0.0596)
Constant	−0.0661	0.936	
	(0.708)	(0.6620)	
N	456	456	409

Note: Standard errors in parentheses.
*p < .10. **p < .05. ***p < .01.

TABLE A.6. Effects of Suspicion (Out to Get) on Transgression Credit / Black Protectionism (Vote Intention)

	Vote Intention		
Variable	b	OR	ME
Suspicion (out to get)	3.126***	22.8***	0.431***
	(0.788)	(17.9)	(0.105)
Guilt	−0.309	0.733	−0.0255
	(0.842)	(0.617)	(0.0756)
Party ID (Dem)	−0.660	0.516	−0.0513
	(0.685)	(0.353)	(0.0521)
Age	−0.0807	0.922	−0.00627
	(0.232)	(0.213)	(0.0179)
Income	−0.384**	0.68**	−0.0299**
	(0.170)	(0.115)	(0.0119)
Sex (male)	−0.175	0.839	−0.0136
	(0.641)	(0.538)	(0.0491)
Constant	−0.566	0.567	
	(1.066)	(0.605)	
N	360	360	260

Note: Standard errors in parentheses.
*p < .10. **p < .05. ***p < .01.

TABLE A.7. Effects of Suspicion (Less Hard) on Transgression Credit / Black Protectionism (Vote Intention)

Variable	Vote Intention		
	b	OR	ME
Suspicion (less hard)	1.793***	6.00***	0.192***
	(0.423)	(2.54)	(0.0440)
Guilt	−0.934**	0.393	−0.106*
	(0.429)	(0.168)	(0.0573)
Party ID (Dem)	−0.0949	0.909	−0.00878
	(0.490)	(0.445)	(0.0455)
Age	0.178	1.19	0.0164
	(0.180)	(0.214)	(0.0167)
Income	−0.364***	0.694	−0.0337***
	(0.123)	(0.085)	(0.0115)
Sex (male)	0.396	1.48	0.0367
	(0.402)	(0.597)	(0.0367)
Constant	−1.012	0.363	
	(0.888)	(0.322)	
N	465	465	418

Note: Standard errors in parentheses.
*p < .10. **p < .05. ***p < .01.

NOTES

PROLOGUE

1. Aaron Kase, "Is Philadelphia the Most Corrupt City in America?," *Vice*, March 28, 2017.
2. Lincoln Steffens, *The Shame of the Cities* (Forgotten Books, 1902).
3. Maria Pulcinella and Aaron Moselle, "Bobby Henon Resigns, Two Months after Bribery Conviction," *WHYY*, January 20, 2022, https://whyy.org; Jeremy Roebuck, "Prosecutors Say Councilmember Kenyatta Johnson Accepted Eagles Tickets from Local 98, Too," *Philadelphia Inquirer*, January 24, 2022.
4. Aaron Moselle, "Judge Declares a Mistrial in Philadelphia Councilmember Kenyatta Johnson Trial," *WHYY*, April 19, 2022, https://whyy.org.
5. "Philadelphia Traffic Court Abolished," *WHYY*, June 19, 2013, https://whyy.org.
6. Graig McCoy, "Longest-Serving Philly Sheriff Is Sentenced to 5 Years in Prison for $675K Bribery Scheme," *Philadelphia Inquirer*, August 1, 2019, www.inquirer.com.
7. Stephanie Farr, "Philly's Fraud Street Run Will Go from the 'Famous Four Seasons Total Landscaping' to 'the Lesser-Known Four Seasons Hotel,'" *Philadelphia Inquirer*, November 12, 2020, www.inquirer.com.
8. Lorraine Minnite, *The Myth of Voter Fraud* (Cornell University Press, 2010).
9. Niara Savage, "'It Feels Racial': Trump Calls Philadelphia and Detroit 'Most Corrupt' Places in the Country, Accused of Singling Out Black Cities," *Atlanta Black Star*, November 6, 2020.
10. Minnite, *Myth of Voter Fraud*, 92.
11. John Koenig, *The Dictionary of Obscure Sorrows* (Simon & Schuster, 2021).
12. Barnes and Beaulieu, "Gender Stereotypes and Corruption"; Beaulieu, "From Voter ID to Party ID."
13. Gordon, "Assessing Partisan Bias."
14. Warner, *Dilemma of Black Politics*; Musgrove, *Rumor, Repression, and Racial Politics*; Fiske, "Surveilling the City."
15. McIlwain and Caliendo, *Race Appeal*, 40.
16. Keiser, "Why Machines vs. Reform Has Still Not Withered Away," 109.
17. Robert Strauss and Dan Eggen, "Philadelphia Mayor Finds Office Bugged," *Washington Post*, October 9, 2003, www.washingtonpost.com.
18. Thomas Fitzgerald, "FBI Bug Turns Out to Be a Boon," *Philadelphia Inquirer*, October 30, 2003.

19 Thomas Fitzgerald, "Poll Shows Slim Lead for Street," *Philadelphia Inquirer*, October 26, 2003.
20 Tom Barnes, "FBI Bug Helps Street Win Re-election as Philadelphia Mayor," *Pittsburgh Post-Gazette*, November 5, 2003, www.post-gazette.com.
21 Taylor, "Political Culture," 491.
22 Taylor, "Political Culture," 493.

INTRODUCTION

1 Gradel and Simpson, *Corrupt Illinois*, 5.
2 Torry and Morin, "Half of U.S. Believes D.C. Is Most Corrupt."
3 Emily Lane, "Public Corruption in Louisiana 'Can't Get Much Worse,' Says Outgoing FBI New Orleans Director," *Times-Picayune*, July 7, 2021, www.nola.com.
4 Robert Snell, Sarah Rahal, and George Hunter, "FBI Raids Detroit's City Hall, Council Members' Homes as It Focuses on Towing Operations," *Detroit News*, August 25, 2021, www.detroitnews.com.
5 Cordis and Milyo, "Measuring Public Corruption."
6 Transparency International, "The ABCs of the CPI: How the Corruption Perceptions Index Is Calculated" (n.d.), www.transparency.org.
7 The CPI was 75 in 2017 and declined during the Trump administration.
8 Johnston, "Right and Wrong in American Politics"; Peters and Welch, "Political Corruption in America"; Redlawsk and McCann, "Popular Interpretations."
9 Johnston, "Right and Wrong in American Politics"; Redlawsk and McCann, "Popular Interpretations."
10 Wilson and King-Meadows, "Perceived Electoral Malfeasance"; Udani and Kimball, "Immigrant Resentment."
11 Holbrook, "Source of Perceptions of Local Political Corruption."
12 Musgrove, *Rumor, Repression, and Racial Politics*; Meier and Holbrook, "'I Seen My Opportunities and I Took 'Em'"; Warner, *Dilemma of Black Politics*.
13 Meier and Holbrook, "'I Seen My Opportunities and I Took 'Em,'" 151.
14 Holbrook, "Source of Perceptions of Local Political Corruption."
15 Schneider and Bos, "Exploration of the Content of Stereotypes." The authors used an experimental design to examine stereotypes by varying the characteristics of a politician. For example, they compared trait assessments about a "Black politician" to those about a "Black professional" and a generic "politician."
16 Gordon, "Assessing Partisan Bias"; Musgrove, *Rumor, Repression, and Racial Politics*; Warner, *Dilemma of Black Politics*; Zilber and Niven, *Racialized Coverage of Congress*; Zilber and Niven, "Stereotypes in the News"; Niven, "Fair Test of Media Bias."
17 Crawford, "'It's a Racist Plot.'"
18 The author goes on to say, "But it didn't have to do with race tensions so much as this: It helped humanize the man."

19 Taylor, "Political Culture."
20 Abrams, Randsley de Moura, and Travaglino, "Double Standard."
21 Bhavnani and Condra, "Why People Vote for Corrupt Politicians"; see also, e.g., Kurer, "Why Do Voters Support Corrupt Politicians?"
22 Gardiner, *Politics of Corruption*, 234.
23 Foner, *Reconstruction*, 388.
24 Adida, Davenport, and McClendon, "Ethnic Cueing across Minorities."
25 Taylor, "Political Culture."
26 Skolnick and Shaw, "O. J. Simpson Criminal Trial Verdict."
27 Adida, Davenport, and McClendon. "Ethnic Cueing across Minorities."
28 Adida, Davenport, and McClendon. "Ethnic Cueing across Minorities."
29 Adam Clayton Powell Jr. (NY), "Resolution Authoring and Directing the Oath of Office to Be Administered to Adam Clayton Powell" (1967), 23, *Congressional Record Permanent Digital Collection*, www.congress.gov.
30 "The House's Refusal to Seat Adam Clayton Powell, Jr. of New York | US House of Representatives: History, Art & Archives" (n.d.), https://history.house.gov.
31 Jack Maskell, "Expulsion, Censure, Reprimand, and Fine: Legislative Discipline in the House of Representatives" (Congressional Research Service, June 27, 2016), 26.
32 Taylor, "Political Culture."
33 Muñoz, Anduiza, and Gallego, "Why Do Voters Forgive Corrupt Mayors?"
34 Banfield and Wilson, *City Politics*, 40.
35 De Sousa and Moriconi, "Why Voters Do Not Throw the Rascals Out?," 490.
36 Gibson and Nelson, *Black and Blue*; Peffley and Hurwitz, *Justice in America*.
37 Weaver and Lerman, "Political Consequences of the Carceral State."
38 Adida, Davenport, and McClendon, "Ethnic Cueing across Minorities."
39 Abrams, Randsley de Moura, and Travaglino, "Double Standard"; Johnston, "How Do I Vote the Scoundrels Out?"; Kurer, "Why Do Voters Support Corrupt Politicians?"; Rundquist, Strom, and Peters, "Corrupt Politicians and Their Electoral Support; de Sousa and Moriconi, "Why Voters Do Not Throw the Rascals Out?": Winters and Weitz-Shapiro, "Lacking Information or Condoning Corruption."
40 Rottinghaus, "Surviving Scandal."
41 Alford et al., "Overdraft"; but see Basinger, "Scandals and Congressional Elections"; Maier, "Impact of Political Scandals"; Praino, Stockemer, and Moscardelli, "Lingering Effect of Scandals"; Welch and Hibbing, "Effects of Charges of Corruption."
42 Russell-Brown, "Black Protectionism as a Civil Rights Strategy."
43 Keiser, "Why Machines vs. Reform Has Still Not Withered Away"; Krase and LaCerra, *Ethnicity and Machine Politics*, 102; Morel, *Takeover*; Wolfinger and Field, "Political Ethos and the Structure of City Government."
44 Banfield and Wilson, *City Politics*, 40.
45 Banfield and Wilson, *City Politics*, 121.

46 Benson, Maaranen, and Heslop, *Political Corruption in America*, 24.
47 Benson, Maaranen, and Heslop, *Political Corruption in America*, 24.
48 Foner, *Reconstruction*, xxv.
49 Prior to the Seventeenth Amendment, senators were selected by the state legislature.
50 Foner, *Reconstruction*, 387–89.
51 Foner, *Reconstruction*, 387–89.
52 Foner, *Reconstruction*, 389.
53 "Guthrie and Dockery: The Greatest Convention Yet."
54 Schragger, "Can Strong Mayors Empower Weak Cities?," 2544.
55 Nelson and Meranto, *Electing Black Mayors*; Browning, Marshall, and Tabb, *Racial Politics in American Cities*.
56 Kaufmann, *Urban Voter*.
57 Howell, *Race, Performance, and Approval of Mayors*; Howell and Perry, "Black Mayors/White Mayors"; Kraus and Swanstrom, "Minority Mayors and the Hollow-Prize Problem."
58 Morel, *Takeover*; Morel and Nuamah, "Who Governs?"
59 Hajnal, *Changing White Attitudes*, 11.
60 Stokes, *Promises of Power*, 230.
61 "Investigation of Mayor Bradley," *Los Angeles Times*, September 21, 1989; Tracy Wood and Rich Connell, "City Atty. to File Counts Against Bradley Today," *Los Angeles Times*, September 13, 1989.
62 Henry Weinstein and Ronald J. Ostrow, "Justice Department Ends Bradley Probe, Won't Seek Indictment," *Los Angeles Times*, December 21, 1991.
63 Gale Scott, "Newark Mayor, 2 Others Indicted in Payroll Case," *Washington Post*, April 1, 1982, www.washingtonpost.com.
64 "Mayor Gibson Stalls Character Assassination," *Philadelphia Tribune*, October 29, 1982.
65 According to a memo regarding "election year sensitivities" from the U.S. Attorney General to all department employees, March 9, 2012, www.justice.gov.
66 Vincent Gray, "I Know What It's Like When Law Enforcement Intervenes in an Election. It Happened to Me," *Washington Post*, November 2, 2016.
67 Harris-Lacewell, "Heart of the Politics of Race."
68 Dincer and Gunalp, "Corruption, Income Inequality, and Poverty."
69 Thompson, *Political Scandal*, 29.
70 Thompson, *Political Scandal*, 24.
71 "Their occurrence or existence involves the transgression of certain values, norms or moral codes; Their occurrence or existence involves elementary of secrecy or concealment, but they are known or strongly believed to exist by individuals other than those involved; Some non-participants disapprove of the action of events and may be offended by the transgression; Some non-participants express their disapproval by publicly denouncing the actions or events; The disclosure and

condemnation of the actions or events may damage the reputation of individuals responsible for them" (Thompson, *Political Scandal*, 24).
72 Albanese, Artello, and Nguyen, "Distinguishing Corruption in Law and Practice"; Hoffman and Sorensen, *Public Corruption and the Law*.
73 Thompson, *Political Scandal*, 13–14.
74 Coleman, *Designing Experiments for the Social Sciences*, 4.

1. PERILOUS NEGRO RULE

1 Cunningham, "'Well, It Is Because He's Black.'"
2 Shelly Tan, "Who Can Be President? According to the Movies, It's Still White Men," *Washington Post*, September 30, 2020, www.washingtonpost.com.
3 David Banks, Jeffrey Barron, Booker Bradshaw, and John Moffitt, "Pilot," *The Richard Pryor Show* (Burt Sugarman Production, September 1977).
4 Strickland, "Sounding White," finds that it can be "concluded that to sound 'white' means to speak 'proper' English, talk in an educated manner, or overly formal." See also Johnson and Buttny, "White Listeners' Responses."
5 This translates roughly to "and unto you peace."
6 "Nation of Islam," FBI file for Nation of Islam, pt. 1, unknown document no., June 6, 1955, https://vault.fbi.gov.
7 "Nation of Islam."
8 Pew Research Center, "Republicans Believe Obama Is a Muslim," September 13, 2010, www.pewresearch.org.
9 *New Yorker*, July 21, 2008, www.newyorker.com.
10 Phoenix, *Anger Gap*.
11 Elizabeth Grace Cheshire, "African American English (AAE) in Key Peele's 'Obama's Anger Translator,'" *Compass*, March 28, 2019, https://wp.nyu.edu.
12 Rich, *David Dinkins and New York City Politics*, 102.
13 Smith, *Whitelash*, 3.
14 McIlwain and Caliendo, *Race Appeal*, 40.
15 Thompson, *Political Ethics and Public Office*, 7.
16 Hilton, Fein, and Miller, "Suspicion and Dispositional Inference," 502.
17 Russell-Brown, "Black Protectionism as a Civil Rights Strategy"; Russell-Brown, *Protecting Our Own*.
18 Abrams, Randsley de Moura, and Travaglino, "Double Standard."
19 Amanda Holpuch, "Tim Scott Becomes First Black Senator Elected in South since Reconstruction," *Guardian*, November 5, 2014, www.theguardian.com.
20 William Sturkey, "Perspective | Warnock's Win Was 150 Years in the Making—but History Tells Us It Is Fragile," *Washington Post*, January 18, 2021, www.washingtonpost.com.
21 Zucchino, *Wilmington's Lie*, 68.
22 Equal Justice Initiative, "Reconstruction in America | EJI Report" (n.d.), https://eji.org.

23 Foner, "Rooted in Reconstruction," 30.
24 Equal Justice Initiative, "Reconstruction in America."
25 Zucchino, *Wilmington's Lie*, 66; Foner, *Reconstruction*.
26 National Endowment for the Humanities, "Reconstruction vs. Redemption" (February 11, 2014), www.neh.gov.
27 Zucchino, *Wilmington's Lie*, 69.
28 Jones, *Race, Sex, and Suspicion*, 6–7.
29 Williams, "War in Black and White," 10.
30 Williams, "War in Black and White," 11.
31 Pollard, *MLK/FBI*.
32 "Negro Rule Shall It Last Longer in North Carolina," *Charlotte Observer*, September 10, 1898.
33 Negro Judges of Election, *Caucasian*, July 19, 1990, 1–3.
34 See also Lynch, *Before Obama*.
35 Dunning, "Undoing of Reconstruction," 438.
36 Foner, "Rooted in Reconstruction," 32.
37 Foner, "Black Reconstruction"; Holt, *Black over White*; Vincent, *Black Legislators in Louisiana during Reconstruction*, 306.
38 Bailey, *Neither Carpetbaggers nor Scalawags*, xi.
39 Andrews, "Negro in Politics," 425.
40 Andrews, "Negro in Politics," 425.
41 Foner, *Reconstruction*, 389.
42 Du Bois, *Black Reconstruction in America*, 637.
43 Sidanius and Pratto, *Social Dominance*, 104.
44 Levine, *Black Culture and Black Consciousness*, 452.
45 Williams, Logan, and Hardy, "Persistence of Historical Racial Violence"; Logan, "Whitelashing."
46 Umfleet, "1898 Wilmington Race Riot Report," 1.
47 Umfleet, "1898 Wilmington Race Riot Report," 222.
48 Umfleet, "1898 Wilmington Race Riot Report," 34, 255.
49 Johnson, *Rough Tactics*.
50 Emerson, "FBI as a Political Police," 239.
51 Ellis, "J. Edgar Hoover," 41.
52 Churchill and Vander Wall, *COINTELPRO Papers*, 91.
53 Hansford, "Jailing a Rainbow," 48.
54 From FBI files quoted in Churchill and Vander Wall, *COINTELPRO Papers*.
55 O'Reilly, *Racial Matters*.
56 Potash, *FBI War on Tupac Shakur*.
57 Tromblay, *U.S. Domestic Intelligence Enterprise*.
58 U.S. Senate, "Intelligence Activities and the Right of Americans Book 11: Final Report of the Select Committee Study Governmental Operations with Respect to Intelligence Activities" (Report No. 94-755) (U.S. GPO, 1976), www.intelligence

.senate.gov; Andrew Rosenthal, "The FBI's Black Phantom Menace," *New York Times*, October 19, 2017.
59 O'Reilly, *Racial Matters*; Garrow, *FBI and Martin Luther King, Jr.*; Churchill and Vander Wall, *COINTELPRO Papers*; Friedly and Gallen, *Martin Luther King, Jr.*
60 Notable Senate Investigations, "Senate Select Committee."
61 Hoffman and Sorensen, *Public Corruption and the Law*; Albanese, Artello, and Nguyen, "Distinguishing Corruption in Law and Practice."
62 Clay, *Just Permanent Interests*, 315.
63 Amick, *American Way of Graft*, 223.
64 Ehrenhalt, "Justice and Ambition"; Jed Shugerman, "The Rise of the 'Prosecutor Politician'" (Prison Policy Initiative, July 13, 2017), www.prisonpolicy.org.
65 Maass, "Bad Federal Policy on Local Corruption," 21.
66 Stokes, *Promises of Power*, 230.
67 Young and Wheeler, *Hard Stuff*, 268.
68 Vincent C. Gray, "I Know What It's Like When Law Enforcement Intervenes in an Election. It Happened to Me," *Washington Post*, November 2, 2016.
69 Baxter, "Federal Discretion in the Prosecution of Local Political Corruption"; Henning, "Federalism and the Federal Prosecution of State and Local Corruption"; Hills, "Corruption and Federalism"; Ruff, "Federal Prosecution of Local Corruption"; Whitaker, "Federal Prosecution of State and Local Bribery"; Maass, "Bad Federal Policy on Local Corruption."
70 Roberts and Doss, "Federalization of 'Grass Roots' Corruption."
71 Theft or Bribery Concerning Programs Receiving Federal Funds, 18 U.S.C. § 666.
72 Congressional Research Service, "Federal Grants to State and Local Governments: A Historical Perspective on Contemporary Issues" (September 30, 2019), https://fas.org.
73 Hoffman and Sorensen, *Public Corruption and the Law*; Albanese, Artello, and Nguyen, "Distinguishing Corruption in Law and Practice."
74 Meier and Holbrook, "'I Seen My Opportunities and I Took 'Em.'" But see Taylor and Cobb, "Individual-Level Origins"; see also Warner, *Dilemma of Black Politics*; Musgrove, *Rumor, Repression, and Racial Politics*; Gordon, "Assessing Partisan Bias."
75 Peter Applebome, "Black Officials Charge Harassment," *New York Times*, June 26, 1989.
76 Gordon, "Assessing Partisan Bias."
77 Gwen Ifill, "Black Officials: Probes and Prejudice: Is There a Double Standard for Bringing Indictments? The Jury's Still Out on Probes and Prejudice," *Washington Post*, February 28, 1988.
78 Musgrove, *Rumor, Repression, and Racial Politics*.
79 Wilson and Lynxwiler, "Federal Government and the Harassment of Black Leaders."
80 Musgrove, *Rumor, Repression, and Racial Politics*, 6.

81 Russell-Brown, "Black Protectionism as a Civil Rights Strategy."
82 Fein, Hilton, and Miller, "Suspicion of Ulterior Motivation"; Hilton, Fein, and Miller, "Suspicion and Dispositional Inference"; Fein, McCloskey, and Tomlinson, "Can the Jury Disregard That Information?"
83 Fein, McCloskey, and Tomlinson, "Can the Jury Disregard That Information?"
84 Skolnick and Shaw, "O. J. Simpson Criminal Trial Verdict."
85 Skolnick and Shaw, "O. J. Simpson Criminal Trial Verdict."
86 Wilson, *Moral Judgment*, 111.
87 Wilson, *Moral Judgment*, 111.
88 Wilson, *Moral Judgment*, 111; Henry, *Culture and African American Politics*, 48.
89 Fein, McCloskey, and Tomlinson, "Can the Jury Disregard That Information?"; Hilton, Fein, and Miller, "Suspicion and Dispositional Inference"; Fein, Hilton, and Miller, "Suspicion of Ulterior Motivation"; Fein et al., "Hype and Suspicion."
90 Nunnally, *Trust in Black America*, 69.
91 Russell-Brown, "Black Protectionism as a Civil Rights Strategy," 22.
92 Hubbell, Mitchell, and Gee, "Relative Effects of Timing of Suspicion"; Fein, Hilton, and Miller, "Suspicion of Ulterior Motivation"; Hilton, Fein, and Miller, "Suspicion and Dispositional Inference"; Fein, "Effects of Suspicion on Attributional Thinking," 1164; Fein et al., "Hype and Suspicion"; Fein, McCloskey, and Tomlinson, "Can the Jury Disregard That Information?"; Fein and Hilton, "Judging Others in the Shadow of Suspicion."
93 Fiske, "Surveilling the City," 71.
94 Thompson, *Political Scandal*; Nyhan, "Scandal Potential"; Botero et al., "Says Who?"; Niven, "Fair Test of Media Bias."
95 Clay, *Just Permanent Interests*.
96 Niven, "Fair Test of Media Bias."
97 Clay, *Just Permanent Interests*, 315.
98 Young and Wheeler, *Hard Stuff*, 266.
99 Thompson, *Political Ethics and Public Office*, 4.
100 Abrams, Randsley de Moura, and Travaglino, "Double Standard"; Marques et al., "Social Categorization."
101 Doherty, Dowling, and Miller, "Are Financial or Moral Scandals Worse?"; Funk, "Impact of Scandal on Candidate Evaluations"; Winter, *Dangerous Frames*; Herrick, "Who Will Survive?"
102 Johnston, "How Do I Vote the Scoundrels Out?," 508.
103 Berinsky et al., "Sex and Race"; Adida, Davenport, and McClendon, "Ethnic Cueing across Minorities"; Lyle, "If Models, Then Malfeasants."
104 Michener, "Policy Feedback in a Racialized Polity."
105 Epp, Maynard-Moody, and Haider-Markel, *Pulled Over*.
106 Weaver and Lerman, "Political Consequences of the Carceral State."
107 Brotherton, *Suspicious Minds*, 64.
108 Parsons et al., "Test of the Grapevine."

109 Crocker et al., "Belief in U.S. Government Conspiracies"; Goertzel, "Belief in Conspiracy Theories."
110 Simmons and Parsons, "Beliefs in Conspiracy Theories."
111 Crocker et al., "Belief in U.S. Government Conspiracies," 943.
112 Davis, Wetherell, and Henry, "Social Devaluation of African Americans."
113 Douglas et al., "Understanding Conspiracy Theories," 4.
114 Douglas et al., "Understanding Conspiracy Theories," 4.
115 DeHaven-Smith and Witt, "Conspiracy Theory Reconsidered," 268.
116 DeHaven-Smith and Witt, "Conspiracy Theory Reconsidered," 268, 269.
117 Watters and Gillers, *Investigating the FBI*; Churchill and Vander Wall, *COINTELPRO Papers*; Musgrove, *Rumor, Repression, and Racial Politics*; O'Reilly, *Racial Matters*.
118 Oliver and Wood, "Conspiracy Theories"; Radnitz and Underwood, "Is Belief in Conspiracy Theories Pathological?"; van Prooijen and Jostmann, "Belief in Conspiracy Theories."

2. BLACK SUSPICION, BLACK PROTECTION

1 Brotherton, *Suspicious Minds*, 21.
2 Clay, *Just Permanent Interests*, 315.
3 Peters and Welch, "Political Corruption in America"; Redlawsk and McCann, "Popular Interpretations."
4 Dagnes, *Sex Scandals in American Politics*; Dagnes and Sachleben, *Scandal!*
5 Churchill and Vander Wall, *COINTELPRO Papers*, 91.
6 Ellis, *Race, War, and Surveillance*, xvi.
7 Davis, "Race Menace in Bootlegging," 339.
8 Russell-Brown, "Black Protectionism as a Civil Rights Strategy."
9 Epp, Maynard-Moody, and Haider-Markel, *Pulled Over*; Baumgartner, Epp, and Shoub, *Suspect Citizens*; Schmitt, Reedt, and Blackwell, "Demographic Differences in Sentencing."
10 Adam Clayton Powell Jr., "Resolution Authoring and Directing the Oath of Office to Be Administered to Adam Clayton Powell" (1967), 23, Congressional Record Permanent Digital Collection, www.congress.gov.
11 Nunnally, *Trust in Black America*; Philpot and White, *African-American Political Psychology*.
12 Collier and Horowitz, *Race Card*; Elder, *Stupid Black Men*; Ford, *Race Card*.
13 McIlwain and Caliendo, *Race Appeal*.
14 Elder, *Stupid Black Men*, 101.
15 Crawford, "Of Suspicious Minds"; Ford, *Race Card*.
16 Crawford, "'It's a Racist Plot.'"
17 Campbell was charged under the Racketeer Influenced and Corrupt Organizations Act (RICO) and for tax violations. Indictment, *United States of America v. William C. Campbell*.

18 "Atlanta Ex-Mayor Is Indicted after Corruption Investigation," *New York Times*, August 31, 2004, www.nytimes.com.
19 David Firestone, "Atlanta Mayor Denounces F.B.I. Inquiry," *New York Times*, September 22, 2000, www.nytimes.com.
20 William Greider, "Mayor Restores Detroit's Faith," *Washington Post*, June 25, 1978, www.washingtonpost.com.
21 Young and Wheeler, *Hard Stuff*, 268.
22 Lee Becker, Thomas A. Schwartz, and Sharon West, "The Report on Media Coverage of Magnum and Vista: Is the Public Good Being Served?," *Detroit Free Press*, February 9, 1984.
23 "Birmingham Mayor Says He Was Target of FBI Harassment," *Philadelphia Tribune*, October 2, 1990.
24 "Birmingham Mayor Says He Was Target."
25 "Birmingham Mayor Says He Was Target."
26 Ronald Smothers, "Charge Against Mayor Strikes Chord in Birmingham: A Southern City Once Torn by Racism Faces New Accusations," *New York Times*, January 20, 1992.
27 James was charged with conspiracy and schemes to defraud the City of Newark. Indictment, *United States of America v. Sharpe James and Tamika Riley*.
28 Christopher J. Christie, "Former Newark Mayor James Indicted; Allegedly Traveled, Spent Lavishly on Newark Credit Cards, and Engaged in Fraudulent Land 'Flipping' with Companion" (press release, July 12, 2007), www.justice.gov.
29 "Lynching Is Still Legal in America," *Michigan Chronicle*, October 26–November 1, 2005, http://gregghenson.typepad.com.
30 David Runk, "Lynching Ad Roils Detroit Race," *Washington Post*, October 30, 2005.
31 "Timeline of Kilpatrick Scandals," *Crain's Detroit Business*, August 7, 2008, www.crainsdetroit.com.
32 Kilpatrick was charged with multiple crimes. Indictment, *United States v. Kwame M. Kilpatrick*.
33 Steven Yaccino, "Kwame M. Kilpatrick, Former Detroit Mayor, Sentenced to 28 Years in Corruption Case," *New York Times*, October 10, 2013, www.nytimes.com.
34 Eric Pianin and Courtland Milloy, "Barry's Racial Defense Wins Some Backers," *Washington Post*, August 26, 1984, www.washingtonpost.com.
35 Jon Nordheimer, "Federal Judge, Facing Impeachment, Ties Woes to Racism and Vows Fight," *New York Times*, November 29, 1987, www.nytimes.com.
36 John Conyers (MI), "Impeachment of Judge Alcee L. Hastings" (1989), 24962, *Congressional Record Permanent Digital Collection*, www.govinfo.gov.
37 Elise Viebeck and David Weigel, "Rep. John Conyers Jr. Resigns over Sexual Harassment Allegations after a Half-Century in Congress," *Washington Post*, December 5, 2017, www.washingtonpost.com; Alex Isenstadt and John Bresnahan, "Conyers's Wife Pleads Guilty," *Politico*, June 26, 2009, www.politico.com; Matt

Laslo, "Rep. John Conyers' Resignation Reverberates through Congress," *Rolling Stone*, December 5, 2017, www.rollingstone.com.
38 William M. Kunstler, "Opinion | Racism Figured in Hastings Impeachment," *New York Times*, August 27, 1988, www.nytimes.com.
39 Kunstler, "Opinion."
40 Ronald Smothers, "Charge Against Mayor Strikes Chord in Birmingham: A Southern City Once Torn by Racism Faces New Accusations," *New York Times*, January 20, 1992.
41 "Magnum Again: The Press and the Professors Would Differ on the Grade," *Detroit Free Press*, February 9, 1984.
42 Lee B. Becker, Thomas A. Schwartz, and Sharon West, "The Report on Media Coverage of Magnum and Vista: Is the Public Good Being Served?," *Detroit Free Press*, February 9, 1984; David Lawrence Jr., "Free Press Editor Responds," *Detroit Free Press*, February 9, 1984.
43 R. H. Melton, "Wilder to Blacks: Don't Be Patsies: Wants NO Excuses Made for Leaders in Trouble," *Washington Post*, July 7, 1987.
44 Wantchekon and Serra, *New Advances in Experimental Research on Corruption*.
45 Funk, "Impact of Scandal on Candidate Evaluations."
46 Botero et al., "Says Who?"
47 Smith, Powers, and Suarez, "If Bill Clinton Were a Woman"; Chanley et al., "Lust and Avarice in Politics Damage Control."
48 McDermott, Schwartz, and Vallejo, "Talking the Talk but Not Walking the Walk."
49 Miller, "Effects of Scandalous Information."
50 Chanley et al., "Lust and Avarice in Politics Damage Control."
51 Christensen, *Experimental Methodology*, 84.
52 Adida, Davenport, and McClendon, "Racial Priming across Minorites"; see also, e.g., Berinsky et al., "Sex and Race."
53 For a defense of this approach, see Christensen, *Experimental Methodology*, 85.
54 Kinder and Palfrey, *Experimental Foundations of Political Science*, 7.
55 All variables are rescaled to range from 0 to 1, with higher values indicating more serious.
56 I map the answer onto an interval scale that ranges from 0 to 1, with higher values indicating greater suspicion ($M = 0.32$, $SD = 0.25$).
57 Jirard, "It May Be Wrong."
58 Zaller, "Monica Lewinsky's Contribution to Political Science"; Doherty, Dowling, and Miller, "Are Financial or Moral Scandals Worse?"
59 That is not to suggest that elected officials beset with questions of moral character do not have to navigate challenging political and media terrain.
60 All variables were coded on a 10-point scale and later recoded to range from 0 to 1.
61 Alpha = .92.
62 Kelly Phillips Erb, "Former Detroit Mayor Found Guilty on Multiple Counts, Including Tax Charges," *Forbes*, March 11, 2013, www.forbes.com.

63 See also Carlson, Ganiel, and Hyde, "Scandal and Political Candidate Image."
64 Thompson, *Political Scandal*.
65 Russell-Brown, "Black Protectionism as a Civil Rights Strategy."
66 Fein et al., "Hype and Suspicion"; "Can the Jury Disregard That Information?"
67 Steven Yaccino, "Kwame M. Kilpatrick, Former Detroit Mayor, Sentenced to 28 Years in Corruption Case," *New York Times*, October 10, 2013, www.nytimes.com.
68 De Sousa and Moriconi, "Why Voters Do Not Throw the Rascals Out?," 490.
69 Weaver and Lerman, "Political Consequences of the Carceral State"; Gibson and Nelson, *Black and Blue*; Soss and Weaver, "Police Are Our Government"; Burch, *Trading Democracy for Justice*; Walker, *Mobilized by Injustice*.
70 Mary Warner, "Harassment of African American Officials" (C-SPAN video clip, September 29, 1990), www.c-span.org.
71 Bobo and Gilliam, "Race, Sociopolitical Participation, and Black Empowerment"; Howell, *Race, Performance, and Approval of Mayors*; Howell and Fagan, "Race and Trust in Government"; Howell and Perry, "Black Mayors/White Mayors"; Marschall and Ruhil, "Pomp of Power."
72 Abrams, Randsley de Moura, and Travaglino, "Double Standard"; Fein, McCloskey, and Tomlinson, "Can the Jury Disregard That Information?"; Russell-Brown, "Black Protectionism as a Civil Rights Strategy"; Russell-Brown, *Protecting Our Own*; Skolnick and Shaw, "O. J. Simpson Criminal Trial Verdict."
73 Russell-Brown, "Black Protectionism as a Civil Rights Strategy"; Russell-Brown, *Protecting Our Own*; Russell-Brown, *Color of Crime*.

3. "BITCH SET ME UP"

1 Christina Cauterucci, "Marion Barry, the Butt of a Thousand Televised Crack Jokes," *Washington City Paper*, November 24, 2014.
2 Chris Rock, M. Rothenberg, and Sandy Chanley, executive producers, *Chris Rock: Bring the Pain* (HBO, 1996).
3 Michael Janofsky, "The 1994 Campaign: The Comeback Man in the News; From Disgrace to 'Amazing Grace': Marion Shepilov Barry Jr.," *New York Times*, September, 14, 1994.
4 R. H. Melton, "Barry Comes Roaring Back in D.C.," *Washington Post*, September 14, 1994.
5 When Barry won a city council seat only months after returning from federal prison, D.C. was a city under siege by the crack epidemic. It was lost on many that the mayor could himself succumb to the vice that gripped his city. Richard L. Berke, "The 1994 Campaign: The Nation; Barry Wins in Washington 4 Years after Drug Violation," *New York Times*, September 14, 1994.
6 Jeff Smith, "Anatomy of a Comeback (or a Few)," *Politico*, November 23, 2014.
7 Smith and Seltzer, *Contemporary Controversies*, 119.
8 Smith and Seltzer, *Contemporary Controversies*, 119.
9 Barry and Tyree, *Mayor for Life*, 247.

10 Bart Barnes, "Marion Barry Dies at 78; 4-Term D.C. Mayor Was the Most Powerful Local Politician of His Generation," *Washington Post*, November 23, 2014, www.washingtonpost.com.
11 Gillette, "Protest and Power in Washington, D.C.," 202.
12 Wilmer, "Marion Barry, Jr.," 64.
13 Wilmer, "Marion Barry, Jr."; Fauntroy, "Home Rule for the District of Columbia."
14 Wilmer, "Marion Barry, Jr." The five terms spanned 1974–78, 1992–94, and 2004–14.
15 "The Next Mayor . . . ," *Washington Post*, September 10, 1982, www.washingtonpost.com.
16 Wilmer, "Marion Barry, Jr.," 78.
17 Vernon Loeb, "Barry Brings Halt to Turbulent D.C. Saga," *Washington Post*, May 22, 1998, www.washingtonpost.com.
18 Steve Daley, "Crucial Tape Shows Barry Inhaling Crack," *Chicago Tribune*, June 29, 1990.
19 Sandy Sardella, "Drug Dealer Testifies He Sold Drugs to D.C. Mayor," *UPI*, November 6, 1989, www.upi.com.
20 Mike York, "Excerpts from Videotape of Barry's Arrest at the Vista Hotel," *Washington Post*, June, 29 1990.
21 York, "Excerpts from Videotape of Barry's Arrest."
22 Michael Melton, "Barry Tape Provides New Details: Informant Called Mayor 'Chicken' Before He Took Pipe," *Washington Post*, May 10, 1990.
23 For emphasis on the mayor's response, the communications of the arresting officer are edited out.
24 Hay, "Sting Operations, Undercover Agents, and Entrapment," 387.
25 Paul Ruffin, "The Black Press Dilemma: How the Barry Case Divided D.C. Journalists," *Washington Post*, July 8, 1990.
26 Ruffin, "Black Press Dilemma."
27 Gillette, "Protest and Power in Washington, D.C.," 208.
28 Smith and Seltzer, *Contemporary Controversies*, 109.
29 Chuck Stone, "A Dream Deferred: A Black Mayor Betrays the Faith," *Washington Monthly*, July–August 1986.
30 Costas-Pérez, Solé-Ollé, and Sorribas-Navarro, "Corruption Scandals, Voter Information, and Accountability"; Johnston, "How Do I Vote the Scoundrels Out?"; Nyhan, "Scandal Potential"; Rundquist, Strom, and Peters, "Corrupt Politicians and Their Electoral Support."
31 De Sousa and Moriconi, "Why Voters Do Not Throw the Rascals Out?," 484.
32 Senator John Danforth (R-MO), quoted in Jaffe and Sherwood, *Dream City*.
33 Smith and Seltzer, *Contemporary Controversies*, 114.
34 See, e.g., Smith and Seltzer, *Contemporary Controversies*, 114.
35 Smith and Seltzer, *Contemporary Controversies*; Crawford, "Of Suspicious Minds."
36 Russell-Brown, "Black Protectionism as a Civil Rights Strategy," 23.

37 Gwen Ifill, "Black Officials: Probes and Prejudice: Is There a Double Standard for Bringing Indictments? The Jury's Still Out on Probes and Prejudice," *Washington Post*, February 28, 1988.
38 "ABC News / *Washington Post* Poll," ABC News and *Washington Post*, September 1987 (Inter-university Consortium for Political and Social Research, 2008-05-15), https://doi.org/10.3886/ICPSR08891.v1.
39 "*Washington Post* Mayor Barry Poll," *Washington Post*, January 1990 (Inter-university Consortium for Political and Social Research, 2015-04-14), https://doi.org/10.3886/ICPSR09437.v2.
40 Moreover, I include a measure of perceived guilt as a control variable to capture concerns about legal culpability in the analysis of Mayor Barry.
41 Michener, "Policy Feedback in a Racialized Polity."
42 Clay, *Just Permanent Interests*; Cobb and Taylor, "Absence of Malice"; Musgrove, *Rumor, Repression, and Racial Politics*; Stokes, *Promises of Power*; Warner, *Dilemma of Black Politics*; Young and Wheeler, *Hard Stuff*.
43 Russell-Brown, "Black Protectionism as a Civil Rights Strategy."
44 Crawford, "Of Suspicious Minds."
45 Michael Abramowitz and R. H. Melton, "From the Cabinet and Advisers: Straight Talk, Call for Resignation," *Washington Post*, January 21, 1990; Richard Morin, "57 Percent of Poll Respondents Say the Mayor Should Resign; Law Enforcement Tried to 'Get' Barry, DC Residents Say," *Washington Post*, January 21, 1990.
46 "Mayor Barry Should Resign," *Washington Post*, January 20, 1990.
47 "Mayor Barry Should Resign," *Washington Post*, September 10, 1989.
48 Fed. R. Crim. P. 9-16.100.
49 Michael York, "Barry Won't Resign, His Attorney Says: Mayor Pleads Not Guilty," *Washington Post*, March 1, 1990.
50 Nat Hentoff, "Of Course It Was Entrapment," *Washington Post*, January 24, 1990, www.washingtonpost.com.
51 "Aides Urge Barry Against Reelection Bid," *Los Angeles Times*, January 21, 1990.
52 R. H. Melton, "Barry Announces He Won't Seek a 4th Term, Calls for the City's Political 'Healing' to Begin: Mayor Says Idea of Resigning Would Be Too 'Disruptive,'" *Washington Post*, June 14, 1990.
53 Melton, "Barry Announces He Won't Seek a 4th Term."
54 Marschall, "Study of Local Elections"; Marschall, Shah, and Ruhil, "Study of Local Elections"; Trounstine, "All Politics Is Local."
55 B. Drummond Ayres Jr., "The 1990 Campaign; Marion Barry's Toughest Campaign: A Bid for Respect as Well as Office," *New York Times*, November 3, 1990, www.nytimes.com.
56 M. Abramowitz, "For Barry, Defeat Is Alien," *Washington Post*, November 7, 1990.
57 Wire Services, "Barry Begins Prison Term for Cocaine Conviction," *Los Angeles Times*, October 27, 1991.

58 Courtland Milloy, "Barry's 'Double-Dog' Dare," *Washington Post*, September 20, 1990, www.washingtonpost.com.
59 Jonathan David Farley, "Preventing the Rise of a 'Messiah,'" *Guardian*, April 4, 2008.
60 Brown and Shaw, "Separate Nations," 23.
61 Julian Bond, "SNCC: What We Did," *Monthly Review* (blog), October 1, 2000, https://monthlyreview.org.
62 Lillian Wiggins, "Lack of Strategy Really Hurts," *Washington Afro-American*, October 14, 1978.
63 Lillian Wiggins, "Who Really Did 'Take a Stand'?," *Washington Afro-American*, October 7, 1978.
64 Wiggins, "Who Really Did 'Take a Stand'?"
65 Wiggins, "Who Really Did 'Take a Stand'?"
66 Milton Coleman, "The Post and the Conspiracy," *Washington Post*, December 20, 1979.
67 Wiggins, "Who Really Did 'Take a Stand'?"
68 Matthew Cooper and Elahe Izadi, "Can DC Really Handle a White Mayor?," *Atlantic*, October 17, 2013.

CONCLUSION

Epigraph: Ta-Nehisi Coates, *Between the World and Me* (Random House, 2015), 22.
1 Russell-Brown, "Black Protectionism as a Civil Rights Strategy."
2 Digeser, "Forgiveness and Politics," 700.
3 Digeser, "Forgiveness and Politics," 706; Wilson, *Moral Judgment*.
4 Wamble, "Chosen One."
5 Solomon Jones, "Seth Williams Is Guilty, but the Black Community Has Been Punished," *WHYY*, June 29, 2017, https://whyy.org.
6 Keeanga-Yamahtta Taylor, "Opinion | The End of Black Politics," *New York Times*, June 13, 2020, www.nytimes.com; Matt Bai, "Post-race—Is Obama the End of Black Politics?," *New York Times*, August 6, 2008, www.nytimes.com.
7 Reed, *Stirrings in the Jug*.
8 Taylor, "Opinion."
9 This was evident in the sexual assault and sexual harassment charges against R&B singer R. Kelly and America's favorite dad Bill Cosby. Both were accused of serious sex crimes.
10 Howell, *Race, Performance, and Approval of Mayors*; Howell and Perry, "Black Mayors/White Mayors."
11 Kraus and Swanstrom, "Minority Mayors and the Hollow-Prize Problem"; Friesema, "Black Control of Central Cities."
12 Steven Yaccino, "Kwame M. Kilpatrick, Former Detroit Mayor, Sentenced to 28 Years in Corruption Case," *New York Times*, October 10, 2013, www.nytimes.com.
13 Bunche, "Review," 70.

14 Gosnell, *Negro Politicians*, 145.
15 Stone, *Black Political Power in America*, 10.
16 Krase and LaCerra, *Ethnicity and Machine Politics*, xi.
17 Gosnell, *Negro Politicians*; Reed, *Stirrings in the Jug*.
18 Bunche, "Review," 70.
19 Russell-Brown, "Black Protectionism as a Civil Rights Strategy," 59.
20 Wilson, *Moral Judgment*, 111.
21 Wilson, *Moral Judgment*, 111.
22 Russell-Brown, "Black Protectionism as a Civil Rights Strategy."

EPILOGUE

1 Angela Couloumbis and Craig R. McCoy, "Fourth Defendant in Sting Case Pleads Guilty," *Philadelphia Inquirer*, June 8, 2015, www.inquirer.com.
2 Luis Ferré-Sadurní and Jesse McKinley, "Rochester Mayor Is Indicted, Throwing City into Further Turmoil," *New York Times*, October 2, 2020, www.nytimes.com.
3 Barnes and Beaulieu, "Gender Stereotypes and Corruption"; Watson and Moreland, "Perceptions of Corruption"; Swamy et al., "Gender and Corruption"; Esarey and Schwindt-Bayer, "Women's Representation."
4 Smith, Smith Powers, and Suarez, "If Bill Clinton Were a Woman," 126.
5 Carlson, Ganiel, and Hyde, "Scandal and Political Candidate Image."
6 Saxton and Barnes, "Sex and Ideology"; Barnes, Beaulieu, and Saxton, "Sex and Corruption"; see also Stilwell and Utych, "Gender and Justification in Political Scandal."
7 Eggers, Vivyan, and Wagner, "Corruption, Accountability, and Gender."
8 See, e.g., Claudine Gay and Katherine Tate, "Doubly Bound"; Brown, "Black Women's Pathways to the Statehouse"; Smooth, "Intersectionality in Electoral Politics"; Simien, "Race, Gender, and Linked Fate."
9 Philpot and Walton, "One of Our Own."
10 I made one attempt at an experiment that was ultimately underpowered.
11 Dixon was charged with multiple crimes. Indictment, *State of Maryland v. Sheila Ann Dixon*.
12 Ian Urbina, "Baltimore's Mayor Is Convicted," *New York Times*, December 1, 2009, www.nytimes.com.
13 "Baltimore Mayor Sheila Dixon Resigns as Part of Plea Deal," *Christian Science Monitor*, January 6, 2010, www.csmonitor.com.
14 Basinger, "Scandals and Congressional Elections"; Rottinghaus, "Surviving Scandal."
15 Luke Broadwater and Yvonne Wenger, "Votes for City Mayor Fell along Racial Lines: Pugh Won White Precincts, Dixon Took Black Areas," *Baltimore Sun*, May 11, 2016.

16 "Sheila Dixon Officially Announces She's Running for Baltimore Mayor," *CBS News*, July 1, 2015, www.cbsnews.com.
17 Yvonne Wenger, "Baltimore Mayor Stephanie Rawlings-Blake Won't Seek Re-election." *Baltimore Sun*, September 11, 2015, www.baltimoresun.com.
18 Luke Broadwater, "Sheila Dixon Is Early Front-Runner in Baltimore's Mayoral Race, New Poll Shows," *Baltimore Sun*, November 21, 2015, www.baltimoresun.com.
19 J. B. Wogan, "In Baltimore Mayor's Race, Sheila Dixon Seeks Forgiveness and a Second Chance," *Governing*, March 23, 2016, www.governing.com.
20 "Sheila Dixon Denounces Fake Mug Shot Flyer as 'Downright Ugly' Tactic," *Fox Baltimore*, April 6, 2016, https://foxbaltimore.com.
21 Jessica Anderson and Colin Campbell, "Catherine Pugh Campaign Blames Misunderstanding for Upset Baltimore Workers," *Baltimore Sun*, April 26, 2016, www.baltimoresun.com.
22 Stephanie Hanes, "Jury Selection Key in Trial of Baltimore Mayor Sheila Dixon," *Christian Science Monitor*, November 9, 2009.
23 Luke Broadwater, "Still Under Fire, Former Baltimore Mayor Sheila Dixon Eyes a Comeback," *Baltimore Sun*, March 17, 2016.
24 "Baltimore's Mayor Is Convicted," *New York Times*, December 1, 2009.
25 Indictment, *United States of America v. Catherine Elizabeth Pugh*.
26 "Catherine Pugh Indictment," *Washington Post*, November 20, 2019; Luke Broadwater, Ian Duncan, and Jean Marbella, "Baltimore Mayor Pugh Resigns amid Growing Children's Book Scandal," *Baltimore Sun*, May 2, 2019.
27 *United States of America v. Catherine Elizabeth Pugh*, 7.
28 Justin Fenton, "Former Mayor Catherine Pugh en Route to Alabama to Report to Prison Friday," *Baltimore Sun*, June 25, 2020.
29 Luke Broadwater, "Leading Candidates Attacked in Fliers Dixon Camp and Pugh Supporters Engage in Negative Campaigning," *Baltimore Sun*, April 6, 2016.
30 Heidi Mitchell, "Meet Marilyn Mosby: The Baltimore Prosecutor in the Eye of the Storm," *Vogue*, June 23, 2015, www.vogue.com.
31 Paul Gessler, "Marilyn Mosby Discusses Election, Her Federal Case and Tension with Police Union," *CBS News*, July 8, 2022, www.cbsnews.com. The six cops were charged, but none were found guilty.
32 U.S. Attorney's Office, District of Maryland, "Baltimore City State's Attorney Marilyn Mosby Facing Perjury and False Mortgage Application Charges Related to Her Purchase of Two Vacation Properties" (January 13, 2022), www.justice.gov.
33 *Baltimore Sun* Staff, "Read the Indictment Against Baltimore State's Attorney Marilyn Mosby," *Baltimore Sun*, January 13, 2022, www.baltimoresun.com.

APPENDIX

1 Botero et al., "Says Who?"; Nyhan, "Scandal Potential"; Puglisi and Snyder, "Newspaper Coverage of Political Scandals"; Thompson, *Political Scandal*.

2 "ABC News / *Washington Post* Poll," ABC News and *Washington Post*, September 1987 (Inter-university Consortium for Political and Social Research, 2008-05-15), https://doi.org/10.3886/ICPSR08891.v1.

3 "*Washington Post* Mayor Barry Poll," *Washington Post*, January 1990 (Inter-university Consortium for Political and Social Research, 2015-04-14), https://doi.org/10.3886/ICPSR09437.v2.

BIBLIOGRAPHY

Abrams, Dominic, Georgina Randsley de Moura, and Giovanni A. Travaglino. "A Double Standard When Group Members Behave Badly: Transgression Credit to Ingroup Leaders." *Journal of Personality and Social Psychology* 105, no. 5 (November 2013): 799–815. https://doi.org/10.1037/a0033600.

Adida, Claire L., Lauren D. Davenport, and Gwyneth McClendon. "Ethnic Cueing across Minorites: A Survey Experiment on Candidate Evaluation in the United States." *Public Opinion Quarterly* 80, no. 4 (December 1, 2016): 815–36. https://doi.org/10.1093/poq/nfw029.

———. "Racial Priming across Minorites: A Survey Experiment of Candidate Evaluations in the U.S." Unpublished manuscript, 2013.

Albanese, Jay S., Kristine Artello, and Linh Thi Nguyen. "Distinguishing Corruption in Law and Practice: Empirically Separating Conviction Charges from Underlying Behaviors." *Public Integrity* 21, no. 1 (January 2, 2019): 22–37. https://doi.org/10.1080/10999922.2018.1423859.

Alford, John, Holly Teeters, Daniel S. Ward, and Rick K. Wilson. "Overdraft: The Political Cost of Congressional Malfeasance." *Journal of Politics* 56, no. 3 (August 1994): 788–801. https://doi.org/10.2307/2132193.

Amick, George. *The American Way of Graft: A Study of Corruption in State and Local Government, How It Happens, and What Can Be Done about It*. Center for Analysis of Public Issues, 1976.

Andrews, Norman P. "The Negro in Politics." *Journal of Negro History* 5, no. 4 (October 1920): 420–36. https://doi.org/10.2307/2713677.

Bailey, Richard. *Neither Carpetbaggers nor Scalawags: Black Officeholders during the Reconstruction of Alabama, 1867–1878*. R. Bailey, 1993.

Banfield, Edward C., and James Q. Wilson. *City Politics*. Vintage, 1963.

Barnes, Bart. "Marion Barry Dies at 78; 4-Term D.C. Mayor Was the Most Powerful Local Politician of His Generation." *Washington Post*, November 23, 2014, sec. Obituaries. www.washingtonpost.com.

Barnes, Tiffany D., and Emily Beaulieu. "Gender Stereotypes and Corruption: How Candidates Affect Perceptions of Election Fraud." *Politics & Gender* 10, no. 3 (September 2014): 365–91. https://doi.org/10.1017/S1743923X14000221.

Barnes, Tiffany D., Emily Beaulieu, and Gregory W. Saxton. "Sex and Corruption: How Sexism Shapes Voters' Responses to Scandal." *Politics, Groups, and Identities* 8, no. 1 (January 1, 2020): 103–21. https://doi.org/10.1080/21565503.2018.1441725.

Barry, Marion, and Omar Tyree. *Mayor for Life: The Incredible Story of Marion Barry, Jr.* Simon & Schuster, 2014.
Basinger, Scott J. "Scandals and Congressional Elections in the Post-Watergate Era." *Political Research Quarterly* 66, no. 2 (June 1, 2013): 385–98. https://doi.org/10.1177/1065912912451144.
Baumgartner, Frank R., Derek A. Epp, and Kelsey Shoub. *Suspect Citizens: What 20 Million Traffic Stops Tell Us about Policing and Race.* Cambridge University Press, 2018. https://doi.org/10.1017/9781108553599.
Baxter, Andrew. "Federal Discretion in the Prosecution of Local Political Corruption." *Pepperdine Law Review* 10, no. 2 (February 11, 2013). http://digitalcommons.pepperdine.edu.
Beaulieu, Emily. "From Voter ID to Party ID: How Political Parties Affect Perceptions of Election Fraud in the U.S." *Electoral Studies* 35 (2014): 24–32.
Becker, Lee, Thomas A. Schwartz, and Sharon West. "The Report on Media Coverage of Magnum and Vista: Is the Public Good Being Served?" *Detroit Free Press*, February 9, 1984.
Benson, George Charles Sumner, Steven A. Maaranen, and Alan Heslop. *Political Corruption in America.* Lexington Books, 1978.
Berinsky, Adam J., Vincent L. Hutchings, Tali Mendelberg, Lee Shaker, and Nicholas A. Valentino. "Sex and Race: Are Black Candidates More Likely to Be Disadvantaged by Sex Scandals?" *Political Behavior* 33, no. 2 (August 17, 2010): 179–202. https://doi.org/10.1007/s11109-010-9135-8.
Bhavnani, Rikhil, and Luke Condra. "Why People Vote for Corrupt Politicians: Evidence from Survey Experiments in Afghanistan." IGC. www.theigc.org.
Bobo, Lawrence, and Franklin D. Gilliam. "Race, Sociopolitical Participation, and Black Empowerment." *American Political Science Review* 84, no. 2 (June 1990): 377–93. https://doi.org/10.2307/1963525.
Bond, Julian. "Monthly Review | SNCC: What We Did." *Monthly Review*, October 1, 2000. https://monthlyreview.org.
Botero, Sandra, Rodrigo Castro Cornejo, Laura Gamboa, Nara Pavao, and David W. Nickerson. "Says Who? An Experiment on Allegations of Corruption and Credibility of Sources." *Political Research Quarterly* 68, no. 3 (September 1, 2015): 493–504. https://doi.org/10.1177/1065912915591607.
Brotherton, Rob. *Suspicious Minds: Why We Believe Conspiracy Theories.* Bloomsbury, 2015.
Brown, Nadia E. "Black Women's Pathways to the Statehouse: The Impact of Race/Gender Identities." In *Black Women in Politics: Identity, Power, and Justice in the New Millennium*, edited by Michael Mitchell and David Covin, 81–96. Routledge, 2014.
Brown, Robert A., and Todd C. Shaw. "Separate Nations: Two Attitudinal Dimensions of Black Nationalism." *Journal of Politics* 64, no. 1 (2002): 22–44. https://doi.org/10.1111/1468-2508.00116.

Browning, Rufus P., Dale Rogers Marshall, and David H. Tabb. *Racial Politics in American Cities*. Longman, 1990.

Bunche, Ralph. "Review: Negro Politicians." *Journal of Negro History* 21, no. 6 (1936): 66–70.

Burch, Traci. *Trading Democracy for Justice: Criminal Convictions and the Decline of Neighborhood Political Participation*. University of Chicago Press, 2013.

Carlson, James, Gladys Ganiel, and Mark S. Hyde. "Scandal and Political Candidate Image." *Southeastern Political Review* 28, no. 4 (December 1, 2000): 747–57. https://doi.org/10.1111/j.1747-1346.2000.tb00798.x.

Chanley, Virginia, John L. Sullivan, Marti Hope Gonzales, and Margaret Bull Kovera. "Lust and Avarice in Politics Damage Control by Four Politicians Accused of Wrongdoing (or, Politics as Usual)." *American Politics Research* 22, no. 3 (July 1, 1994): 297–333. https://doi.org/10.1177/1532673X9402200303.

Christensen, Larry B. *Experimental Methodology*. Pearson/Allyn & Bacon, 2007.

Churchill, Ward, and Jim Vander Wall. *The COINTELPRO Papers: Documents from the FBI's Secret Wars against Dissent in the United States*. South End Press, 2002.

Clay, William L. *Just Permanent Interests: Black Americans in Congress, 1870–1991*. Amistad Press, 1992.

Cobb, Michael D., and Andrew J. Taylor. "An Absence of Malice: The Limited Utility of Campaigning Against Party Corruption." *American Politics Research* 43, no. 6 (November 1, 2015): 923–51. https://doi.org/10.1177/1532673X15570470.

Coleman, Renita. *Designing Experiments for the Social Sciences: How to Plan, Create, and Execute Research Using Experiments*. SAGE, 2018.

Collier, Peter, and David Horowitz. *The Race Card: White Guilt, Black Resentment, and the Assault on Truth and Justice*. Prima Lifestyles, 1997.

Cordis, Adriana S., and Jeffrey Milyo. "Measuring Public Corruption in the United States: Evidence from Administrative Records of Federal Prosecutions." *Public Integrity* 18, no. 2 (April 2, 2016): 127–48. https://doi.org/10.1080/10999922.2015.1111748.

Costas-Pérez, Elena, Albert Solé-Ollé, and Pilar Sorribas-Navarro. "Corruption Scandals, Voter Information, and Accountability." *European Journal of Political Economy* 28, no. 4 (December 2012): 469–84. https://doi.org/10.1016/j.ejpoleco.2012.05.007.

Crawford, Nyron N. "'It's a Racist Plot': An Experimental Test of the Racial Defense." *Urban Affairs Review* 58, no. 5 (2022): 1277–1304. https://doi.org/10.1177/10780874211016937.

———. "Of Suspicious Minds: Race, Scandal, and the DC Mayoralty." *Journal of Urban Affairs* 41, no. 5 (July 4, 2019): 679–99. https://doi.org/10.1080/07352166.2018.1514263.

Crocker, Jennifer, Riia Luhtanen, Stephanie Broadnax, and Bruce Evan Blaine. "Belief in U.S. Government Conspiracies Against Blacks among Black and White College Students: Powerlessness or System Blame?" *Personality and Social Psychology Bulletin* 25, no. 8 (August 1999): 941–53. https://doi.org/10.1177/01461672992511003.

Cunningham, Phillip. "'Well, It Is Because He's Black': A Critical Analysis of the Black President in Film and Television." PhD diss., Bowling Green State University, 2011. https://scholarworks.bgsu.edu/acs_diss/69.

Dagnes, Alison. *Sex Scandals in American Politics: A Multidisciplinary Approach to the Construction and Aftermath of Contemporary Political Sex Scandals*. Continuum, 2011.

Dagnes, Alison, and Mark Sachleben, eds. *Scandal! An Interdisciplinary Approach to the Consequences, Outcomes, and Significance of Political Scandals*. Bloomsbury, 2014.

Davis, Charles Hall. "The Race Menace in Bootlegging." *Virginia Law Register* 7, no. 5 (1921): 337–44. https://doi.org/10.2307/1107371.

Davis, James, Geoffrey Wetherell, and P. J. Henry. "Social Devaluation of African Americans and Race-Related Conspiracy Theories." *European Journal of Social Psychology* 48, no. 7 (2018): 999–1010. https://doi.org/10.1002/ejsp.2531.

deHaven-Smith, Lance, and Matthew T. Witt. "Conspiracy Theory Reconsidered: Responding to Mass Suspicions of Political Criminality in High Office." *Administration & Society* 45, no. 3 (April 1, 2013): 267–95. https://doi.org/10.1177/0095399712459727.

de Sousa, Luís, and Marcelo Moriconi. "Why Voters Do Not Throw the Rascals Out?—A Conceptual Framework for Analysing Electoral Punishment of Corruption." *Crime, Law and Social Change* 60, no. 5 (December 1, 2013): 471–502. https://doi.org/10.1007/s10611-013-9483-5.

Digeser, Peter. "Forgiveness and Politics: Dirty Hands and Imperfect Procedures." *Political Theory* 26, no. 5 (October 1, 1998): 700–724. https://doi.org/10.1177/0090591798026005004.

Dincer, Oguzhan C., and Burak Gunalp. "Corruption, Income Inequality, and Poverty in the United States." FEEM Working Paper no. 54.2008, July 11, 2008. https://doi.org/10.2139/ssrn.1158446.

Doherty, David, Conor M. Dowling, and Michael G. Miller. "Are Financial or Moral Scandals Worse? It Depends." *PS: Political Science & Politics* 44, no. 4 (October 2011): 749–57. https://doi.org/10.1017/S1049096511001247.

Douglas, Karen M., Joseph E. Uscinski, Robbie M. Sutton, Aleksandra Cichocka, Turkay Nefes, Chee Siang Ang, and Farzin Deravi. "Understanding Conspiracy Theories." *Political Psychology* 40, no. S1 (2019): 3–35. https://doi.org/10.1111/pops.12568.

Du Bois, W. E. B. *Black Reconstruction in America: Toward a History of the Part Which Black Folk Played in the Attempt to Reconstruct Democracy in America, 1860–1880*. Routledge, 2017.

Dunning, William E. "The Undoing of Reconstruction." *Atlantic*, October 1901.

Eggers, Andrew C., Nick Vivyan, and Markus Wagner. "Corruption, Accountability, and Gender: Do Female Politicians Face Higher Standards in Public Life?" *Journal of Politics* 80, no. 1 (January 1, 2018): 321–26. https://doi.org/10.1086/694649.

Ehrenhalt, Alan. "Justice and Ambition: U.S. Attorneys Can Do What They Want in Prosecuting Public Corruption. Is That Wise?" *Governing* 2, no. 12 (1989): 38–44. https://librarysearch.temple.edu/articles/gale_ofa7948149.

Elder, Larry. *Stupid Black Men: How to Play the Race Card—and Lose*. Macmillan, 2008.

Ellis, Mark. "J. Edgar Hoover and the 'Red Summer' of 1919." *Journal of American Studies* 28, no. 1 (1994): 39–59.

———. *Race, War, and Surveillance: African Americans and the United States Government during World War I*. Indiana University Press, 2001.

Emerson, Thomas. "The FBI as a Political Police." In *Investigating the FBI*, edited by Pat Watters and Stephen Gillers, 239. Doubleday, 1973.

Epp, Charles R., Steven Maynard-Moody, and Donald P. Haider-Markel. *Pulled Over: How Police Stops Define Race and Citizenship*. University of Chicago Press, 2014.

Esarey, Justin, and Leslie A. Schwindt-Bayer. "Women's Representation, Accountability and Corruption in Democracies." *British Journal of Political Science* 48, no. 3 (July 2018): 659–90. https://doi.org/10.1017/S0007123416000478.

Fauntroy, Michael. "Home Rule for the District of Columbia." In *Democratic Destiny and the District of Columbia: Federal Politics and Public Policy*, edited by Ronald W. Walters and Toni-Michelle Travis, 21–44. Lexington Books, 2010.

Fein, Steven. "Effects of Suspicion on Attributional Thinking and the Correspondence Bias." *Journal of Personality and Social Psychology* 70, no. 6 (1996): 1164–84.

Fein, Steven, and James L. Hilton. "Judging Others in the Shadow of Suspicion." *Motivation and Emotion* 18, no. 2 (1994): 167–98.

Fein, Steven, James L. Hilton, and Dale T. Miller. "Suspicion of Ulterior Motivation and the Correspondence Bias." *Journal of Personality and Social Psychology* 58, no. 5 (May 1990): 753–64.

Fein, Steven, Allison L. McCloskey, and Thomas M. Tomlinson. "Can the Jury Disregard That Information? The Use of Suspicion to Reduce the Prejudicial Effects of Pretrial Publicity and Inadmissible Testimony." *Personality and Social Psychology Bulletin* 23, no. 11 (November 1, 1997): 1215–26. https://doi.org/10.1177/01461672972311008.

Fein, Steven, Seth J. Morgan, Michael I. Norton, and Samuel R. Sommers. "Hype and Suspicion: The Effects of Pretrial Publicity, Race, and Suspicion on Jurors' Verdicts." *Journal of Social Issues* 53, no. 3 (October 1, 1997): 487–502. https://doi.org/10.1111/j.1540-4560.1997.tb02124.x.

Fiske, John. "Surveilling the City: Whiteness, the Black Man and Democratic Totalitarianism." *Theory, Culture & Society* 15, no. 2 (1998). https://doi.org/10.1177/026327698015002003.

Foner, Eric. "Black Reconstruction: An Introduction." *South Atlantic Quarterly* 112, no. 3 (July 1, 2013): 409–18. https://doi.org/10.1215/00382876-2146368.

———. *Reconstruction: America's Unfinished Revolution, 1863–1877*. HarperCollins, 2011.

———. "Rooted in Reconstruction: The First Wave of Black Congressmen." *The Nation*, October 15, 2008. www.thenation.com.

Ford, Richard Thompson. *The Race Card: How Bluffing about Bias Makes Race Relations Worse*. Macmillan, 2008.
Friedly, Michael, and David Gallen. *Martin Luther King, Jr: The FBI File*. Carroll & Graf, 1993.
Friesema, H. Paul. "Black Control of Central Cities: The Hollow Prize." *Journal of the American Institute of Planners* 35, no. 2 (March 1, 1969): 75–79. https://doi.org/10.1080/01944366908977576.
Funk, Carolyn L. "The Impact of Scandal on Candidate Evaluations: An Experimental Test of the Role of Candidate Traits." *Political Behavior* 18, no. 1 (March 1996): 1–24. https://doi.org/10.1007/BF01498658.
Gardiner, John A. *The Politics of Corruption: Organized Crime in an American City*. Russell Sage Foundation, 1970.
Garrow, David J. *The FBI and Martin Luther King, Jr.: From "Solo" to Memphis*. Open Road Media, 2015.
Gay, Claudine, and Katherine Tate. "Doubly Bound: The Impact of Gender and Race on the Politics of Black Women." *Political Psychology* 19, no. 1 (1998): 169–84. https://doi.org/10.1111/0162-895X.00098.
Gibson, James L., and Michael Nelson. *Black and Blue: How African Americans Judge the U.S. Legal System*. Oxford University Press, 2018. https://doi.org/10.1093/oso/9780190865214.001.0001.
Gillette, Howard. "Protest and Power in Washington, D.C.: The Troubled Legacy of Marion Barry." In *African-American Mayors: Race, Politics, and the American City*, edited by Jeffrey S. Adler, 200–226. University of Illinois Press, 2001.
Goertzel, Ted. "Belief in Conspiracy Theories." *Political Psychology* 15, no. 4 (1994): 731–42.
Gordon, Sanford C. "Assessing Partisan Bias in Federal Public Corruption Prosecutions." *American Political Science Review* 103, no. 4 (2009): 534–54.
Gosnell, Harold. *Negro Politicians: The Rise of Negro Politics in Chicago*. University of Chicago Press, 1935.
Gradel, Thomas J., and Dick Simpson. *Corrupt Illinois: Patronage, Cronyism, and Criminality*. University of Illinois Press, 2015.
"Guthrie and Dockery: The Greatest Convention Yet—The Representatives of the People Come Together in the Grandest Phalanx on Record." *Caucasian*, August 20, 1896.
Hajnal, Zoltan L. *Changing White Attitudes toward Black Political Leadership*. Cambridge University Press, 2007.
Hansford, Justin. "Jailing a Rainbow: The Marcus Garvey Case." *Georgetown Journal of Modern Critical Race Perspectives* 2 (2009). https://papers.ssrn.com/abstract=1321527.
Harris-Lacewell, Melissa V. "The Heart of the Politics of Race: Centering Black People in the Study of White Racial Attitudes." *Journal of Black Studies* 34, no. 2 (November 1, 2003): 222–49. https://doi.org/10.1177/0021934703255596.

Hay, Bruce. "Sting Operations, Undercover Agents, and Entrapment." *Missouri Law Review* 70 (2005): 387–432.
Henning, Peter J. "Federalism and the Federal Prosecution of State and Local Corruption." SSRN, December 7, 2003. https://papers.ssrn.com/abstract=476241.
Henry, Charles P. *Culture and African American Politics*. Indiana University Press, 1990.
Herrick, Rebekah. "Who Will Survive? An Exploration of Factors Contributing to the Removal of Unethical House Members." *American Politics Research* 28, no. 1 (January 1, 2000): 96–109. https://doi.org/10.1177/1532673X00028001006.
Hills, Roderick M., Jr. "Corruption and Federalism: (When) Do Federal Criminal Prosecutions Improve Non-federal Democracy? The Role and Limits of Legal Regulation of Conflicts of Interest (Part I)." *Theoretical Inquiries in Law* 6 (2005): 113–54.
Hilton, James L., Steven Fein, and Dale T. Miller. "Suspicion and Dispositional Inference." *Personality and Social Psychology Bulletin* 19, no. 5 (October 1, 1993): 501–12. https://doi.org/10.1177/0146167293195003.
Hoffman, David H., and Juliet Sorensen. *Public Corruption and the Law: Cases and Materials*. West, 2017.
Holbrook, Thomas. "Source of Perceptions of Local Political Corruption." Unpublished manuscript, 2014.
Holt, Thomas. *Black over White: Negro Political Leadership in South Carolina during Reconstruction*. University of Illinois Press, 1979.
Howell, Susan E. *Race, Performance, and Approval of Mayors*. Palgrave Macmillan, 2007.
Howell, Susan E., and Deborah Fagan. "Race and Trust in Government: Testing the Political Reality Model." *Public Opinion Quarterly* 52, no. 3 (September 21, 1988): 343–50. https://doi.org/10.1086/269111.
Howell, Susan E., and Huery L. Perry. "Black Mayors/White Mayors: Explaining Their Approval." *Public Opinion Quarterly* 68, no. 1 (March 1, 2004): 32–56. https://doi.org/10.1093/poq/nfh003.
Hubbell, Anne P., Monique M. Mitchell, and Jenifer C. Gee. "The Relative Effects of Timing of Suspicion and Outcome Involvement on Biased Message Processing." *Communication Monographs* 68, no. 2 (June 1, 2001): 115–32. https://doi.org/10.1080/03637750128056.
Jaffe, Harry, and Tom Sherwood. *Dream City: Race, Power, and the Decline of Washington, DC*. Simon & Schuster, 1994.
Jirard, Stephanie. "It May Be Wrong, But It Is Not a Crime: The Negligible Legal Consequences for the Amoral Sexual Activity of Men in Public Office." In *Sex Scandals in American Politics: A Multidisciplinary Approach to the Construction and Aftermath of Contemporary Political Sex Scandals*, edited by Alison Dagnes, 134–51. Continuum, 2011.
Johnson, Fern L., and Richard Buttny. "White Listeners' Responses to 'Sounding Black' and 'Sounding White': The Effects of Message Content on Judgments about Language." *Communications Monographs* 49, no. 1 (1982): 33–49.

Johnson, Mark A. *Rough Tactics: Black Performance in Political Spectacles, 1877–1932*. University Press of Mississippi, 2021.

Johnston, Michael. "How Do I Vote the Scoundrels Out? Why Voters Might Not Punish Corrupt Politicians at the Polls." *Crime, Law and Social Change* 60, no. 5 (December 1, 2013): 503–14. https://doi.org/10.1007/s10611-013-9477-3.

——. "Right and Wrong in American Politics: Popular Conceptions of Corruption." *Polity* 18, no. 3 (1986): 367–91.

Jones, D. Marvin. *Race, Sex, and Suspicion: The Myth of the Black Male*. Praeger, 2005.

Kaufmann, Karen M. *The Urban Voter: Group Conflict and Mayoral Voting Behavior in American Cities*. University of Michigan Press, 2004.

Keiser, Richard. "Why Machines vs. Reform Has Still Not Withered Away: Regime Conflict after The First (and Second) Black Mayor." Paper, Midwest Political Science Association, Chicago, 2011.

Kinder, Donald R., and Thomas R. Palfrey. *Experimental Foundations of Political Science*. University of Michigan Press, 1993.

Krase, Jerome, and Charles LaCerra. *Ethnicity and Machine Politics*. University Press of America, 1991.

Kraus, Neil, and Todd Swanstrom. "Minority Mayors and the Hollow-Prize Problem." *PS: Political Science & Politics* 34, no. 1 (2001): 99–105.

Kurer, Oskar. "Why Do Voters Support Corrupt Politicians?" In *The Political Economy of Corruption*, edited by Arvind K. Jain, 63–86. Routledge, 2001. https://doi.org/10.4324/9780203468388.

Levine, Lawrence W. *Black Culture and Black Consciousness: Afro-American Folk Thought from Slavery to Freedom*. Oxford University Press, 2007.

Logan, Trevon D. "Whitelashing: Black Politicians, Taxes, and Violence." Working paper, National Bureau of Economic Research, June 2019. https://doi.org/10.3386/w26014.

Lyle, Monique. "If Models, Then Malfeasants: Implications of Political Scandal for Stereotype Threat and Stereotype Lift." Unpublished manuscript, 2015.

Lynch, Matthew. *Before Obama: A Reappraisal of Black Reconstruction Era Politicians*. ABC-CLIO, 2012.

Maass, Arthur. "Bad Federal Policy on Local Corruption." *Spectrum: The Journal of State Government* 66, no. 1 (1993): 17–26.

Maier, Jürgen. "The Impact of Political Scandals on Political Support: An Experimental Test of Two Theories." *International Political Science Review* 32, no. 3 (June 1, 2011): 283–302. https://doi.org/10.1177/0192512110378056.

Marques, José M., Dominic Abrams, Dario Páez, and Michael A. Hogg. "Social Categorization, Social Identification, and Rejection of Deviant Group Members." In *Blackwell Handbook of Social Psychology: Group Processes*, edited by Michael A. Hogg and R. Scott Tindale, 400–424. Blackwell, 2001.

Marschall, Melissa J. "The Study of Local Elections in American Politics." In *The Oxford Handbook of American Elections and Political Behavior*, edited by Jan E. Leighley, 471–92. Oxford University Press, 2010.

Marschall, Melissa J., and Anirudh V. S. Ruhil. "The Pomp of Power: Black Mayoralties in Urban America." *Social Science Quarterly* 87, no. 4 (December 1, 2006): 828–50. https://doi.org/10.1111/j.1540-6237.2006.00438.x.

Marschall, Melissa J., Paru Shah, and Anirudh Ruhil. "The Study of Local Elections: Editors' Introduction: A Looking Glass into the Future." *PS: Political Science & Politics* 44, no. 1 (January 2011): 97–100. https://doi.org/10.1017/S1049096510001940.

McDermott, Monika L., Douglas Schwartz, and Sebastian Vallejo. "Talking the Talk but Not Walking the Walk: Public Reactions to Hypocrisy in Political Scandal." *American Politics Research* 43, no. 6 (November 1, 2015): 952–74. https://doi.org/10.1177/1532673X15577830.

McIlwain, Charlton D., and Stephen M. Caliendo. *Race Appeal: How Candidates Invoke Race in U.S. Political Campaigns*. Temple University Press, 2011.

Meier, Kenneth J., and Thomas M. Holbrook. "'I Seen My Opportunities and I Took 'Em': Political Corruption in the American States." *Journal of Politics* 54, no. 1 (1992): 135–55. https://doi.org/10.2307/2131647.

Michener, Jamila. "Policy Feedback in a Racialized Polity." *Policy Studies Journal* 47, no. 2 (2019): 423–50. https://doi.org/10.1111/psj.12328.

Miller, Beth. "The Effects of Scandalous Information on Recall of Policy-Related Information." *Political Psychology* 31, no. 6 (2010): 887–914. https://doi.org/10.1111/j.1467-9221.2010.00786.x.

Minnite, Lorraine C. "What Happened to Hope and Change? A Poll of 2008 Voters." *Project Vote*, September 2010, 22–23.

Morel, Domingo. *Takeover: Race, Education, and American Democracy*. Oxford University Press, 2018.

Morel, Domingo, and Sally A. Nuamah. "Who Governs? How Shifts in Political Power Shape Perceptions of Local Government Services." *Urban Affairs Review* 56, no. 5 (September 1, 2020): 1503–28. https://doi.org/10.1177/1078087419855675.

Muñoz, Jordi, Eva Anduiza, and Aina Gallego. "Why Do Voters Forgive Corrupt Mayors? Implicit Exchange, Credibility of Information and Clean Alternatives." *Local Government Studies* 42, no. 4 (July 3, 2016): 598–615. https://doi.org/10.1080/03003930.2016.1154847.

Musgrove, George Derek. *Rumor, Repression, and Racial Politics: How the Harassment of Black Elected Officials Shaped Post–Civil Rights America*. University of Georgia Press, 2012.

Nelson, William, and Phillip Meranto. *Electing Black Mayors: Political Action in the Black Community*: Ohio State University Press, 1977.

Niven, David. "A Fair Test of Media Bias: Party, Race, and Gender in Coverage of the 1992 House Banking Scandal." *Polity* 36, no. 4 (2004): 637–49.

Notable Senate Investigations. "Senate Select Committee to Study Governmental Operations with Respect to Intelligence Activities." U.S. Senate Historical Office, 1976.

Nunnally, Shayla C. *Trust in Black America: Race, Discrimination, and Politics*. New York University Press, 2012.

Nyhan, Brendan. "Scandal Potential: How Political Context and News Congestion Affect the President's Vulnerability to Media Scandal." *British Journal of Political Science* 45, no. 2 (April 2015): 435–66. https://doi.org/10.1017/S0007123413000458.

Oliver, J. Eric, and Thomas J. Wood. "Conspiracy Theories and the Paranoid Style(s) of Mass Opinion." *American Journal of Political Science* 58, no. 4 (2014): 952–66. https://doi.org/10.1111/ajps.12084.

O'Reilly, Kenneth. *Racial Matters: The FBI's Secret File on Black America, 1960–1972*. Repr. ed. Free Press, 1991.

Parsons, Sharon, William Simmons, Frankie Shinhoster, and John Kilburn. "A Test of the Grapevine: An Empirical Examination of Conspiracy Theories among African Americans." *Sociological Spectrum* 19, no. 2 (1999): 201–22.

Peffley, Mark, and Jon Hurwitz. *Justice in America: The Separate Realities of Blacks and Whites*. Cambridge University Press, 2010.

Peters, John G., and Susan Welch. "Political Corruption in America: A Search for Definitions and a Theory, or If Political Corruption Is in the Mainstream of American Politics Why Is It Not in the Mainstream of American Politics Research?" *American Political Science Review* 72, no. 3 (September 1978): 974–84. https://doi.org/10.2307/1955115.

Philpot, Tasha S., and Hanes Walton. "One of Our Own: Black Female Candidates and the Voters Who Support Them." *American Journal of Political Science* 51, no. 1 (2007): 49–62.

Philpot, Tasha S., and Ismail K. White, eds. *African-American Political Psychology: Identity, Opinion, and Action in the Post–Civil Rights Era*. Springer, 2010.

Phoenix, Davin L. *The Anger Gap: How Race Shapes Emotion in Politics*. Cambridge University Press, 2019.

Pollard, Sam, dir. *MLK/FBI*. Field of Vision, 2020.

Potash, John. *The FBI War on Tupac Shakur: The State Repression of Black Leaders from the Civil Rights Era to the 1990s*. Microcosm, 2021.

Praino, Rodrigo, Daniel Stockemer, and Vincent G. Moscardelli. "The Lingering Effect of Scandals in Congressional Elections: Incumbents, Challengers, and Voters." *Social Science Quarterly* 94, no. 4 (December 1, 2013): 1045–61. https://doi.org/10.1111/ssqu.12046.

Puglisi, Riccardo, and James M. Snyder. "Newspaper Coverage of Political Scandals." *Journal of Politics* 73, no. 3 (July 1, 2011): 931–50. https://doi.org/10.1017/S0022381611000569.

Radnitz, Scott, and Patrick Underwood. "Is Belief in Conspiracy Theories Pathological? A Survey Experiment on the Cognitive Roots of Extreme Suspicion." *British Journal of Political Science* 47, no. 1 (2017): 113–29.

Redlawsk, David P., and James A. McCann. "Popular Interpretations of 'Corruption' and Their Partisan Consequences." *Political Behavior* 27, no. 3 (September 1, 2005): 261–83. https://doi.org/10.1007/s11109-005-4469-3.

Reed, Adoph. *Stirrings in the Jug: Black Politics in the Post-Segregation Era*. University of Minnesota Press, 1999.

Rich, Wilbur C. *David Dinkins and New York City Politics: Race, Images, and the Media*. State University of New York Press, 2012.

Roberts, Robert, and Marion T. Doss. "The Federalization of 'Grass Roots' Corruption." *Spectrum: The Journal of State Government* 66, no. 1 (1993): 6–16.

Rottinghaus, Brandon. "Surviving Scandal: The Institutional and Political Dynamics of National and State Executive Scandals." *PS: Political Science & Politics* 47, no. 1 (January 2014): 131–40. http://dx.doi.org/10.1017/S1049096513001509.

Ruff, Charles F. C. "Federal Prosecution of Local Corruption: A Case Study in the Making of Law Enforcement Policy." *Georgetown Law Journal* 65 (1977): 1171–1228.

Ruffin, Paul. "The Black Press Dilemma: How the Barry Case Divided D.C. Journalists." *Washington Post*, July 8, 1990.

Rundquist, Barry S., Gerald S. Strom, and John G. Peters. "Corrupt Politicians and Their Electoral Support: Some Experimental Observations." *American Political Science Review* 71, no. 3 (September 1977): 954–63. https://doi.org/10.1017/S0003055400265179.

Russell-Brown, Katheryn. "Black Protectionism as a Civil Rights Strategy." *UF Law Faculty Publications*, January 1, 2005. https://scholarship.law.ufl.edu/facultypub/82.

———. *The Color of Crime: Racial Hoaxes, White Fear, Black Protectionism, Police Harassment and Other Macroaggressions*. 2nd ed. New York University Press, 2009.

———. *Protecting Our Own: Race, Crime, and African Americans*. Rowman & Littlefield, 2006.

Saxton, Gregory W., and Tiffany D. Barnes. "Sex and Ideology: Liberal and Conservative Responses to Scandal." *Journal of Elections, Public Opinion and Parties* 32, no. 2 (2022): 396–407. https://doi.org/10.1080/17457289.2020.1800713.

Schmitt, Glenn, Louis Reedt, and Kevin Blackwell. "Demographic Differences in Sentencing." U.S. Sentencing Commission, November 13, 2017. www.ussc.gov.

Schneider, Monica C., and Angela L. Bos. "An Exploration of the Content of Stereotypes of Black Politicians." *Political Psychology* 32, no. 2 (April 1, 2011): 205–33. https://doi.org/10.1111/j.1467-9221.2010.00809.x.

Schragger, Richard C. "Can Strong Mayors Empower Weak Cities? On the Power of Local Executives in a Federal System." *Yale Law Journal* 115, no. 9 (2006): 2542–78.

Sidanius, Jim, and Felicia Pratto. *Social Dominance: An Intergroup Theory of Social Hierarchy and Oppression*. Cambridge University Press, 1999.

Simien, Evelyn M. "Race, Gender, and Linked Fate." *Journal of Black Studies* 35, no. 5 (May 1, 2005): 529–50. https://doi.org/10.1177/0021934704265899.

Simmons, William Paul, and Sharon Parsons. "Beliefs in Conspiracy Theories among African Americans: A Comparison of Elites and Masses." *Social Science Quarterly* 86, no. 3 (September 1, 2005): 582–98. https://doi.org/10.1111/j.0038-4941.2005.00319.x.

Skolnick, Paul, and Jerry I. Shaw. "The O. J. Simpson Criminal Trial Verdict: Racism or Status Shield?" *Journal of Social Issues* 53, no. 3 (1997): 503–16. https://doi.org/10.1111/j.1540-4560.1997.tb02125.x.

Smith, Elizabeth S., Ashleigh Smith Powers, and Gustavo A. Suarez. "If Bill Clinton Were a Woman: The Effectiveness of Male and Female Politicians' Account Strategies Following Alleged Transgressions." *Political Psychology* 26, no. 1 (2005): 115–34. https://doi.org/10.1111/j.1467-9221.2005.00411.x.

Smith, Robert C., and Richard Seltzer. *Contemporary Controversies and the American Racial Divide*. Rowman & Littlefield, 2000.

Smith, Terry. *Whitelash: Unmasking White Grievance at the Ballot Box*. Cambridge University Press, 2020.

Smooth, Wendy. "Intersectionality in Electoral Politics: A Mess Worth Making." *Politics & Gender* 2, no. 3 (2006): 400–414.

Soss, Joe, and Vesla Weaver. "Police Are Our Government: Politics, Political Science, and the Policing of Race–Class Subjugated Communities." *Annual Review of Political Science* 20, no. 1 (2017): 565–91. https://doi.org/10.1146/annurev-polisci-060415-093825.

Stilwell, Ashley, and Stephen Utych. "Gender and Justification in Political Scandal." *American Politics Research* 50, no. 1 (January 1, 2022): 131–43. https://doi.org/10.1177/1532673X211041145.

Stokes, Carl B. *Promises of Power: A Political Autobiography*. New York: Simon & Schuster, 1973.

Stone, Chuck. *Black Political Power in America*. Dell, 1970.

Strickland, Amanda L. "'Sounding White': African American Attitudes toward 'Whiteness' in Speech of African Americans." PhD diss., Purdue University, 2010.

Swamy, Anand, Stephen Knack, Young Lee, and Omar Azfar. "Gender and Corruption." *Journal of Development Economics* 64, no. 1 (February 2001): 25–55. https://doi.org/10.1016/S0304-3878(00)00123-1.

Taylor, Andrew J., and Michael D. Cobb. "The Individual-Level Origins of Congressional Corruption Scandals." *American Politics Research* 48, no. 4 (2020): 442–54. 1532673X1985009. https://doi.org/10.1177/1532673X19850093.

Taylor, Steven. "Political Culture and African Americans' Forgiveness of Elected Officials." *Polity* 37, no. 4 (2005): 491–510.

Thompson, Dennis Frank. *Political Ethics and Public Office*. Harvard University Press, 1987.

Thompson, John B. *Political Scandal: Power and Visibility in the Media Age*. Wiley, 2000.

Torry, Saundra, and Richard Morin. "Half of U.S. Believes D.C. Is Most Corrupt." *Washington Post*, March 23, 1989.

Tromblay, Darren E. *The U.S. Domestic Intelligence Enterprise: History, Development, and Operations*. CRC Press, 2015.

Trounstine, Jessica. "All Politics Is Local: The Reemergence of the Study of City Politics." *Perspectives on Politics* 7, no. 3 (September 2009): 611–18. https://doi.org/10.1017/S1537592709990892.

Udani, Adriano, and David C. Kimball. "Immigrant Resentment and Voter Fraud Beliefs in the U.S. Electorate." *American Politics Research* 46, no. 3 (2018): 402–33. https://doi.org/10.1177/1532673X17722988.

Umfleet, LeRae. "1898 Wilmington Race Riot Report." 1898 Wilmington Race Riot Commission, 2006. https://digital.ncdcr.gov.

Van Prooijen, Jan-Willem, and Nils B. Jostmann. "Belief in Conspiracy Theories: The Influence of Uncertainty and Perceived Morality." *European Journal of Social Psychology* 43, no. 1 (2013): 109–15. https://doi.org/10.1002/ejsp.1922.

Vincent, Charles. *Black Legislators in Louisiana during Reconstruction*. Louisiana State University Press, 1976.

Walker, Hannah L. *Mobilized by Injustice: Criminal Justice Contact, Political Participation, and Race*. Oxford University Press, 2020.

Wamble, Julian. "The Chosen One: How Community Commitment Makes Certain Representatives More Preferable." Unpublished manuscript, 2019.

Wantchekon, Leonard, and Danila Serra, eds. *New Advances in Experimental Research on Corruption*. Emerald Books, 2012.

Warner, Mary R. *The Dilemma of Black Politics: A Report on Harassment of Black Elected Officials*. M. R. Warner, 1977.

Watson, David, and Amy Moreland. "Perceptions of Corruption and the Dynamics of Women's Representation." *Politics & Gender* 10, no. 3 (September 2014): 392–412. https://doi.org/10.1017/S1743923X14000233.

Watters, Pat, and Stephen Gillers. *Investigating the FBI*. Doubleday, 1973.

Weaver, Vesla M., and Amy E. Lerman. "Political Consequences of the Carceral State." *American Political Science Review* 104, no. 4 (November 2010): 817–33. https://doi.org/10.1017/S0003055410000456.

Welch, Susan, and John R. Hibbing. "The Effects of Charges of Corruption on Voting Behavior in Congressional Elections, 1982–1990." *Journal of Politics* 59, no. 1 (February 1997): 226–39. https://doi.org/10.2307/2998224.

Whitaker, Charles N. "Federal Prosecution of State and Local Bribery: Inappropriate Tools and the Need for a Structured Approach." *Virginia Law Review* 78, no. 7 (1992): 1617–54. https://doi.org/10.2307/1073355.

Williams, Jhacova A., Trevon D. Logan, and Bradley L. Hardy. "The Persistence of Historical Racial Violence and Political Suppression: Implications for Contemporary Regional Inequality." *Annals of the American Academy of Political and Social Science* 694, no. 1 (March 2021): 92–107. https://doi.org/10.1177/00027162211016298.

Williams, Rachel Marie-Crane. "A War in Black and White: The Cartoons of Norman Ethre Jennett and the North Carolina Election of 1898." *Southern Cultures* 19, no. 2 (2013): 7–31. https://doi.org/10.1353/scu.2013.0014.

Wilmer, Leon. "Marion Barry, Jr.: A Politician for the Times." In *Democratic Destiny and the District of Columbia: Federal Politics and Public Policy*, edited by Ronald W. Walters and Toni-Michelle Travis, 61–85. Lexington Books, 2010.

Wilson, David C., and Tyson King-Meadows. "Perceived Electoral Malfeasance and Resentment over the Election of Barack Obama." *Electoral Studies* 44 (December 1, 2016): 35–45. https://doi.org/10.1016/j.electstud.2016.07.003.

Wilson, James Q. *Moral Judgment: Does the Abuse Excuse Threaten Our Legal System?* Basic Books, 1997.

Wilson, Michele, and John Lynxwiler. "The Federal Government and the Harassment of Black Leaders: A Case Study of Mayor Richard Arrington Jr. of Birmingham." *Journal of Black Studies* 28, no. 5 (1998): 540–60.

Winter, Nicholas J. G. *Dangerous Frames: How Ideas about Race and Gender Shape Public Opinion*. University of Chicago Press, 2008.

Winters, Matthew S., and Rebecca Weitz-Shapiro. "Lacking Information or Condoning Corruption: When Do Voters Support Corrupt Politicians?" *Comparative Politics* 45, no. 4 (2013): 418–36.

Wolfinger, Raymond E., and John Osgood Field. "Political Ethos and the Structure of City Government." *American Political Science Review* 60, no. 2 (1966): 306–26. https://doi.org/10.2307/1953358.

Young, Coleman A., and Lonnie Wheeler. *Hard Stuff: The Autobiography of Coleman Young*. Viking, 1994.

Zaller, John R. "Monica Lewinsky's Contribution to Political Science." *PS: Political Science & Politics* 31, no. 2 (June 1998): 182–89. https://doi.org/10.2307/420248.

Zilber, Jeremy, and David Niven. *Racialized Coverage of Congress: The News in Black and White*. Greenwood, 2000.

———. "Stereotypes in the News: Media Coverage of African-Americans in Congress." *Harvard International Journal of Press/Politics* 5, no. 1 (2000): 32–49.

Zucchino, David. *Wilmington's Lie: The Murderous Coup of 1898 and the Rise of White Supremacy*. Atlantic Monthly Press, 2020.

INDEX

Page numbers in *italics* indicate figures and tables

ABC News / *Washington Post* poll, 92, 94, 96, 133; racialized suspicion and, 134; suspicion and, 95, 109
accountability, 114, 115; democratic, 101; race card and, 64; for scandals, 56–57
Adida, Claire, 10, 11
African Americans: corruption effect on, 20; forgiveness by, 110; political thought of, xvi–xvii, 113; racialized suspicion and, 91, 107–9; stereotypes of, 32; suspicion and, *100*, 140; trust of, 31; in Wilmington, 38–39. *See also* Black Americans
Alabama, Birmingham, 70
Andrews, Norman P., 37
anticorruption activities, racial bias in, 3–4
Arrington, Richard, Jr., surveillance of, 66–67

"bad nigger" trope, 38
Bailey, Richard, 37
Baltimore, Maryland, 24; BCPS in, 124; mayoral election in, 120–22, 123, *123*; mayor of, 118–19, *120*
Baltimore City Public Schools (BCPS), 124
Baltimore Sun (newspaper), 120, 122
Banfield, Edward C., 12, 15
Barry, Marion S., Jr., xi, xvii, 69, 102, 136–37, 158n40; Black political power and, 99; Black voters relation to, 88–90; city council election of, 83–84, 103–4, 156n5; diGenova relation to, 68; drug-related activity of, 23, 82, 100–101, 138–39; entrapment of, 13; racialized suspicion and, 84, 91, 93, *97*, 137; resignation relation to, 99; in SNCC, 85, 104; sting operation against, 86–88. *See also* Mayor Barry Poll
BCPS. *See* Baltimore City Public Schools
Becker, Lee, 66, 70
Berke, Richard L., 84
bias: in-group, 15; juror, 50–51; of media, 88; racial, 3–4
Biden, Joe, 134
Big Lie, Trump and, xiii–xiv
bin Laden, Osama, 27
Birmingham, Alabama, 70
The Birth of a Nation (Griffith), 25
Black Americans: Black politicians relation to, 111, 113; conspiracy theories of, 58–59; discrimination and, 7; mass incarceration of, 42; racial discrimination and, 53, 54; racialized suspicion and, 14, 29–30, 52, 80; surveillance of, 40, 41; suspicion and, 107; trust and, 13; in U.S., 9–10; White Americans compared to, 19
Black civil right leaders, FBI surveillance of, 14
Black elites, 60; harassment of, 29; as targeted people, 30; Whitelash effect on, 28
Black mayors: financial crime and, 76; law enforcement relation to, 65; racialized suspicion and, 74, 75; scandals of, 17–18, 24, 72–73

177

Black officials, 46, 47
Black Panther Party, 27
Black political experience, in U.S., 19
Black political power, 111; Barry and, 99; criminality effect on, 48; mayors and, 17; political harassment and, 62; during Reconstruction, 31–32; in Washington, D.C., 104–5
Black politicians: Black Americans relation to, 111, 113; Black protectionism of, 71; Black voters relation to, 7–8, 12, 16, 28–29, 60; discrimination of, 50; harassment of, 30; integrity of, 4, 6; as judges, 34–35; law enforcement relation to, 95; in municipal government, 45; political harassment of, 91, 93; racialized suspicion and, 92, 95, 135, 136; scandals of, 64–65; stereotypes of, 4, 27–28, 146n15; surveillance of, 107; in U.S. Senate, 31; White-dominated institutions relation to, 7, 14; White politicians compared to, 114
Black politics: African American political thought and, xvi–xvii, 113; ethics in, 81; racialized suspicion and, 125
Black presidents, in disaster genre, 25
Black prosecutors, 110–11
Black protectionism, 8, 9, 98, 111, 114; of Black politicians, 71; Black voters and, 23; Black women and, 117, 118, 126; character relation to, 77; integrity relation to, 109–10; law enforcement relation to, 109–10; political judgment relation to, 76; racialized suspicion and, 15, 29, 48, 49, 50, 61, 115, 117; racism relation to, 63; suspicion relation to, 104, *143*, *144*; transgression credit as, 30, 82, 91, 95, 100, 106, 108, 131; trigger questions for, 52
Black racism: discrimination and, 13; jurors and, 10, 51
Black radical politics, 26

Black Reconstruction (Du Bois), 38
Black voters: Barry relation to, 88–90; Black politicians relation to, 7–8, 12, 16, 28–29, 60; Black protectionism and, 23; corruption and, 19; double standards and, 21; law enforcement and, 8–9; racialized suspicion and, 57, 71, 108; scandals and, xvii–xviii; sex scandals and, 75; transgression credits and, 108; White voters compared to, 10
Black women, 110; Black protectionism for, 117, 118, 126; as mayor, 24. *See also* Dixon, Sheila; Pugh, Catherine
blame, 131; suspicion effect on, *78*
Blind Institute for White Children, 32
Bork, Robert, 133
Bos, Angela L., 4
Bradley, Tom, xi, 17
bribery, *46*; Conyers, M. and, 69–70; federal statutes for, 21; illegal gratuities and, 22; prosecution for, 47; during Reconstruction, 16
Bring the Pain (television show), 83
Broadwater, Luke, 122
Brotherton, Rob, 61
Brown, Byron W., xi, 114–15
Brownlee, Michelle, 118
Bubala, Mary, 124
Bunche, Ralph J., 20–21, 112, 113, 114
Burleigh, H. T., 6
Bush, George W., 27–28

Caliendo, Stephen, 64
California, Los Angeles, 17
California Fair Political Practices Commission, 17
Campbell, Bill, 65
Caucasian (newspaper), 16, 34–35
CBC. *See* Congressional Black Caucus
Center for American Women and Politics, 117

Chappelle, Dave, 27–28
character: perceptions of, 131; racialized suspicion relation to, 77; suspicion effect on, *78*
Charlotte-Observer (newspaper), 34
Chicago, Illinois, 1, 19
Chicago Tribune (newspaper), 86
Christie, Chris, 67
Cianci, Buddy, xvii
City Bureau, 19
city council, Barry elected to, 83–84, 103–4, 156n5
civil rights era, COINTELPRO in, 40
Clay, William Lacy, 42; media relation to, 55
Clean Slate Baltimore PAC, 121
Cleveland, Ohio, 17
Coates, Ta-Nehisi, 107
COINTELPRO. *See* counterintelligence program
communication intelligence (COMINT), 40
concealment, 148n71
Congressional Black Caucus (CBC), 11; double standards of, 70
conspiracy theories: of Black Americans, 58–59; race related, 50
Conyers, John, 69–70
Conyers, Monica, 118; bribery and, 69–70
corruption, 112–13; Black women mayors and, 24; criminal statute 18 U.S.C. 666 and, 44; double standards and, 92; electoral punishment for, 60; federal prosecution of, *18*; in local government, 18, 19; novel survey experiment to study, 71, 72, *72*; perceptions of, 3, 5, 7, *20*, 23; in Philadelphia, xiii–xiv, 1; in political machines, 15–16; prosecution of, 44, 45, *45*; prosecutors relation to, 42–43; in public opinion, 4; in public programs, 20; racism relation to, xiv; during Reconstruction, 36–38; scandals relation to, 21–22; tolerance for, 8–9, 11; Trump and, xv; in U.S., 1–2, 35
corruption convictions, 4, 6
Corruption Perception Index (CPI), 1–2
corruption-related probes, by federal government, 30
Cosby, Bill, 159n9
counterintelligence program (COINTELPRO), 39, 41, 61, 111; in civil rights era, 40; integrity and, 9; law enforcement and, 14
Couric, Katie, xvi
CPI. *See* Corruption Perception Index
Craven County, North Carolina, 34
crime: corruption-related, 22; financial, 73, 76, 109, 131; racialization of, 55; racialized suspicion and, 80–81
criminality: Black political power affected by, 48; suspicion of, 59
criminal justice system: racial discrimination in, 14; racism in, 51–52, 65
criminal statute 18 U.S.C. 666, of the U.S. Code, 43, 44
Crocker, Jennifer, 59
Cumming, Ken, 84
Cunningham, Phillip, 25

Daley, Steve, 86
Davis, Charles Hall, 63
decentralization, 57
deception, in sting operations, 41
deHaven-Smith, Lance, 59
democratic accountability, 101
Department of Justice (DOJ), 68, 99
Detroit, Michigan, 66; corruption in, 1; municipal bankruptcy of, 112; Young, C., as mayor of, 6
Detroit Free Press (newspaper), 66, 70
diGenova, Joseph E., 68
Digeser, Peter, 110
The Dilemma of Black Politics (Warner), 81, 113

disaster genre, Black presidents in, 25
discrimination: Black Americans and, 7; of Black politicians, 50; Black racism and, 13; by government, 114; racial, 14, 52, 53, 54
disproportionality, 98; in punishment, 63
District of Columbia Home Rule Act (1973), 85
Dixon, Sheila, xi, 126; in Baltimore mayoral election, 120–22, 123; resignation of, 119
DOJ. *See* Department of Justice
Donaldson, Frank, 70
double standards, 94–95; Black voters and, 21; of CBC, 70; corruption and, 92; integrity and, 114; in law enforcement, 98; racial disproportionality and, 63–64; racism and, 47, 50
double system, of justice, 52
Douglas, Karen, 59
drug-related activity, of Barry, 23, 82, 100–101, 138–39
Du Bois, W. E. B., 38, 113; on double system of justice, 52; surveillance of, 62
Dunning, William, 35, 36
duty, 115

Ebony (magazine), 26
Elder, Larry, 64
elections, mayoral, xv–xvi, 120–22, 123, *123*
electoral outcomes, 80
electoral punishment, for corruption, 60
Ellis, Mark, 39
Ellison, Charles, 47
Emerson, Thomas, 39
entrapment, of Barry, 13
ethical lapses, 56
ethics: in Black politics, 81; judgments relation to, 29; reputation relation to, 77; scandals relation to, 4, 6, 11; suspicion and, 24

Farrakhan, Louis, 26
Fattah, Chaka, xiii
favoritism: lawbreaking compared to, 2, 3; nepotism as, 21
favors, integrity and, 12
FBI, 92; Black civil right leaders surveilled by, 14; COINTELPRO of, 9, 14, 39–41, 61, 111; Moore relation to, 86–87; NOI and, 26; Street relation to, 7–8
federal funds, law enforcement and, 44
federal government: corruption-related probes by, 30; surveillance by, 62. *See also* FBI; United States (U.S.)
federal prosecution, of corruption, *18*
federal prosecutors, 43, 44
federal statutes, for bribery, 21
Fein, Steven, 30, 78; on juror bias, 50–51
female politicians, sex scandals of, 117
financial crime, 73; Black mayors and, 76; sex scandals compared to, 109, 131
Fiske, John, 54
Fitzgerald, F. Scott, 84
Foner, Eric, 16, 31, 36–37
forgiveness, 9; justice relation to, 110
Four Seasons Total Landscaping, xiv
fraud: mail and wire, 22; voter, xiii, xiv–xv, 3
Fraud Street Run, xiv

Garvey, Marcus, 39; surveillance of, 62
generalized suspicion: race and, 96–97, 98; vote intention and, 102
gentrification, 105
Gibson, Kenneth, xi, 17
Gillette, Howard, Jr., 85
Gillum, Andrew, xi, 114–15
Gilman, Leonard, 43
Giuliani, Rudy, xiv
Gosnell, Harold, 20, 112–13
government: discrimination by, 114; federal, 30, 52; local, 18, 19; mistrust of, 50; municipal, 45; racism of, 61

Gradel, Thomas J., 1
Gray, Freddie, 120, 125
Gray, Vincent, xi, 18, 43, 110–11; media relation to, 56; racialized suspicion and, 53
Griffith, D. W., 25
guilt, 158n40

Hansford, Justin, 39
harassment: of Black elites, 29; of Black politicians, 30; political, 28, 42, 62, 91, 93, 96, 97, 126; race and, 49, 58; racial, xv; state-sanctioned, 81, 82
harassment ideology, 48
Harris, Kamala, 117
Hastings, Alcee L., xi, 69–70
Hay, Bruce, 88
Healthy Holly, 123–24
Henon, Bobby, xiii
Henry, Charles P., 52
Highton, Daniel (hypothetical mayor), 72, 76, 78, 131, 132
Hilton, James, 29
Hobbs Act, 22
Holbrook, Thomas, 3, 4; on prosecution of corruption, 45
Hoover, J. Edgar, 39, 41, 104
House Banking Scandal, 55
House Ethics Committee, 12–13
House of Representatives, U.S., 69; Black women in, 117; Ways and Means Committee of, 11
human intelligence (HUMINT), 40–41

ideology, harassment, 48
Ifill, Gwen, 47, 92
illegal gratuities, bribery and, 22
Illinois, Chicago, 1, 19
immigrants, 15–16
implicit-exchange theory, 11
indictment, of mayors, 42–43
information processing, suspicion relation to, 81–82
in-group bias, 15
In Living Color (sketch-comedy show), 83
institutional racism, 69
integrity, 115; of Black politicians, 4, 6; Black protectionism relation to, 109–10; COINTELPRO and, 9; double standards and, 114; favors and, 12; of public institutions, 42
Iron-Contra Affair, 2

Jackson, Jesse, 134, 137
Jackson, Thomas Penfield, 103
James, Sharpe, xi, 67; financial crime conviction of, 73
Jennett, Norman, 32–33, 33, 34, 35; "The Vampire That Hovers over North Carolina (Negro Rule)" of, 36, 36
Jet (magazine), 26
"Jim Young, the Negro Politician, at Head of the Committee on Education at the Blind Institution for Women and Children at Raleigh" (drawing), 33
"Jim Young, the Negro Politician, Inspecting Apartments in White Blind Institution" (drawing), 34
Johnson, Andrew, 25, 35
Johnson, Kenyatta, xiii
Johnston, Michael, 57
Jones, Solomon, 111
judges, Black politicians as, 34–35
judgments: ethics relation to, 29; racialized suspicion relation to, 78–79, 104; suspicion effect on, 102
judicial system, trust in, 13
jurors: bias of, 50–51; Black racism and, 10, 51; suspicion of, 78
justice: double system of, 52; forgiveness relation to, 110

Kase, Aaron, xiii
Kaufmann, Karen, 4
Keiser, Richard, xvi

Kelly, R., 159n9
Key, Keegan-Michael, 27
Kilpatrick, Kwame, xi, 47, 112; financial crime conviction of, 73, 76; media relation to, 68; punishment of, 79
Kinder, Donald R., 73
King, Martin Luther, Jr., 40, 61; surveillance of, 62
Koenig, John, xiv
Kunstler, William M., 70

The Larry Young Morning Show (television show), 120
lawbreaking, favoritism compared to, 2, 3
law enforcement: Black mayors relation to, 65; Black politicians relation to, 95; Black protectionism relation to, 109–10; Black voters and, 8–9; COINTELPRO and, 14; double standards in, 98; federal funds and, 44; motivations of, 81; racialized suspicion relation to, 57–58; racism in, 54–55; suspicion of, 102
Lawrence, David, Jr., 70
Lead Charge in Prosecution, *43*
Leno, Jay, 83
Letterman, David, 83
Levine, Lawrence, 38
Lewis, Charles, 86
local government, corruption in, 18, 19
Los Angeles, California, 17

Maass, Arthur, 42
Magnum case, 66
mail and wire fraud, 22
mass incarceration, of Black Americans, 42
mayoral election: in Baltimore, 120–22, 123, *123*; in Philadelphia, xv–xvi
Mayor Barry Poll, 92–93, 94–95, 109, 136–37; racialized suspicion in, 139, 140, 141; resignation calls in, *100*; suspicion measured in, *97*, *103*; vote intention in, 138

mayors: of Baltimore, 118–19, *120*; Black political power and, 17; Black women, 24; indictment of, 42–43; race of, 132; scandals of, 17–18, 24, 72–73
McDonnell, Bob, 47
McDonnell v. United States, 47
McIlwain, Charlton, 64
media: bias of, 88; Kilpatrick relation to, 68; scandals relation to, 55; sex scandals relation to, 75; Young, C. relation to, 56, 66
Meier, Kenneth, 3; on prosecution of corruption, 45
Michener, Jamila, 98
Michigan, Detroit, 1, 6, 66, 112
Michigan Chronicle (newspaper), 68
mistrust, of government, 50
MLK/FBI (documentary), 33
Moore, Rasheeda, 86–87
Moriconi, Marcelo, 13, 89–90
Morrison, Toni, 7
Mosby, Marilyn, xi, 125–26
Mosby, Nick, 125
motivations: of law enforcement, 81; suspicion and, 77
motives, racialized suspicion relation to, 54–55
Muhammad, Faraji, 120
municipal bankruptcy, 112
municipal government, Black politicians in, 45
Murch, Donna, 33
Musgrove, Derek, 48

Nation of Islam (NOI), 26
Negro Politicians (Gosnell), 20, 112
nepotism, 21
Newark, New Jersey, 17
New Orleans, corruption in, 1
News and Observer (newspaper), 32
Newton, Huey, 26
New Yorker (magazine), 27

New York Times (newspaper), 65, 122; Barry in, 83–84
The Nine Lives of Marion Barry (documentary), 89
Nixon, Richard, xi, 14; Watergate scandal and, 2
NOI. *See* Nation of Islam
North Carolina: Craven County, 34; Wilmington, 32, 38–39
novel survey experiment, 71, 72, 72

Obama, Barack, 26–27
Ohio, Cleveland, 17

PAC. *See* political action committee
Palfrey, Thomas R., 73
paranoia, racial, 81
Parsons, Sharon, 58
party affiliation, 134–35, 139
Peele, Jordan, 27
perceptions: of character, 131; of corruption, 3, 5, 7, 20, 23; race relation to, 7
Philadelphia, 113; corruption in, xiii–xiv, 1; mayoral election in, xv–xvi
Philadelphia Inquirer (newspaper), xvi, 7–8
political action committee (PAC), 120–21
political harassment, 28; Black political power and, 62; of Black politicians, 91, 93; of Black women, 126; racialized suspicion about, 96, 97; surveillance and, 42
political judgment, Black protectionism relation to, 76
political machines, corruption in, 15–16
political thought, African American, xvi–xvii, 113
Politico (newspaper), 84
Powell, Adam Clayton, Jr., xi, 11, 47, 63
Powell v. McCormack, 11
Pratt, Sharon, 84, 89
prosecution: for bribery, 47; of corruption, 44, 45, 45; racism of, 88

prosecutors, 54–55; Black, 110–11; corruption relation to, 42–43; federal, 43, 44
Pryor, Richard, 25–26
public institutions, integrity of, 42
public opinion, 126; corruption in, 1–2, 4; race and, 23
public programs, corruption in, 20
public trust, 56
Pugh, Catherine, xi, 120, 121, 123; resignation of, 124–25
punishment, 131; disproportionality in, 63; resignation demand as, 99; suspicion effect on, 78–79, 79

race: conspiracy theories related to, 50; generalized suspicion and, 96–97, 98; harassment and, 49, 58; of mayors, 72, 132; perceptions relation to, 7; public opinion and, 23; scandals relation to, 57; suspicion relation to, 73, 74, 75, 94–95, 136, 140
race card, accountability and, 64
racial bias, in anticorruption activities, 3–4
racial discrimination, 52, 54; Black Americans and, 53, 54; in criminal justice system, 14
racial disproportionality, double standards and, 63–64
racial harassment, xv
racialization, of crime, 55
racialized suspicion, 8, 9, 49, 101; ABC News / *Washington Post* poll and, 134; African Americans and, 91, 107–9; Barry and, 84, 91, 93, 97, 137; Black Americans and, 14, 29–30, 52, 80; Black mayors and, 74, 75; Black politicians and, 92, 95, 135, 136; Black politics and, 125; Black protectionism and, 15, 29, 48, 49, 50, 61, 115, 117; Black voters and, 57, 71, 108; Black women and, 126; character relation to, 77;

racialized suspicion (*cont.*)
crime and, 80–81; generalized suspicion compared to, 96–97; Gray, V. and, 53; judgments relation to, 78–79, 104; law enforcement relation to, 57–58; in Mayor Barry Poll, 139, 140, 141; motives relation to, 54–55; about political harassment, 96, 97; racism relation to, 63; reputation and, 76–77; scandals and, 61; transgression credit relation to, 82, 91, *133*; trigger questions for, 50; in Washington D.C., 23; White-dominated institutions and, 29, 61, 64, 104
racial paranoia, 81
racial violence, in Wilmington, North Carolina, 38–39
racial voting, 101
racism, 65, 70; Black, 10, 13, 51; Black protectionism relation to, 63; in criminal justice system, 51–52, 65; double standards and, 47, 50; of government, 61; institutional, 69; in law enforcement, 54–55; of prosecution, 88; voter fraud and, xiv–xv, 3; against Young, C., 66
Racketeer Influenced and Corrupt Organizations Act (RICO), 22
racketeering activity, 65
Rangel, Charles R., xii, 12–13; scandals of, 11
Rawlings-Blake, Stephanie, 120
Reagan, Ronald, 133; diGenova appointed by, 68
Reconstruction, U.S.: Black political power during, 31–32; bribery during, 16; corruption during, 36–38
Reconstruction Amendments, 31
reputation, 76, 131, 148n71; ethics relation to, 77
resignation: Barry relation to, 99; of Dixon, 119; of Pugh, 124–25; suspicion and, *100*, *141*, *142*

Revels, Hiram Rhodes, 16
Rich, Wilbur, 27
The Richard Pryor Show (television show), 25–26
RICO. *See* Racketeer Influenced and Corrupt Organizations Act
Rock, Chris, 83
Ruffin, Paul, 88
Russell-Brown, Katheryn, 8, 15, 30; on Black protectionism, 77, 98, 108, 114; on Black women, 117; on racialized suspicion, 52; trigger questions of, 50

Saturday Night Live (sketch-comedy show), 83
"Scandalize My Name" (song), 6
scandals: accountability for, 56–57; of Barry, 89; of Black politicians, 64–65; Black voters and, xvii–xviii, 10; corruption relation to, 21–22; of mayors, 17–18, 24, 72–73; media relation to, 55; novel survey experiment to study, 71, 72, *72*; racialized suspicion and, 61; of Rangel, 11; seriousness of, 73, *73*; sex, 22–23, 62, 75, 109, 118, 131, 159n9; suspicion and, 75, 80; of Young, C., 66
Schneider, Monica C., 4
Scott, Tim, 31
Seltzer, Richard, 84, 89
Senate, U.S., 69; Black politicians in, 31
Senate Select Committee to Study Governmental Operations with Respect to Intelligence Activities, 62
seriousness, of scandals, 73, *73*
sex scandals, 22–23, 62, 159n9; of female politicians, 117; financial crime compared to, 109, 131; media relation to, 75
The Shame of the Cities (Steffens), 18
Shaw, Jerry I., 10, 51
signals intelligence (SIGINT), 40–41
Simmons, William, 58

Simpson, Dick, 1
Simpson, O. J., 51, 110–11
Skinner, Harry, 16
Skolnick, Paul, 10, 51
Smith, Jeff, 84
Smith, Robert C., 84, 89
Smith, Terry, 28
SNCC. *See* Student Nonviolent Coordinating Committee
de Sousa, Luís, 13, 89–90
state legislatures, Black women in, 117
state-sanctioned harassment, 81, 82
Steffens, Lincoln, xiii, 18
stereotypes: of African Americans, 32; of Black politicians, 4, 27–28, 146n15
Stern, Ronald, 87
sting operation: against Barry, 86–88; against Brownlee, 118; deception in, 41
Stokes, Carl, xii, 17; on prosecutors, 42–43
Stone, Chuck, 113
Street, John F., xii; FBI relation to, 7–8; mayoral election of, xv–xvi
Student Nonviolent Coordinating Committee (SNCC), 85, 104
Supreme Court, U.S., *Powell v. McCormack* in, 11
surveillance: of Arrington, 66–67; of Barry, 86–87; of Black Americans, 40, 41; of Black politicians, 107; by federal government, 62; political harassment and, 42; of Young, C., 66
suspicion, *78, 97, 107*; ABC News / *Washington Post* poll and, 95, 109; African Americans and, *100*, 140; Black Americans and, 107; Black protectionism relation to, 104; of criminality, 59; ethics and, 24; generalized, 96–97, 98, 102; information processing relation to, 81–82; motivations and, 77; race relation to, 73, 74, *75*, 94–95, *136*, 140; resignation and, *100, 141, 142*; scandals and, *75*, 80; transgression credit and, 109, *143, 144*; vote intention affected by, 78–79, *79*, 80, *103*. *See also* racialized suspicion

targeted people, Black elites as, 30
Taylor, Steven, xvii, 11; on scandals, 10
Thompson, John B., 21, 23, 29
tolerance, for corruption, 8–9, 11
Tonight Show (television show), 83
transgression credit, 76–77, *78*; Black protectionism and, 30, 82, 91, 95, 100, 106, 108, 131; forgiveness as, 110; in Mayor Barry Poll, 138; racialized suspicion relation to, 82, 91, *133*; suspicion and, 109, *143, 144*
Transparency International, CPI of, 1–2
trigger questions: for Black protectionism, 52; for racialized suspicion, 50
Trump, Donald J., xii; Big Lie and, xiii–xiv; corruption and, xv
trust, 120; of African Americans, 31; in judicial system, 13; public, 56
Turner, Maurice, 137

UMES. *See* Urban Mayor Election Study
United States (U.S.): Black Americans in, 9–10; Black political experience in, 19; corruption in, 1–2, 35; House of Representatives of, 11, 69, 117; Reconstruction in, 16, 31–32, 36–38; Senate of, 31, 69
Urban Mayor Election Study (UMES), 4
U.S. *See* United States
U.S. Code, criminal statute 18 U.S.C. 666 of, 43, 44

"The Vampire That Hovers over North Carolina (Negro Rule)" (drawing), 36
violence, racial, 38–39
Virginia Law Register (journal), 63
Vista case, 66

vote intention, 131, 141; generalized suspicion and, 102; in Mayor Barry Poll, 138; suspicion effect on, 78–79, 79, 80, *103*
voter fraud, xiii; racism and, xiv–xv, 3

Wamble, Julian, 111
Warner, Mary R., 81, 113
"A Warning" (drawing), *35*
Warnock, Raphael, 31
Warren, Lovely, 118
Washington, D.C.: Black political power in, 104–5; city council of, 83–84, 103–4, 156n5; corruption in, 1; Gray, V., as mayor of, 18; racialized suspicion in, 23
Washington Afro-American (newspaper), 104–5
Washington City Paper (newspaper), 84
Washington Post (newspaper), 18, 23, 70, 91; ABC News poll with, 92, 94, 95, *96*, 109, 133, 134; on Barry, 68, 84, 85, 102, 103; Ifill in, 47; as White power broker, 105; on Young, C., 66. *See also* Mayor Barry Poll
Water Filter Company, 65
Watergate scandal, 2
Ways and Means Committee, of U.S. House of Representatives, 11
Wells, Ida B., surveillance of, 62
White Americans, Black Americans compared to, 19

White-dominated institutions, 52, 81; Black Americans suspicious of, 54; Black politicians relation to, 7, 14; discrimination by, 50; racialized suspicion and, 29, 61, 64, 104
Whitelash, 28
White politicians, Black politicians compared to, 114
White power brokers, 105
White supremacy, 32; racial violence and, 38
White voters, 34–35; in Birmingham, 70; Black voters compared to, 10; Whitelash and, 28
Wiggins, Lillian, 104–5
Wilder, Douglas, 70–71
Williams, Rachel Marie-Crane, 33
Williams, R. Seth, 110, 111
Williams, Seth, xiii
Wilmington, North Carolina, 32; racial violence in, 38–39
Wilson, James Q., 12, 15, 51–52, 114; on decentralization, 57
The Wire (HBO series), 12, 15
Witt, Matthew, 59
WJZ-TV, 124–25
Wright, Jeremiah, 26

Young, Coleman, xii, 6, 42, 70; on Gilman, 43; media relation to, 56, 66
Young, Jim, 32–33, *33*, 34

ABOUT THE AUTHOR

NYRON N. CRAWFORD is Associate Professor of Political Science and Faculty Fellow in the Public Policy Lab at Temple University.

www.ingramcontent.com/pod-product-compliance
Lightning Source LLC
Chambersburg PA
CBHW020410080526
44584CB00014B/1261